North Vietnam and the Pathet Lao

North Vietnam and the Pathet Lao

Partners in the Struggle for Laos

Paul F. Langer
and
Joseph J. Zasloff

Harvard University Press

Cambridge, Massachusetts

1970

Preface

In contrast to the mountain of books on the conflict in Vietnam, little has been written about the struggle in Laos. Yet, events there deserve study. Although small, sparsely populated, and weak, its historic connection with Indochina and its central position in Southeast Asia—it borders on China, South and North Vietnam, Cambodia, Thailand, and Burma—give Laos a special significance in the Indochinese conflict.

This book, part of a more comprehensive inquiry which the authors are conducting into the Lao Communist movement, focuses on the role of North Vietnam in Laos. This subject is important for several reasons: The relationship between the North Vietnamese and the Pathet Lao is clearly of interest to those who are searching for a resolution of the war in Southeast Asia, the more so as Hanoi already has sufficient forces in Laos to take over the whole country. An understanding of the present and past role of the North Vietnamese also provides a basis for speculating about their future actions in Laos. Moreover, such analysis will throw light on the indigenous strength of the Lao Communist organization. Finally, and beyond the context of Southeast Asia, an examination of the North Vietnamese role in Laos constitutes a case study of a senior revolutionary partner providing assistance and direction to its junior partner in the conduct of a revolution, thus contributing to our understanding of the interrelationship of Asian revolutionary movements.

While the North Vietnamese have been supporting the Pathet

Lao, the United States has been providing crucial assistance to the Royal Lao Government. (An exploration of US involvement in Laos by a subcommittee of the US Senate Committee on Foreign Relations is now in the public record. See *Hearings Before the Subcommittee on United States Security Agreements and Commitments Abroad*, Committee on Foreign Relations, United States Senate, Ninety-First Congress, First Session, Part 2, October 20, 21, 22, and 28, 1969.) Indeed, during the last decade, the clash of external powers in Laos has in many respects assumed more significance than the competition among internal Lao factions. However, a comprehensive analysis of the international conflict over the future of Laos and particularly of the US involvement is not the task of this book. The authors will be satisfied if they have at least contributed to a better understanding of one important aspect of the struggle in Laos: the role played in it by North Vietnam.

In the intense controversy over American policy in Southeast Asia, readers of a monograph on one aspect of the Indochinese conflict will inevitably wonder about the authors' views on US policy in that region. As our book does not deal with the involvement of the United States and does not offer any policy recommendations, a sentence on this subject might be appropriate. For some years, we have felt strong misgivings about the wisdom and moral acceptability of US policy in Indochina and have favored a rapid and total disengagement from the war. Regardless of these reservations, we believe there is a great need for objective studies on important issues in the Southeast Asian conflict, and in this spirit we have endeavored to provide a dispassionate analysis of North Vietnam's role in the struggle for Laos.

In our research and writing, we have had much friendly assistance and cooperation in Laos, the United States, and elsewhere, and we wish to acknowledge our indebtedness without being able to name each contributor. We single out for special thanks only a few of the friends and colleagues who have rendered guidance by reading and commenting on our drafts: Thomas J. Barnes, Melvin Gurtov, Hans Heymann, Jr., Stephen T. Hosmer,

Konrad Kellen, Mark S. Pratt, and Robert L. Solomon. We are grateful to Sibylle Crane for her editorial assistance. We express our warmest thanks to Tela C. Zasloff for her research, editorial assistance, and administrative management in Laos. Finally, we wish to acknowledge the support given this work by The RAND Corporation under its program of research for the Advanced Research Projects Agency of the Department of Defense. These organizations, and the persons to whom we are indebted for help, do not necessarily share the views we have expressed in this study.

PAUL F. LANGER
JOSEPH J. ZASLOFF

Contents

Appendixes

Maps

Charts

North Vietnam and the Pathet Lao

Abbreviations

CDNI   Comité pour la Défense des Intérêts Nationaux (Committee for the Defense of National Interests)

DRV   Democratic Republic of Vietnam (North Vietnam)

FAR   Forces Armées Royales (Royal Lao Armed Forces)

ICC   International Control Commission

ICP   Indochinese Communist Party

KPL   Khaosan Pathet Lao (Pathet Lao Press)

LPLA   Lao People's Liberation Army (Kongthap Potpoi Pasason Lao)

NLFSV   National Liberation Front of South Vietnam

NLHS   Neo Lao Hak Sat (Lao Patriotic Front)

NVA   North Vietnamese Army

NVN   North Vietnam

PL   Pathet Lao (Land of the Lao; by extension, various components or the totality of the Lao revolutionary movement)

PPL   Phak Pasason Lao (People's Party of Laos)

RLG   Royal Lao Government

I

Introduction

Events in Vietnam overshadow the struggle in Laos — "the forgotten war," as the Lao Prime Minister Souvanna Phouma used to describe it. In Laos, as in South Vietnam, the fighting is in effect a continuation of the war that began when the defeat of the Japanese in the Second World War created a power vacuum in the former French Indochinese states — a vacuum that France was never able to fill. The Lao war, therefore, contains several elements: Vietnam's traditional attempts to assert hegemony over at least parts of what the French in the last century designated as Laos; an extension of the North Vietnamese struggle to take over South Vietnam; and a civil war between Lao Communists and anti-Communists.

North Vietnam's exploitation of the eastern portion of southern Laos — commonly known as the Ho Chi Minh Trail area — is the main reason that Laos has come to play so important a part in the conflict between North Vietnam and the United States over the future of the Indochinese peninsula.

The long struggle in Laos has resulted, essentially, in three areas of control: the Mekong Valley area, in which the non-Communist Royal Lao Government (RLG) maintains primary influence; the sparsely populated Trail area, where the North Vietnamese Army (NVA) operates with virtual autonomy; and the predominantly mountainous regions, where the North Vietnamese and the Lao Communist movement exercise control. Because

I

Laos is thinly populated, each side is able to maintain guerrilla bases behind enemy lines. There are vast areas of no-man's-land, where any platoon that marches through can claim control.

Scholarly studies on Laos are few. Of the available literature, little is concerned with modern Laos and even less with the Lao Communist movement. For Vietnam, the American research establishment has for several years poured vast resources into the study of Viet Cong organization, policies, and operations. No similar effort has been made for Laos. To date, little is known about the origins, evolution, organization, and leadership of the Lao revolutionary movement, still commonly known as the Pathet Lao (Land of the Lao), the name by which the Lao Communists called their armed forces until late 1965.

The term Pathet Lao (PL) was first used in 1950 by those Lao forces that followed the Viet Minh's lead and refused to accept the accommodation with the French to which other Lao nationalists had acceded the previous year. The term gained international currency when it was used at the Geneva Conference of 1954, although representatives of the PL forces were not seated at the conference and it was a Viet Minh general who signed the cease-fire with the French on their behalf. The name remained in common use as a generic term for the Lao Communists despite the fact that a "legal" political party, the Neo Lao Hak Sat (NLHS), the Lao Patriotic Front, was formed in early 1956. Therefore, although Pathet Lao is properly the name only of the armed forces of the Lao Communists between 1950 and 1965, it is colloquially used to include all non-Vietnamese components of the Lao Communist movement to this day. Among them are: Phak Pasason Lao (PPL), the People's Party of Laos, the semisecret Communist Party organization; the Lao Patriotic Front (NLHS), which is the legal front party; the administration in the Communist zone of Laos; the Lao People's Liberation Army (LPLA), the Kongthap Potpoi Pasason Lao, the armed forces under the command of the NLHS Central Committee; and the Dissident Neutralists (or Patriotic Neutralist Forces, as they like to call themselves).

In this study we shall use the terms "Lao Communists" and

"Lao Communist movement" in referring to these organizations. We recognize, however, that there is little Marxist-Leninist content in the thinking of their members and that many of the participants have little or no knowledge of the true leadership of the front organizations to which they belong. In the Lao Communist movement we include the entire Communist apparatus in Laos: the North Vietnamese advisers to the Lao People's Liberation Army, the NLHS administration, and the People's Party of Laos, as well as the North Vietnamese main force units in Laos and the North Vietnamese Army (NVA) personnel for the logistic structure of the Ho Chi Minh Trail.

Prevailing views about the Lao Communist movement tend to reflect more political prejudice than knowledge. Thus, the NLHS — the overt manifestation of the Lao Communist movement — and its chairman, Prince Souphanouvong, are believed by some to be no more than puppets manipulated by Hanoi. Others view them as indigenous nationalists dedicated to the unification of their country, the expulsion of all "neocolonialist" influences, and the realization of a program of social reform. The official line enunciated by the NLHS in three Party programs and repeated in its continuous propaganda is, of course, designed to convey the latter impression. So far, little systematic study has been undertaken to establish the reality behind these conflicting opinions.

In this book, as part of our larger inquiry into the Communist movement in Laos, we examine the role played by the North Vietnamese in the Lao revolutionary struggle since its beginning in the 1940's. Unfortunately, not enough material is available — and what there is is vague and ambiguous — to permit us to trace the role of Lao elements in the Indo-Chinese Communist Party in the period between the latter's inception in 1930 and the formation in the 1940's of Lao liberation groups, some of which were sponsored by the Viet Minh. As we approach the current years, however, we have more concrete data from which to develop more fully the Lao-Vietnamese relationship in this struggle.

Our information gathering for this study involved eight months of field work in Laos, from December 1966 to August 1967. In addition, both before and after this period, we surveyed the literature on Laos and interviewed people, many of them in Washington, who had special knowledge about the country. Earlier research, which had taken the authors to Laos, Vietnam, and elsewhere in Southeast Asia also contributed useful background information and a better appreciation of the forces at work in the two countries.

The dearth of documentation on the early years of the Indochinese Communist Party, the secrecy surrounding Communist operations in Laos, and the lack of prominent defectors from the Communist ranks constituted important handicaps in our inquiry. Furthermore, research in Laos presents the normal difficulties found in a developing country engaged in war, but, there are special obstacles in Laos. Only a very few individuals are responsible for decision-making within the Communist areas, and they are inaccessible to the researcher. The little information about the vital issues of organization and policy that passes beyond that inner circle is diluted as it is transmitted to lower and less sophisticated levels. Thus, the average defector or prisoner from the Pathet Lao ranks has a limited field of vision and finds it hard to place events in broader perspective. Studying the North Vietnamese role in Laos was rendered still more difficult by the assiduous efforts of the Vietnamese to conceal this role.

An analysis of the Lao Communist insurrection and of the part played in it by the North Vietnamese is further complicated by a certain lack of consistency and precision characteristic of the Lao. The confusion over Lao names and nomenclature will serve as an example. An individual name may appear — with or without surname — under a bewildering variety of spellings, so that it is often impossible even for a Lao to identify the person with confidence. A similar situation prevails with respect to the names of organizations and localities, and the dating of events is also often difficult. Moreover, because the Lao language is in a state of flux, the precise meaning of a given statement may at times be in question.

Though at the outset we recognized the need for establishing modest goals with regard to comprehensiveness, depth, and precision, we collected a body of data sufficiently large and reliable to enable us to construct a fairly complete picture of the North Vietnamese role in the Lao Communist movement. We found many Lao, in and out of government, willing to share their relevant experiences. Some had gone to school during the French colonial period with their future Lao or Vietnamese adversaries; others were linked to them by family ties; still others had been associated with them in the same political camp or had confronted them at the conference table. Defectors to the government side had no compunction about talking to us of their past experiences and observations. Interviews with knowledgeable third-country nationals supplemented our information.

More instructive about the Vietnamese role in Laos were the interviews we conducted in Laos with North Vietnamese defectors and prisoners who for the most part had been assigned to Laos during the past several years. Although some of the ordinary Vietnamese soldiers had only limited service in Laos, there were officers with greater experience, who had an understanding of the interaction between the Communist forces of Laos and those of North Vietnam.

The testimony of the North Vietnamese sources we interviewed and a careful examination of the reports released by the Royal Lao Government (RLG) of its interrogations of North Vietnamese prisoners and defectors enabled us to construct a composite of North Vietnamese operations in Laos. In addition, we conducted interviews with former NLHS personnel and studied the interrogation reports issued by the RLG. We supplemented this information with some one hundred and fifty background interviews with individuals of various nationalities, the majority of them Lao.

The comparatively small number of relevant sources who could be interviewed in Laos compelled us to be less systematic and hence less ambitious than we might have been had they been more abundant. This very deficiency, on the other hand, protected us against the temptation of proceeding to a quantitative data analysis that in the circumstances could only have been faulty. Rather than treating the informants as respondents in an interview sample, we questioned each with a view to increasing our fund of knowledge and correcting the often hazy and contradictory notions about the Vietnamese role in the Lao Communist movement.

For historical perspective, we drew, of course, on the substantial literature concerned with Indochina. Unfortunately, however, Lao government archives are still relatively undeveloped. This scarcity of documents reflects not only the low importance assigned to written communications but also the political uncertainties of life in contemporary Laos. A prominent Lao political figure once caustically remarked that the fewer papers in one's possession, "the less to burn in the next coup d'état."

Nevertheless, we were able to examine some captured Communist Lao and Vietnamese documents, including diaries and internal communications, as well as textbooks, newspapers, propaganda literature, and posters that we collected during our field work or acquired subsequently. These materials ranged from a single mimeographed sheet to several hundred handwritten or printed pages. Also useful were Vietnamese, Pathet Lao, Thai, Cambodian, Chinese, and Soviet radio broadcasts, some printed materials emanating from Hanoi, Peking, and Moscow, and a few documents that we were able to obtain from private Lao collections.

Given the uncertainties of political life in Laos, we have considered it prudent not to identify by name those persons who were willing to share with us their experiences and judgments. (Instead, these Lao or Vietnamese informants are keyed by letter and number to the detailed identifications provided in Appendix A.) For the same reason, we have not been able to document every statement. Our text should make the reasons clear.

Part One: The Past

II

The Setting of the Lao
Revolutionary Movement

Any revolutionary movement bears the imprint of its environment: conflict in Laos has been strongly marked by the physical character of the country as well as by the historical and social context. The Lao Communists' relationship to the North Vietnamese Communists — the focus of this study — has developed within this setting. Before examining the Communist movement in Laos, let us therefore look briefly at some relevant characteristics of the country and its people.

The Geographic and Ethnic Factors

A glance at the political map of contemporary Laos shows the country divided into two zones, one controlled by the Communists, the other by the Royal Lao Government, with the exception of some pockets of enemy resistance in each zone. Although there are gray areas not ruled effectively by either side, the boundary of political control extends roughly in a northwesterly-southeasterly direction.

It is significant that topographic and ethnic maps also show two distinct zones and that these zones virtually coincide with the present political division of the country. There is the Laos of the plains, controlled by the Royal Lao Government, and the Laos of the hills and mountain jungles, where Communist authority pre-

MAP I.   The Administrative Divisions of Laos

vails. The plains are the domain of the ethnic Lao; the uplands are distinguished by a heavy concentration of diverse non-Lao ethnic groups, which span the political borders of the country, reaching into neighboring Vietnam, China, Burma, Thailand, and Cambodia. This cultural, linguistic, and racial variety is the result of frequent migrations into Laos from the other countries of the region — migrations which even today continue to complicate any attempt to stabilize the political situation and define the national borders. It is estimated that about half of Laos' approximately three million inhabitants (no precise population figures exist) belong to ethnic minority groups. Apart from the predominant lowland ethnic Lao (the Lao Loum), we can distinguish three major ethnic groups within the territory of present-day Laos: the Meo (or Lao Soung), the Tai,[1] and the Kha (or Lao Theung).

The Meo are of Tibeto-Burman stock and belong to a group that migrated in recent times, mostly during the last hundred years from its original habitat in South China to the adjacent areas of Vietnam, Laos, Burma, and Thailand. Today, roughly a quarter-million Meo live in northern Laos and probably an equal number reside in the Tay Bac Autonomous Zone of North Vietnam, which borders on the Communist-controlled region of Laos. Our research suggests that the Meo, like the related Yao, though often aware of their geographic origins, have little contact with or interest in the three million or so of their relatives who have remained in South China, where they are known as Miao. The Meo of Laos, known for their fighting spirit, are still in a seminomadic state and engage in slash-and-burn agriculture.

The Tai tribes are scattered throughout the mountainous regions of North Vietnam and the adjacent areas of China and Laos as well as through Northeast Burma and northern Thailand. According to the different colors of their upper garment, many subdivisions, such as Black Tai, Red Tai, White Tai, are distinguished. Within Laos, Tai tribes are heavily concentrated in the provinces of Sam Neua (also known as Houa Phan province), Phong Saly, and Xieng Khouang. In addition to their own

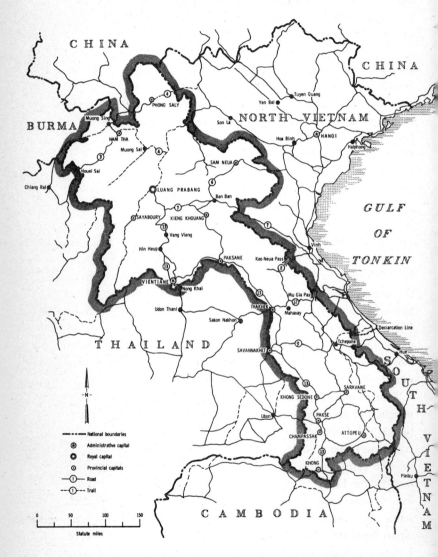

CHINA

CHINA

BURMA

Muong Sing
PHONG SALY
NAM THA
Muong Sai
Houei Sai
Chiang Rai
SAYABOURY
LUANG PRABANG
XIENG KHOUANG
Vang Vieng
Hin Heup
PAKSANE
VIENTIANE
Nong Khai
Udon Thani
Sakon Nakhon
THAKHEK
Mahaxay
SAVANNAKHET
KHONG SEDONE
SARAVANE
Ubon
PAKSE
CHAMPASSAK
ATTOPEU
KHONG

NORTH VIETNAM
Yen Bai
Tuyen Quang
Son La
Hoa Binh
HANOI
Haiphong
SAM NEUA
Ban Ban
Vinh
Keo Neua Pass
Mu Gia Pass
Demarcation Line
Tchepone
Hue

GULF
OF
TONKIN

THAILAND

SOUTH
VIETNAM
Pleiku

CAMBODIA

—N—

————— National boundaries
⊛ Administrative capital
◉ Royal capital
◉ Provincial capitals
—①— Road
- -①- Trail

0   50   100   150
Statute miles

Map II. The Major Roads and Trails of Lao

language, they generally are fluent in Lao and in Vietnamese.

The Kha, or Lao Theung, are of Mon-Khmer origin and live largely in the mountain areas of South Laos. Traditionally they have been dominated and exploited by the lowland Lao; hence their Lao name Kha, meaning "slave."

Throughout much of Laos, it may be said of the major ethnic groups that the Lao Loum prefer the lowlands, the Tai the mountain valleys, the Kha the mid-mountain level, and the Meo the mountain tops, although recent wartime dislocation and socio-economic change have modified this stratification.[2] Lao and non-Lao profess different religions: the Lao are Buddhists, the ethnic minorities, animists. Although through interaction they have influenced each other, they have developed different social and cultural patterns of life.

Because the Communist revolutionaries have been operating chiefly in regions inhabited by non-Lao, many observers contend that the Pathet Lao political movement is based on an amalgam of non-Lao minority interests. They conclude that the civil war in Laos is primarily a reflection of ethnic confrontation. Actually, the majority of the Meo and related Yao tribes in Laos are aligned with the Royal Lao Government against the Communists. Moreover, the distribution of Communist power in the eastern mountain areas of Laos is mainly the result of their proximity to North Vietnam, which has played a vital role in the survival and growth of the Lao Communist movement.

Topographically, Laos is characterized by unusually difficult terrain and an extremely poor system of communications, conditions which foster regional isolationism and separatism. Few roads cut across this landlocked country and fewer yet are passable during the rainy season. Moreover, the rudimentary road system built by the French runs from east to west; that is to say, it leads from Vietnam into Laos and, since Laos is laid out on a north-south axis, neglects communications within the country itself. Apart from the Mekong River, there are virtually no navigable waterways. Railroads are nonexistent. Much of upland Laos can be reached only by narrow trails unsuited to vehicular traffic.

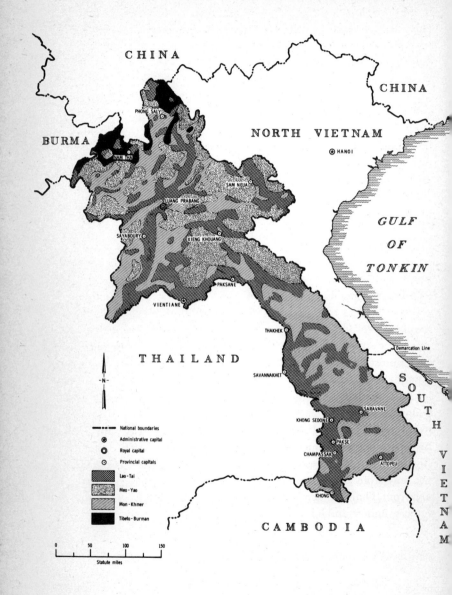

CHINA

CHINA

BURMA

PHONG SALY

NORTH VIETNAM

⊕ HANOI

NAM THA

SAM NEUA

LUANG PRABANG

GULF

OF

TONKIN

SAYABOURY

XIENG KHOUANG

PAKSANE

VIENTIANE

THAILAND

THAKHEK

SAVANNAKHET

Demarcation Line

SARAVANE

KHONG SEDONE

S
O
U
T
H

V
I
E
T
N
A
M

PAKSE

CHAMPASSAK

ATTOPEU

KHONG

CAMBODIA

National boundaries
⊕ Administrative capital
◎ Royal capital
◉ Provincial capitals

Lao - Tai
Meo - Yao
Mon - Khmer
Tibeto - Burman

0   50   100   150

Statute miles

MAP III. The Major Ethnic Groups in Laos

Transportation is particularly awkward in the mountainous zones in the eastern part of the country, bordering on Vietnam. In this part the Communist movement first sank its roots and has continued to rule. This is country which offers ideal conditions for small groups of guerrillas to hide out and survive despite enemy pressure, especially when a Vietnamese sanctuary is available to them.

The very topography of the Communist zone of Laos, stretched out from the borders of southern China and North Vietnam to the boundaries of Cambodia, and the resultant poor internal communications put obstacles in the way of any attempt to integrate this region administratively and govern it from a single center.

Geography affects the complexion of the Lao Communist movement in still other ways. The border areas of Laos provide ideal conditions for infiltration and exfiltration, particularly in the sparsely populated regions bordering on Vietnam. The same ethnic groups are found on both sides of the border, and boundaries, often ill-defined, tend to be ignored. It is not surprising, therefore, that throughout the history of Laos external influences have played a critical role in determining internal development. Following the tradition of Vietnamese rulers who have claimed suzerainty over territory also claimed by the Lao, the Vietnamese Communists today show an intense interest in these regions. Even if political considerations had not drawn the Pathet Lao into cooperation with the Vietnamese Communists, any Lao group competing for power in eastern Laos would have to face the fact that its survival hinges to a large extent upon the attitude of its much stronger Vietnamese neighbor. Because the government draws its strength from the richer valley regions of Laos and derives support not only from the United States and other Western powers but also from Thailand across the Mekong, the Lao Communists, to survive, understandably turn to the Vietnamese.

The Lao-Vietnamese Relationship

For centuries, the Lao have been in conflict with their Thai neighbors across the Mekong. Thai power has often expanded into Laos, and portions of what the Lao regard as their territory have been incorporated into Thailand. In fact, substantially more ethnic Lao now live in northeast Thailand than in Laos itself. But the Thai have by no means been the only enemy endangering the survival of Laos; the Vietnamese threat has also been felt acutely. The Vietnamese have at times extended their control over large areas of Laos, especially in the north, and Lao kings have often paid tribute to the Annamese emperors. Thus, Laos has long been a battleground for the expansionist drives of both the Thai and the Vietnamese.

If cultural affinity alone had determined the political orientation of modern Laos, it probably would have led to an association with Thailand, at least for the ethnic Lao population of the Mekong Valley. The two peoples are believers in Theravada Buddhism, speak a similar language written in a script of Indian derivation, and belong to the Hinduized sphere of civilization. In contrast, the Vietnamese have Sinitic origins and are influenced by a Confucian tradition and a mandarin concept of administration. But the French occupation of the country in the nineteenth century forced Laos into a political grouping with Vietnam and Cambodia as a member of a new political unit known as French Indochina. This union — and decades of French rule from the Governor General's office in Hanoi — brought about some degree of integration among the three culturally and ethnically distinct peoples. At the very least, it produced among the indigenous elites of these countries a feeling of shared destiny and common objectives. French education, French viewpoints, and French civilization became the common heritage of the educated few in Laos, Cambodia, and Vietnam, thereby creating bonds which to a remarkable degree have survived the collapse of the French colonial regime.

Ruling Indochina from Hanoi, France in its colonial policy tended to favor the Vietnamese. They were in any case bound to assume the leading position in the French colonial state because of their numerical superiority and their higher economic and professional development as well as their tough and dynamic national character. When the Vietnamese under Ho Chi Minh launched their anti-French independence movement, it was natural that they should have the support of certain Lao who had particularly close ties to the Vietnamese — the future Lao Communist leaders Kaysone Phomvihan and Nouhak Phomsavan, for example. But even some members of the Lao upper classes, including Prince Souphanouvong (the future titular leader of the revolutionary movement), Phoumi Vongvichit, and Singkapo Chounramany, were ready to accept Vietnamese leadership in the making of their own revolution.

The issue of Vietnamese influence over the Lao revolutionaries — or perhaps one should say the phenomenon of the Lao revolutionaries' willingness to cooperate with and even subordinate themselves to the Vietnamese Communists — raises an important question about Lao attitudes toward their Vietnamese neighbors. A widely accepted thesis holds that the Lao dislike the Vietnamese. Our research points to a more complex relationship. For one thing, the typical lowland Lao rarely exhibits the acute, virulent nationalism and xenophobia so common in contemporary Asia and so often directed against the neighboring people. Among the broader population, therefore, anti-Vietnamese feelings do not appear to be intense. It is true, however, that many members of the Lao elite fear what they perceive as Vietnamese aggressiveness, as well as organization and drive. Often betraying a sense of their own inferiority, the elite see unfortunate implications for Laos in too close an association with a people that has shown tendencies to expand into adjacent, less populated areas. The feeling of inadequacy vis-à-vis the Vietnamese is particularly evident among those educated Lao who were once placed in positions subordinate to the Vietnamese by French colonial officers, whose administrative policies tended to discriminate against the Lao.

Even in the towns on both sides of the Mekong, however, where recent decades have brought an influx of Vietnamese merchants and artisans, one encounters scant evidence of severe Lao-Vietnamese tensions. Despite the gap between the Lao and Vietnamese elites, there have been many cases of intermarriage. While such alliances tend to be frowned upon, the experience of French colonial rule that Lao and Vietnamese have shared has created ties that transcend cultural and national differences. Our research and particularly our interviews with Lao defectors suggest that the present generation of Lao revolutionaries has been able to accept Vietnamese assistance — and even guidance — without feeling the animosity that so often characterizes the donor-recipient relationship. It is open to question whether this will be true of the next generation even if North Vietnam's policy continues to take account of the sensitivities of the Lao allies.

The Role of Nationalism

Nationalism has proved the most potent political force in postwar Asia. Success or failure of Communist movements there has been fundamentally affected by the extent to which the Communists have been able to identify their cause with nationalism. In Laos, the Communists, for many reasons, have not had the success of their Vietnamese counterparts in capturing what there was of nationalism. The powerful Lao state of Lane Xang was the product of a distant golden age, which ended in the seventeenth century. Thereafter, Laos was divided into separate kingdoms and principalities, a condition which encouraged the centrifugal forces of regional separatism rather than sentiments of national identification and unity. This state of affairs did not change fundamentally during the half century of French rule, from 1893 to the end of the Second World War.

In fact, it may be argued that the weakness of Lao nationalism today is due in part to the nature of French colonial rule. The French viewed Laos as a quaint, though attractive, backwater of Southeast Asia, where not much profit could be obtained from modernization. Thus, they built what was, compared with that in Vietnam, a modest French-style educational establishment open primarily to a small urban elite. French rule left little mark on the rest of the population. France administered the country with no more than a few hundred French nationals stationed in all of Laos. Although they introduced French as the language of administration, the colonial authorities did not interfere much with the customs of the country, nor did they collect onerous taxes (except for corvée contributions exacted mainly from ethnic minorities) or make much of an effort to modernize the country. To judge by the reports of the time, traditional life in Laos went on largely undisturbed.

Except for the handful of leaders who were educated in Vietnam or in France, the lowland Lao did not deeply resent French rule, and there was no strong base for nationalism among the common people. Even those of the Lao elite who did resent French colonial domination appreciated the fact that it protected their country from its Vietnamese and Thai neighbors, who had overrun Laos in the past (although they might have had to admit that French policy also had the effect of reducing Laos' traditional cultural ties with Thailand). This explains the acceptance of compromise with France after the war on the part of most of the Lao elite — with the notable exception of Souphanouvong and a few other members of the Lao independence movement, who favored association with the Viet Minh. It also helps us understand why some Lao notables sided with the French during the days of Japanese supremacy even when there was danger in this association. Such sentiments contrasted sharply with the virulent anti-French feelings so common in Vietnam during those same years.

The moderate Lao nationalism is further blunted by the ethnic complexity of contemporary Laos, where half the population is ethnically non-Lao and each group has its own historic and cultural associations and traditions. The Lao revolutionaries, led at the outset principally by members of the lowland Lao elite, could not appeal to Lao nationalist convictions, nonexistent among the tribal peoples who populate the highland areas nominally under their control.

As will be explained later, the breakup of the Lao nationalist independence movement in 1949 clearly left Souphanouvong and his associates in a minority position. Thus the Lao revolutionaries never monopolized the nationalist movement in their country as the Viet Minh did in Vietnam. Moreover, the close relationship between Lao and Vietnamese that had always characterized the Lao revolutionary movement further detracted from the nationalist appeal of the Pathet Lao.

Now that the struggle against "French imperialism" is no longer an issue, "Thai imperialism" and "American imperialism" are the themes that provide the Lao Communists with a political weapon. So skillfully employed by the Communists elsewhere in Asia, this weapon is of less value in Laos, where antiforeign feelings are less intense. The luxurious living (at least by the modest Lao standards), corruption, and accompanying moral decay associated with the sudden pouring in of American aid during the 1950s did arouse resentment, which the Lao Communists used against the "American imperialists." Nevertheless, in our interviews with some of the Lao elite we found a forthright awareness of the fact that, to survive and develop in the modern world, Laos will require outside assistance for a long time to come. On the other hand, this same realization also makes it easy for the Lao revolutionaries to accept without resentment substantial aid and advice from the Vietnamese Communists.

Social and Political Conditions

Contemporary Laos is not characterized by such gross inequities as maldistribution of land or abject poverty alongside great and conspicuous wealth. To this day Laos remains a country of isolated hamlets and villages where the government official is rarely seen. Regionalism rather than centralized authority determines the pattern of social, economic, and political life. In the Lao countryside — and even in the country's few towns — the ordinary citizen shows little concern about affairs transcending his immediate interests and limited horizon. His level of participation in national life is minimal, partly because of the primitive state of communications and the widespread illiteracy of the population. Despite the existence of a National Assembly, broadly based political organizations — with the exception of the revolutionary movement's Neo Lao Hak Sat — exist in name only. Even more than other developing nations of Asia, contemporary Laos looks to an extremely small group whose social status and educational background, combined with the requisite political ambitions and skills, qualify it for the role of leadership.

This elite is interrelated to an unusual degree, and family ties are generally strong enough to prevent complete alienation even among politically competing elements. In studying the Lao revolutionary movement we found that virtually every one of its leaders had close relatives on the government side. Except during periods of strenuous fighting, family bonds tend to remain intact. At least among the older generation, amicable relations with family members who are political enemies are acceptable in Laos all through the hierarchy, as was shown in the relationship between Prime Minister Souvanna Phouma and his political rival Prince Souphanouvong, who is his half-brother.

An example from our interview with a conservative Lao minister illustrates this point. His wife, he told us, is a close relative of Prince Souphanouvong, whose mother lived in the minister's household until her death in 1963. While Souphanouvong was in Vientiane, participating in the coalition government, he frequently visited his mother. During this period, the minister, by his own account, would often launch political attacks on the floor of the National Assembly against his leftist relative in the morning and invite him to a family dinner in the evening. Taking down from the wall a picture showing the Communist Prince with his conservative relatives, the minister told us that relations within the family had remained quite affectionate. When asked whether their political differences didn't get in the way of their family relationship, he dismissed the question with good humor. "After all," he said, "family ties have nothing to do with politics."

In contrast to the Vietnamese, rarely are the educated Lao intellectuals or even avid readers. The desire for intellectual achievement, in the Western sense, plays little part in the life of the Lao elite. Our study of the Lao revolutionary movement's propaganda and of its internal communications thus revealed not only few traces of Marxist ideology but hardly any attempt to apply systematic analysis and "scientific thought" to the social, economic, and political problems of contemporary Laos. Thus, the public speeches of the movement's leaders are remarkable for their lack of ideological content and terminology. One can only conclude that ideology, for the revolutionary as well as for the nonrevolutionary Lao, plays a distinctly subordinate role.

III

The Growth of the Lao Revolutionary Movement and the Vietnamese Role

The Vietnamese revolutionary independence movement was the catalyst for the first Lao attempts to gain independence from France. From its inception, the Lao nationalist movement was confronted with the need to clarify its position toward Vietnam. It was over this issue — whether the Lao nationalists should enlist Vietnamese aid even at the risk of inviting Vietnamese influence over Laos — that the Lao independence movement split in 1949. The group around Prince Souphanouvong, as well as a "Vietnam faction" in Laos that included most of the future Lao Communist leaders (especially Kaysone Phomvihan and Nouhak Phomsavan), favored close alliance with the Vietnamese Communists and broke away from their more conservative compatriots in the Lao Issara movement. In due time, these two groups evolved into a single Communist-led and Vietnamese-sponsored Lao revolutionary movement, commonly called the Pathet Lao.

Stirrings of Lao Nationalism

When in 1893 the French placed Laos under their rule,[1] they probably saved the Lao from being absorbed by their stronger and more vigorous neighbors, the Thai and the Vietnamese, who had long been making inroads into Lao territory. Under the pro-

23

tective umbrella of French colonial power, Laos remained until well into the twentieth century the stagnant backwater of France's Indochinese empire. After the Second World War, Nhouy Abhay, one of the small number of educated Lao, expressed concern about his country's future, with some justification:

One can state with confidence that until 1940 the Lao with a few extremely rare exceptions scarcely interested themselves in the affairs of their own country: obscurantism, the lack of communications facilities, and fifty years of [French] protectorate rule had marked the Lao soul and had put it to sleep in the soft bed of irresponsibility.[2]

Perhaps Nhouy Abhay did not sufficiently stress the connection between French policy and the conditions he deplored in Laos.

Colonial policy toward Laos was formulated and directed from the Governor General's residence in Hanoi. With Vietnam and the Vietnamese forming the cornerstone of its Indochinese empire, France viewed Laos and the Lao as of secondary importance. Administered under French supervision largely by Vietnamese bureaucrats, Laos often appeared to the Lao themselves as a Vietnamese colony. This situation was reflected especially in education. There were very few schools in Laos as compared to Vietnam, and these few institutions not only were headed by French principals but were staffed almost exclusively by French and Vietnamese instructors who tended to favor the advancement of their young compatriots over that of their Lao pupils. This discriminatory treatment was the more pronounced, the higher the level of education. Such conditions were responsible for the latent anti-French and anti-Vietnamese feeling among some of the young Lao.

Many Lao and certainly the small elite must have been exposed, if only vicariously, to the ferment of the Vietnamese revolutionary independence movement; Vietnamese civil servants staffed the administration of Laos and Vietnamese students attended the country's one institution of secondary education (a limited one at that), the Collège (later, Lycée) Pavie in Vientiane.

There Lao students were actually a minority. For example, in the decade of the nineteen thirties, only fifty-two Lao (and not a single member of the ethnic minorities) figured in the diploma lists as against ninety-six Vietnamese.[3] A few young Lao went on to a full secondary education at the lycées of Saigon and Hanoi. A very few even traveled to France to obtain a university education. But there is no firm evidence of Lao participation in early revolutionary activity in France or in Indochina.

The beginnings of a documented Lao independence movement, which eventually gave rise to a Lao revolutionary organization, go back no further than the Second World War. The fall of France in 1940 for the first time confronted the Lao with the possibility that the French protective umbrella might be withdrawn and that the future of Laos would have to be determined by the Lao themselves. In that same year, as one of the leading participants in the adventure told us,[4] a group of some fifty Lao youths, mostly students at the Collège Pavie, plotted an anti-French coup in the administrative capital of Vientiane. Their amateurish scheme failed entirely, and the youthful Lao activists were forced to seek refuge across the Mekong in Thailand, where they received sympathetic but rather ineffectual support.

In 1945, the Japanese decided to replace Vichy France's administration of Indochina with direct Japanese rule. On March 9, a small Japanese detachment crossed the Mekong from the Thai border post of Nong Khai and, encountering little French resistance, entered Vientiane the following day. In neighboring Vietnam, Emperor Bao Dai responded to Japanese intervention by declaring his country's independence from France. In Vientiane, meanwhile, the Japanese, to the accompaniment of three banzai, proclaimed an end to colonial rule over Laos and told the populace that Japan was leading the fight against the white imperialists and bringing independence to the peoples of Asia.

It is a significant indication of the difference in political consciousness between the Vietnamese and the Lao that the first in Laos to respond to the Japanese proclamation were the Vietnamese residents of Vientiane. Here, as in most other small urban centers along the Mekong, the Vietnamese colony had steadily grown under French rule, until in 1945 it was actually larger than the Lao population.[5] Its numbers had been further swelled by the influx from Thailand of many Vietnamese who had lived in exile across the Mekong during the war. On March 23 a mammoth demonstration by Vietnamese residents in Vientiane celebrated the independence of Vietnam. Although held on Lao soil, it ended with the hoisting of the Japanese and Vietnamese flags.

Lao eyewitnesses and former participants in the Lao independence movement have told us that at this point many Lao first felt concern that Vietnamese domination might come to replace French. Available evidence suggests that some of the several small political groups which sprang up in Laos during the spring of 1945 owed their origin almost as much to the fear of overwhelming Vietnamese influence as to the desire for independence from the French.

Direct Japanese rule in Laos was of short duration, as Japan capitulated to the Allies in August 1945. In Vietnam, Ho Chi Minh established his People's National Liberation Committee, Emperor Bao Dai abdicated, and on September 2 Ho Chi Minh proclaimed the independence of the Democratic Republic of Vietnam (DRV).

Laos had neither the organization nor the experienced, sophisticated leadership that existed in Vietnam. Opinion was divided as to how Laos could best preserve its integrity against the certainty of external threats. These concerns and the differences in the situations of Laos and Vietnam were clearly stated by the most prestigious Lao of the time, the Premier and Viceroy, Prince Phetsarath:

Nourished by French civilization, I have not the slightest desire at my age to return to school to learn Chinese or Russian . . . Our [Lao and Vietnamese] policies are not the same. Vietnamese policy seeks to rid itself entirely of the French, whereas ours seeks to obtain independence within the framework of the French Union . . . We still have need to lean on a strong power in order to protect ourselves against the designs of our neighbors both in the east and in the west, in the north and in the northwest.[6]

But the Prince's views were not shared by all the leaders of his time. Some, like Oun (later known as Oun Sananikone) and the group of young Lao nationalists returning from exile in Thailand, favored reliance on Thailand, or even a closer association with that kindred nation, both to prevent France from returning to Laos and to bar further Vietnamese expansion westward. Others sought to avoid dependence on either Thailand or Vietnam and hoped to convince the French of the wisdom of gradually transferring political power to the Lao leadership. Still others thoroughly distrusted the Thai and at the same time refused to entertain the thought of even temporary French participation in Lao affairs. To them, already influenced by the Vietnamese Communists, the struggle was essentially an anticolonial one, with racial (anti-white) overtones. Not surprisingly, supporters of this viewpoint, who favored a greater degree of domestic political and social change than did the other, more conservative factions, saw much in the Viet Minh movement to admire and were inclined to seek its assistance for what appeared to them a common goal: absolute independence from France. Such assistance was gladly given by the Viet Minh, who actively sought out sympathetic elements in Laos.

For a while, the disparate Lao political groups were able to agree on a common program and on a person who could implement their consensus — Prince Phetsarath. On September 1, 1945, the Prince announced Laos' independence from France, and two weeks later, in the name of the King, he proclaimed the unification of Laos through the merger of north and south under a single regime. On October 12, the Prince, although disavowed by the King (then under the thumb of the French in Luang Prabang) and stripped by him of all titles and prerogatives, lent his support and prestige to a new constitution, which made Laos for the first time a constitutional monarchy.[7] That same day, a provisional government of Laos was set up in Vientiane with his backing. This new government, which was soon to be ousted by the returning French forces, enjoyed the support of the major Lao political groups, none of which, it is true, represented more than a handful of men at the outset.[8]

Meanwhile, in the outlying areas of Laos, other factions and groups had made their appearance. One was centered in Savannakhet, an important Mekong town at the end of the strategic Route 9, which leads out of Vietnam through Tchepone. This group was led by Prince Souphanouvong, Prince Phetsarath's youngest brother, who had just returned from almost a decade in Vietnam. As a political figure, first in his brother's Lao Issara government and later as the titular chief of an independent political movement, the Neo Lao Issara (later renamed Neo Lao Hak Sat and more commonly known as the Pathet Lao), Souphanouvong has played a conspicuous role in the political struggle over the future of Laos. His real influence, however, has been increasingly eclipsed by that of his associates Nouhak Phomsavan and the half-Vietnamese Kaysone Phomvihan. Lacking Souphanouvong's aristocratic lineage and having close ties to Ho Chi Minh, they have enjoyed more fully the confidence of the Vietnamese Communists.[9] An examination of the Prince's early political career will shed some light on the beginnings of the revolutionary movement in Laos and on its increasingly close association with the Viet Minh.

The Early Career of Prince Souphanouvong

A good many legends have grown up around the personality and past of the "Red Prince." In the Communist literature he has emerged as something of a folk hero, a man who spends much of his life outside his own country on secret missions to Hanoi and Peking or leading guerrilla movements in the more remote mountain regions of Laos. The known facts about Souphanouvong's career cast a more ambiguous light, however. Although his biography contains some undocumented stretches, its general outline can be pieced together from official records scattered in Vientiane files, interviews with former classmates and associates, and his own official and private statements.

A notarized document, signed by the Prince, shows that he was born on July 13, 1909, in the royal capital of Luang Prabang, as the twentieth and youngest son of the Viceroy, Bounkhong,[10] and the latter's minor wife — or perhaps concubine — (Mom) Khamouane.[11] Three of his brothers were to play leading roles in the history of contemporary Laos: the previously mentioned Prince Phetsarath, acknowledged chief of the Free Laos movement and the second man in the realm; Prince Souvannarath, in 1947 the first Prime Minister of an independent Laos; and Prince Souvanna Phouma, who was to emerge sometimes as the political rival, sometimes as the ally, of Souphanouvong.

While the brothers were all scions of an illustrious Lao family, Souphanouvong suffered from several disadvantages: Not only was he the youngest, but his mother, it seems, was not of royal blood.[12] His remarkable vigor, his combative, adventurous, and romantic spirit, and his strong desire to excel — qualities attested to by those we interviewed who knew him well — may not be unrelated to the pressures he felt from an early age to make up for the handicap of being the son of a minor, if viceroyal, wife in a royal household.

Like Kaysone, Phoumi Vongvichit, and most of the other leaders of the Lao Communist movement, Prince Souphanouvong received his education largely in Vietnam. He attended the Lycée Albert Sarraut in Hanoi and reportedly was one of a very small number of upper-class Lao who could successfully compete with the young Vietnamese intellectual elite and with French students attending this institution, known for its high intellectual standards. A Vientiane notable and former classmate of the Prince confirms what other sources report: Souphanouvong impressed all who had contact with him as an intelligent, ambitious, and extremely vain young man with a tendency to play to the gallery. His outstanding scholastic record, his reported ability to handle eight or more languages (including Russian and classical Greek), and his ostentatious vegetarianism tend to bear out this generally accepted description of the Prince.

Several Lao who knew him cite a number of reasons why Souphanouvong should have developed a strong resentment against the established order and French rule even before he came under the influence of Ho Chi Minh and other Vietnamese revolutionaries. They point to the circumstances of his childhood as well as to the discrimination he suffered in Hanoi.[13]

Probably more important for the Prince's future and his political orientation were his stay in France, where his brother Phetsarath sent him for further study, and the discriminatory treatment he received during his professional career after his return to Indochina. In France, Souphanouvong attended a first-rate engineering school, Ecole Nationale des Ponts et Chaussées, graduating in 1937 with an excellent academic record.[14] It is fairly well established that, unlike other scions of prominent Lao families, he did not choose to lead a life of relative ease in France.[15]

Souphanouvong's student days coincided with the height of the popular-front movement in France. It would be hard to imagine, therefore, that he did not have some exposure to the political currents that were sweeping the country. Indeed, Wilfred Burchett asserts that "he had already some political convictions through contact with progressives in France." [16]

It is not clear whether Souphanouvong's presumed involvement with Communists and Marxists during his stay in France was a superficial one or a deeper, ideological one.[17] At any rate, after his return to Laos the Prince gave no evidence of having become steeped in Marxist theory, and no concern with Marxism is reflected in his writings and speeches[18] — one reason perhaps why in later years the Vietnamese Communists apparently did not consider him fit to be more than the titular head of the Lao revolutionary movement. (Where the Prince professes to stand today, however, is not in doubt: in 1967 he publicly proclaimed himself a Marxist-Leninist.)

Souphanouvong's experience after his return to Indochina in 1938 must have heightened his resentment of French colonial rule, for despite his good professional qualifications the French assigned him to a relatively subordinate and poorly paid job in the colonial administration.[19] Whatever disappointment or resentment he may have felt,[20] however, he continued, until his return to Laos in 1945, to go about his civil engineering work in central Vietnam. It was here that he made the acquaintance of his future wife, Le Thi Ky-Nam, and that his involvement with the Vietnamese Communists had its real beginning.

Prince Souphanouvong and the Vietnamese

In view of Souphanouvong's eventual close association with the Viet Minh, his attitude toward the Vietnamese is of particular interest. One must remember that his formative years and, until he returned to Laos in 1945, most of his adult life were spent outside his native country, for the most part in Vietnam; he actually had more frequent contact with Vietnamese than with his Lao contemporaries. Also, it should be recalled, the Prince had received the same French education as the Vietnamese elite, and he spoke fluent Vietnamese. He may have felt more of an intellectual tie with the educated Vietnamese than with the upper-class Lao, whom, to judge by his letters,[21] he did not consider his equals. He was quite critical of the Lao for their inertia and political apathy, and the dynamism of the Vietnamese must have struck a responsive chord in him. No doubt he viewed the Lao as "poor revolutionary material," badly in need of guidance — his own guidance as well as that of the experienced Vietnamese.

That the Prince took a Vietnamese rather than a Lao wife made him suspect to some of his compatriots who feared the Vietnamese influence over Laos.[22] An exceptionally attractive and very strong-minded woman[23] who is said to have had pronounced Viet Minh sympathies, Le Thi Ky-Nam undoubtedly helped strengthen the bonds between her Lao husband and the Vietnamese Communists. Many Lao are convinced that in the early stages of his career and at least as early as his marriage Prince Souphanouvong became a prisoner, so to speak, of the Viet Minh, to whose authority he eventually succumbed completely. His half-brother Souvanna Phouma has said in looking back on the past:

Souphanouvong [in 1946] did not view things the way we did. He was strongly influenced by his Viet Minh friends. Little by little he came completely under their thumb.[24]

Since Souphanouvong's world view, as reflected in his words
and actions at that time, was close to that of the Viet Minh, cooperation with the Vietnamese Communists would not have appeared to him a betrayal of the cause of Lao independence. But if
he threw in his lot with them and came increasingly under their
influence, it may well have been more for pragmatic political reasons than from ideological motives. We know from eyewitness accounts how strong were the Prince's vanity and his urge to excel
and lead. As the youngest brother of the famous Prince Phetsarath and the junior of another able brother, Souvanna Phouma,
he could not, by reason of age and lineage, expect easily to assume
the leading position, especially because his rival brothers had the
backing of the Thai authorities. Only Vietnamese assistance
could provide the politically ambitious Souphanouvong with the
necessary leverage to propel himself to the top leadership of a
Laos independent of France.

To judge by the Prince's own statements during this early period, he viewed Vietnamese assistance as indispensable to his
quest for power in Laos, but was confident at the same time that
he could prevent the Vietnamese from gaining undue influence.
Available documents[25] suggest that the Prince never believed that
Laos alone could achieve independence from France; rather, like
Ho Chi Minh, he subscribed to the notion that the three peoples
of Indochina had to struggle toward that goal in close concert. For
a backward and weak country such as Laos the only hope of modernizing its political and social institutions lay in a strong alliance
with the Vietnamese revolutionaries.

By early 1945, Souphanouvong must have become well acquainted with the Vietnamese independence movement, as he
moved around Vietnam in connection with his engineering
work.[26] His anti-French future wife may have been the first to in-
troduce him to members of the Viet Minh.[27] At any rate, we know
that Souphanouvong made official contact with the Viet Minh at
the time of the Japanese capitulation, in the summer of 1945.

By then, Ho Chi Minh was on his way to Cao Bang in northern
Vietnam (Tonkin), and on August 16 he established the People's

National Liberation Committee, which was to lead the revolution and proclaim the Democratic Republic of Vietnam. Prince Souphanouvong, in the central Vietnamese town of Vinh at the time, apparently was sufficiently moved by these events to ask for an audience with Ho, who encouraged the Prince to launch an independence movement in his native Laos and pledged Viet Minh support.[28] According to the Australian Communist Wilfred G. Burchett, Ho Chi Minh on that occasion exhorted the young Lao visitor to "oust the foreign imperialists."

As a result, Prince Souphanouvong set out for Laos in the fall of 1945, under the protection of guards and guns provided by the Viet Minh, to help advance the independence movement just then getting under way in Vientiane. As he crossed into Laos, he picked up local support, especially among the tribal people, and then descended toward the Mekong River towns, where the Japanese capitulation had created something of a political no-man's-land. In Savannakhet and Thakhek, towns inhabited mainly by Vietnamese, the Prince helped to establish "national liberation committees" on the pattern of those set up by the Viet Minh in Vietnam. Reportedly, Kaysone had already preceded the Prince to his home town of Savannakhet to make contact with Vietnamese residents and Lao nationalist circles there, and it is likely that he played at least as great a role as the Prince in creating the liberation committees. Souphanouvong then continued toward Vientiane to join forces with the new Lao Issara nationalist government, which had been established there a month earlier. He arrived in the capital some time in November, still accompanied by his Vietnamese bodyguards.

Souphanouvong probably had only the vaguest idea of what his next step would be, but he clearly wanted to play a leading part in his country's liberation from French rule. Returning to Laos after all these years, however, he was bound to seem a stranger to his own people and, worse yet, a stranger moving under the escort of armed Vietnamese. After several clashes between his group and Lao activists, Vientiane proved too small to accommodate both Souphanouvong's ambitions and those of his rivals for power. He therefore returned to Savannakhet and then to Thakhek, where he soon created for himself a power base within the Lao community and among the large Vietnamese population sympathetic to the Viet Minh.

Partly in recognition of his ability and perhaps even more as a concession to his brother Prince Phetsarath, who was the real authority behind the Lao Issara government, Souphanouvong was designated Foreign Minister and later also Minister of Defense and Commander-in-Chief of the Issara forces. None of these posts meant much in practice, because the total armed might of the new government probably did not exceed a few hundred men, and they followed their local leaders rather than any so-called Commander-in-Chief. Nevertheless, for a few weeks at least, Souphanouvong exercised control over the Thakhek-Savannakhet area of central Laos.

The re-entry of the French into Laos destroyed, for the time being, any hope that the Prince or the Lao Issara movement might have entertained of creating an independent Laos. In January and February 1946, French forces returned to the northern part of the country; by March, after securing an accord with Ho Chi Minh, they were approaching the Mekong towns of central Laos. Prince Souphanouvong had to fight or flee. He preferred to stand and fight at Thakhek, but his forces were no match for the French, and he suffered a decisive defeat.

In the face of the French reconquest of Laos, the Lao Issara government fled to Thailand. Most of its members remained in exile until the fall of 1949, when a compromise between the French and the moderate Lao nationalists made possible their return. During those three years, the Lao Issara government in Bangkok, grouped around Prince Phetsarath, had little influence on the course of events in Laos. Its financial resources were extremely limited, and the Lao "liberation forces" consisted of small guerrilla bands operating outside the control of the "central" government-in-exile in Bangkok.

Though it is not always possible to pinpoint the movements of Prince Souphanouvong during these years, we know that he spent much time close to the periphery of Laos and some time inside, seeking to organize guerrilla forces against the French. While most of his associates, including his brothers Phetsarath and Souvanna, were satisfied with the life of political refugees in Bangkok, Souphanouvong emerged as the activist of the group, to such a degree that some of his compatriots saw in him "un-Lao" character traits that reminded them of the Vietnamese.[29] Seldom even paying lip service to the authority of his brother Prince Phetsarath, he behaved like an independent leader rather than a member of a coalition government. Arrogant and strong-willed, he frequently displayed contempt for his Lao associates.

Souphanouvong's position was in many ways stronger than that of any of his rivals in Bangkok. By September 1946, all of Laos had reverted to French control. External support for the Lao independence movement was therefore crucial to its survival. The remaining small guerrilla units were poorly armed, poorly led, and badly in need of training and financial support. Between 1946 and 1949, the Viet Minh provided the major share of external support for anti-French activity in Laos, thus playing a critical role in sustaining the revolutionary momentum. Souphanouvong served them as a useful intermediary.

The Prince might have sought to enlist Thai rather than Vietnamese support for his claim to leadership over the Lao Issara.[30] During World War II, the Thai had indeed given some assistance to the Lao nationalists. But Souphanouvong's Vietnamese associations and leftist leanings (even if he was not the revolutionary ideologue that many proclaimed him to be) may have been sufficiently incriminating to make the Thai hesitate to strengthen him rather than the conservative elements of the Issara government, to which they were already giving limited assistance. And if suspicions of the Prince's ties to the Viet Minh were not the overriding factor in the Thai leaders' calculations, practical political considerations probably would have inclined them to continue giving their support to Phetsarath rather than to the young Souphanouvong, whose chances of assuming control of the Lao movement for independence from France, Thailand's archenemy, must have appeared to them very slim.

Practical as well as political considerations thus pointed toward the Viet Minh as the Prince's most plausible source of support. Their policy toward Laos and the Lao independence movement did not openly conflict with the cause of Lao nationalism, and they carefully avoided creating antagonism among Lao leaders who like Souphanouvong were inclined to throw in their lot with the Viet Minh. Acknowledging Prince Souphanouvong as the titular head of the Lao independence movement, the Viet Minh under his prestigious name actively organized Lao resistance groups throughout much of the Laos-Vietnam border region. Within the limits of their own meager resources they supplied their Lao allies with weapons and money.[31] Even Lao Issara leaders in Thailand had to admit that much of the financial support for their movement came from the Viet Minh representative in Bangkok, though most of it was channeled directly to Souphanouvong.

The Revolutionaries in Eastern Laos

Communist accounts of the Lao revolutionary movement place much emphasis on the person and activities of Prince Souphanouvong. There can be no doubt about the Prince's intelligence and ambition, his vigor and colorful personality. Yet it is doubtful whether Souphanouvong's importance in the development of the Lao revolutionary movement was ever as great as Communist propaganda would have it — or as the Prince, who is known for his vanity, believes himself.

Part of Souphanouvong's fame no doubt stems from his aristocratic family background and his, by Lao standards, superior educational and professional training. Nevertheless, the Prince was little known in his own country until late 1945, when Phetsarath, then Laos' leading statesman, made him both a cabinet minister and Commander-in-Chief, the posts in which he rose to prominence. Reports on subsequent developments in Laos naturally drew heavily on news emanating from Phetsarath's government-in-exile in Bangkok. What the outside world knew about the independence movement in Laos, therefore, tended to concentrate on the more accessible regions along the country's western frontier, where the Lao Issara forces, nominally at least under Souphanouvong, were operating during the mid-1940s. One cannot escape the impression that very early the Vietnamese Communists singled out Souphanouvong as the Lao who combined the qualities they considered desirable in a public representative of a Communist-sponsored movement that wished to mask its true complexion.

It is understandable, therefore, that accounts of the early years of the revolutionary movement often give more attention to Souphanouvong's role than it may deserve. Indeed, any documented history of that period runs the risk of overstating the significance of events in the western part of the country. The other side to the story of the Lao revolution, which was centered in the east, probably will never be fully documented. Actually, however, it was more important for the development of the Lao Communist movement than were the activities of Souphanouvong. The rather shadowy figures in the border regions of Laos and Vietnam — Kaysone, Nouhak, certain Vietnamese whose backgrounds and careers remain obscure, and still others — played a central role in shaping the course of events. Our interviews with several Lao revolutionaries who worked with these men enable us to summarize the pertinent developments in eastern Laos and the Vietnamese part in them, though it is still impossible to reconstruct from this evidence the full and chronologically accurate story of events.

In the sparsely populated border regions of Laos and Vietnam, the political situation was extremely confused. A prominent native of Tchepone, whose account is confirmed by other sources, told us that between the end of World War II and 1949, when the Lao Issara movement broke up, numerous small anti-French resistance groups operated in this area.[32] Some of them were in close contact with the Lao Issara government-in-exile in Bangkok; others were only nominally loyal to it; and still others — especially those led by tribal chiefs — operated independently. What they all had in common was their dependence on Viet Minh support. In some cases this assistance took the form of rice, money, arms, and ammunition. In others, Vietnamese advisers attached themselves to the Lao or tribal groups. And at times, the Vietnamese provided military protection for the small bands of Lao conducting ambushes or armed propaganda against the French.

One Lao leader of a resistance unit told us that he met with Ho Chi Minh in Hanoi in 1946 and that Kaysone and Nouhak, already closely associated with the Viet Minh, were present at this meeting, at which he was encouraged to step up his anti-French activities. In the summer of 1946, a Resistance Committee of Eastern Laos came into being under the sponsorship of the Viet Minh, and among its members were several who later became leaders of the Pathet Lao movement. It is from this committee that the small Viet Minh-supported resistance units grew gradually, between 1946 and 1949, especially in the areas near Vietnam. This process was going on quietly in eastern Laos while Souphanouvong, in a more dramatic fashion, was challenging his colleagues in Bangkok.

The Split in the Lao Issara and the Vietnamese Issue

During 1947 and 1948, the Prince visited Vietnam at least once (and probably several times) for talks with Viet Minh leaders. What exactly was agreed on is not known, but Viet Minh support increasingly came to bypass the Lao Issara government-in-exile and to be channeled directly to Souphanouvong and to the small Lao partisan groups that had for some time been operating under Viet Minh guidance along the Lao-Vietnamese border.

Events in 1949 produced the political division in Laos that has continued to this day. French policy having developed to the point where it allowed the Lao a measure of autonomy, the French-sponsored Lao government in Vientiane entered into communication with the nationalist exiles in Bangkok and invited them to participate in the administration of the country. Most Lao nationalists responded favorably and later that year returned home. A notable exception was Prince Souphanouvong, who — taking his cue from his Vietnamese allies — resisted the trend toward accommodation with the French.

According to Vietnamese sources (corroborated by interviews with former members of Souphanouvong's movement), the Lao "liberation forces" — nominally under the Prince's direction but in fact under a variety of leaders who for material and tactical support were dependent on the Vietnamese Communists — had since late 1947 been shifting gradually from western to eastern Laos, that is to say, away from Thailand and closer to Vietnam.[33] Between the end of 1948 and early 1949, they had set up the "military zones" of Southeast and Northeast Laos (primarily Sam Neua province). Here they began to launch armed propaganda activities with the aim of establishing "people's power bases." [34] On January 20, 1949,[35] Souphanouvong made the final break within the Lao nationalist camp by proclaiming the establishment of Lao Issara forces responsible only to him and not to the Bangkok government-in-exile. He had been having increasingly acrimonious exchanges with his erstwhile associates in Bangkok, who were already quietly preparing to return home.

Souphanouvong's letter of March 26, 1949, officially declared an end to his participation in the national coalition. This document,[36] an official copy of which we discovered in a private collection in Laos, clarifies the differences which had come to separate the partners in the Lao independence movement. Souphanouvong lashes out at what he considers the traditional weaknesses of the Lao people — no doubt contrasting these in his own mind with the dynamic leadership qualities he found among the Vietnamese Communists:

The patriot who consciously sacrifices himself for the sake of national liberation is sure to encounter at the end one of these three things: death, prison (and exile), or victory. If you wish only for a riskless victory, then you have embarked on a "gondola of dreams." Then you had better leave the political arena which demands men of action and of self-denial. As for me, I decided at the age of thirteen to rid myself, whatever the cost . . . of this inclination toward letting things drift, . . . of indolence, of this "resting on big words," all so characteristic of our country and of declining races destined to serve as sheep to the hungry wolves.

The Prince sees a clear connection between the regeneration that he urges upon Lao people and government on one hand, and his country's ability to obtain and preserve national independence on the other:

As long as the Lao will not rid themselves of their disastrous inclination to make the least effort [he insists], they will forever be destined to occupy only the lowly position of the coolie, will never enjoy freedom on their own soil, and hence will never achieve national independence.

Souphanouvong rejects the government's concern over his decision to recruit tribal mercenaries, for which he is quite willing to accept full responsibility.[37] He tells his colleagues in Bangkok that they are lacking in "political suppleness," without which any government will end up resembling one of "children or old ladies who repeat endlessly the same rigid principles." He also makes it very clear that he does not see the international situation as do his colleagues in Bangkok. Speaking of the need to 'fight the "French colonialists, docile instruments of the Anglo-Americans," he explains that he does not share Bangkok's apprehension that the French might come to terms with the Vietnamese and Chinese Communists if the Lao Issara should remain stubbornly in opposition. (Significantly, it was over this issue, the role of the Vietnamese, that his major disagreements with the Lao Issara government-in-exile developed.)

The Prince accuses his colleagues of always having suspected him of having sold out his country to Ho Chi Minh's Vietnam. He points out that in the face of French pressure Vietnamese aid had been the only way in which a Lao liberation front could be maintained in the eastern part of the country and that he, Sou-phanouvong, had been instrumental in obtaining this vital assistance. Long before the battle of Thakhek against the French (that is, before March 1946), he had sent his envoy to Ho Chi Minh with a request for the "loan of a million" (presumably, piastres). These Vietnamese funds enabled the Lao resistance movement to operate in Sam Neua, Xieng Khouang, and other provinces of eastern Laos and to help Sithon Khommadam and Khamtay Si-phandone[38] organize resistance against the French in the Sara-vane-Attopeu region of southern Laos. No doubt playing up his own role, for the two men were prominent in their own right and had contacts of their own with the Vietnamese, Souphanouvong calls attention to the fact that the weapons in the hands of these forces are the product of his personal initiative with the Viet Minh.

Souphanouvong singles out the lesson implicit in the experience of the Vietnamese resistance movement:

Our weapons — because weapons, and effective ones at that, are necessary, and so is ammunition, which must be constantly renewed or manufactured — must protect our propaganda, ensure the security of our political leaders and buttress our diplomatic action.

And then he asks rhetorically:

But from where, Your Ministerial Excellencies, do we take these indispensable weapons?

All weapons in their possession have come from the Vietnamese, and to place hope in the vague promises of others seems hardly realistic. Nor is there reason to count on a friendly gesture on the part of the "colonialist hangmen."

Moreover, he points out, it is utterly unrealistic to think of the possibility of obtaining aid from a foreign country, party, or political organization "without serious and duly guaranteed counter-value. You must understand that it is only the Buddha and the true Lao patriots who love and will continue to love the Lao fatherland selflessly (and for its own sake)." Did the Prince consciously pay a political price for the Viet Minh loans, and, if so, what was that price? Neither he nor the available documents tell.

Souphanouvong concludes his long and impassioned letter with the statement that his dignity and political integrity would be injured were he to participate further in the Lao Issara government and that he therefore finds himself compelled to submit his resignation as of the date of the document, March 26, 1949.[39]

A subsequent exchange of letters between the government and the Prince brought to light other, significant points.[40] Katay Sasorith, writing on behalf of the Lao Issara government, states that Souphanouvong had quite consistently acted like an autocrat, seeking to create for himself a power base among his military forces by systematically eliminating from them all former (French-trained) career and noncommissioned officers. Although asked several times to relinquish his position of Commander-in-Chief of the Lao Issara forces, he had not complied with the order and in general had refused to keep the government apprised of his actions and transactions. This applied especially to Souphanouvong's relationship with the Vietnamese, said Katay, and he proposed that "we give the Prince Souphanouvong the opportunity to disengage himself correctly from the Vietnamese on the day when we will be obliged to conclude a compromise with the French."

Katay asserted that Souphanouvong had entered into agreements with Ho Chi Minh and his representatives but had refused to inform the government of the contents of these agreements. "We don't even know to this day," he wrote, "to what point we are under an obligation to the Vietnamese or what obligations we have incurred toward them." Katay's suspicions about the Prince's dealings with the Vietnamese were obviously reinforced by what he called Souphanouvong's "most delicate personal position due to his wife, who actively and openly meddles in political matters . . . the compromising situation resulting from the nationality of origin and political attitude of his wife." Katay added that the prestige of the Lao Issara was not being helped by the fact that the Prince had dispatched into Laos guerrilla forces which were more Vietnamese than Lao, if not entirely Vietnamese, and that he had gone so far as to employ a Cambodian among his unit commanders and also a Lao-Vietnamese métis by the name of Boun Kong, who earlier had been in charge of a Vietnamese unit.

During May 1949 one more round of bitter exchanges centering around the Vietnamese issue took place between Souphanouvong and the spokesman for the government-in-exile in Bangkok. The Prince's views were stated very clearly in his letter of May 13. In it, he pointed out that the members of the Lao Issara government who were now opposing him had distinguished themselves and proved their resistance spirit principally by serving with honor under the French colonial regime — the very regime that the Lao Issara was supposed to be fighting. How could he, the Prince, have confidence in such men? While reiterating his patriotism as a Lao, he suggested that perhaps his own stature was best proved by his fame abroad rather than by his being, like his opponents, "illustrious only within a small enslaved and backward country like Laos." Then, turning to what he termed the "thorny question of Vietnamese financial aid," he refused to explain further his dealings with Ho Chi Minh, since his opponents, "anti-Vietnamese by principle or prejudice," would at any rate never understand them. In strong language he added:

As to the various conventions and agreements entered into with the Ho Chi Minh government, they cannot be placed on the agenda until the day when there will exist a Lao Issara government worthy of that name "Free Laos," that is, a government which has the support of a strong majority of the Lao population engaged in the resistance movement and made up of politicians of some stature. Ho Chi Minh will never talk with bluffers or pseudo-resistance fighters. He would use those simply as instruments of his Indochinese policy or [to advance the cause] of Vietnamese victory.

He went on to argue that, while it was all very well to demand that the Lao resistance forces be made up only of Lao elements, it was first necessary to have such indigenous forces and to have arms. Without them "there is no solution but to resort to a core of foreign support" around which indigenous military strength can be developed.

It is logical to assume that the Prince had thrown in his lot with the Viet Minh convinced that their support was essential, could bring his country independence from the French, and give him the leadership of a free Laos. He did not seem altogether unaware of the strength and the intense ambitions of the Vietnamese Communists — ambitions that might well extend to Laos — but appeared confident of his ability to handle his allies once he had gained uncontested leadership and mass support. Or perhaps he merely had concluded that cooperation with the Vietnamese, particularly under a leader who, like himself, was sympathetic to their goals and strategy, was the only way for weak and backward Laos to survive as a more or less independent political entity, surrounded as it was by stronger and more dynamic neighbors.

This last exchange marked the final parting of the ways of the two schools of thought within the Lao Issara movement. On May 16, 1949, the government officially removed Souphanouvong from his posts. Looking back on events in the spring of 1949, Prince Souvanna Phouma has said:

Dissension had reached such a point that our government tired of the servitude [to the Viet Minh] accepted by Souphanouvong and expelled him in May 1949. His fate from this time on was sealed and he became the creature of the North Vietnamese.[41]

On July 19, 1949, France and Laos signed an agreement providing for the continued membership of Laos in the French Union and giving the Lao limited autonomy. On October 25 the Lao Issara government disbanded, and most of its members (but not Prince Phetsarath) returned to political life in Laos.

Souphanouvong, after his falling out with these former associates, set out with a few followers on a trek to eastern Laos. There he found a Lao "resistance movement" which was sponsored and controlled by the Viet Minh and, at the urging of the Viet Minh, merged his faction with the anti-French resistance groups already operating in eastern Laos. He was allowed to become the titular leader of the coalition, but much power, not surprisingly, remained in the hands of Kaysone and Nouhak, who, thanks to their closer association with the Viet Minh, commanded a stronger power base than the ambitious Prince.

IV

The Drive for Independence:
The Viet Minh and the Pathet Lao,
1949–1954

When the Lao Issara leaders returned from Thailand to Vientiane in 1949, Souphanouvong's dissident faction was clearly a minority within the relatively weak Lao nationalist movement. Lao nationalism was not a potent force, and neither the Lao Issara nor its opponents had succeeded in mobilizing mass support. Yet the new Vientiane government in which the returning Lao Issara exiles participated had some nationalist appeal and could in addition draw upon the traditional claims to obedience that the ruling elite enjoyed within lowland Lao society.

Neither of the contending parties could lay claim to the allegiance of the diverse but important ethnic minorities, whose political orientation was determined by each group's chieftain. It was he to whom and through whom the appeal for allegiance had to be made. Once his support had been won, his group would ordinarily accept his choice. Sithon Khommadam was one such leader whom the Vietnamese Communists apparently identified as a key figure. The son of a Lao Theung nationalist chieftain who had won fame for leading a bitter struggle against the French during the first decade of this century, Sithon enjoyed considerable prestige among the numerous Lao Theung peoples of southern Laos. As he was won over by the Viet Minh, he brought with him substantial tribal support. The Vietnamese were less successful with the Meo in the northern mountain regions (who tended to side with the Vientiane government), but they did enlist one prominent Meo, Faydang (Phaydang), who commanded the loyalty of a minority segment of the Meo population. However, his alliance with the Communists was probably more a reflection of internal feuds among the Meo tribes than the result of ideological conviction.

Not only was Souphanouvong's popular base a small one, but in 1949 he commanded a weak organization, few arms, and little money. It is not surprising, therefore, that when he split with the Lao Issara he felt compelled to shift his operations to the eastern regions of Laos along the borders of Vietnam, there to join other Lao revolutionaries who were already heavily dependent on Viet Minh guidance and support. The Viet Minh organization at that time was itself struggling to expand, having been engaged in a bitter war with the French ever since 1946. Compared to the Lao resistance groups, the Viet Minh was a powerful movement; it had already developed a cohesive corps of leaders, a revolutionary ideology, and an impressive organizational structure, and it enjoyed widespread support among the peasantry. The small rebel faction challenging the legitimacy of the new government of Laos was forced to rely heavily on the Vietnamese for political and military guidance, security, arms and ammunition, food, and money.

The Lao resistance leaders at this stage can be divided into two broad categories: those who, like Prince Souphanouvong and Prince Souk Vongsak, for reasons of birth and education had a claim to status and positions of influence within the Lao society; and others who, like Kaysone and Nouhak, lacked those prerogatives and could attain power only through Vietnamese support. The first group may have had an alternative way of fulfilling its political ambitions, but for a number of reasons chose to align itself with the Viet Minh rather than accept continuing French tutelage. The second, having no choice, developed a close alliance with the Vietnamese Communists and used it to maximum advantage in advancing its aspirations for power in Laos. Not surprisingly, the first group had initially been part of the Lao Issara movement centered in Thailand, whereas the second group from the beginning had built its power base in eastern Laos in a symbiotic relationship with the Vietnamese Communists.

The loyalists who returned to Vientiane have never ceased to criticize Souphanouvong and his associates for throwing in their lot with the Vietnamese, historic enemies who in the long run seemed to them a greater threat to Lao independence than the French.[1] But to the Pathet Lao leaders, continued French influence was the greater danger, and they believed that Lao and Vietnamese interests coincided in the desire to expel France from Indochina. A Lao nationalist who viewed this as the foremost goal for his country had no option but to accept Vietnamese support. (The United States — which Souphanouvong had approached for help — despite its professed anticolonialism was disinclined to exert its power to force out the French. Indeed, after the start of the Korean War in 1950, American material support to the French war effort in Indochina mounted substantially.) The resulting cleavage between those Lao who chose to align themselves with the Vietnamese and those who returned home to semiautonomy under France has remained to this day the basic political division of Laos. As for the Viet Minh, their involvement in developing a Lao Communist movement in southern Laos enhanced their stake in the country and provided a cover under which they could intervene in Laos at will.

There is no doubt that the primary purpose of the Viet Minh was to win independence for Vietnam, after which they would tackle the transformation of the country's economic, social, and political order. Whatever contribution, small though it might be, the Lao could make in weakening the French would serve that purpose. It was in the Viet Minh's interest, therefore, to help build a Lao organization that would cooperate with them in the struggle. Viet Minh leaders may also have been thinking of a future in which Laos would be firmly linked to Vietnam.

At the time that the Pathet Lao, having broken with the Lao Issara, drew closer to the Viet Minh, prospects for the latter's suc-

cess in the war against the French were turning brighter as the result of the consolidation of Communist power in China and the
arrival in 1949 of Chinese Communist troops on the northern
frontiers of Indochina. The victory of a powerful ally who shared
the same ideology and the expectation that Chinese supplies
would be forthcoming raised the morale of the Viet Minh. By the
same token France's anxieties increased with the presence of a
hostile power on the border of its colony. Though the worst
French fears of direct intervention by Chinese troops were not
realized, Chinese supplies indeed began to flow to the Viet Minh
in 1950 and rose to the level of an estimated 4,000 tons per month
by the end of the war.[2] With this assistance the Viet Minh were
soon able to give substantial support to their Lao allies.

Pathet Lao Growth and
Viet Minh Support, 1950–1954

Following the dissolution of the Lao Issara in October 1949,
Souphanouvong journeyed to meet Ho Chi Minh at the Viet
Minh headquarters at Tuyen Quang, North Vietnam, and negotiate for Vietnamese support. The Viet Minh had long envisaged
bringing the disparate Lao resistance groups into a single political
front which with Vietnamese backing could challenge the Vientiane government for political power over Laos. Not long after the
meeting with Ho, Souphanouvong launched an appeal to all militant Lao elements to convene at a First Resistance Congress. And
in the summer of 1950 they met, their 105 representatives[3] including Faydang, Sithon Khommadam, Kaysone, Nouhak, and
Phoumi Vongvichit. (Most of the participants in the 1950 congress now play leading roles in the Lao Communist movement.)
Following this meeting, an announcement was made on August
15, 1950, that the traditional name for the Lao independence
movement, Lao Issara, had been dropped in favor of a new label,
Neo Lao Issara (Free Laos Front).[4] The new political organization, modeled on the Viet Minh Patriotic Front, was headed by
Prince Souphanouvong, who was also a member of its Central

Committee.[5] In addition, the congress announced a new "resistance government," with Souphanouvong as Premier and Phoumi Vongvichit as Deputy Prime Minister and Minister for Internal Affairs. Kaysone and Nouhak held the levers of power — the ministries of Defense and of Finance respectively — and Prince Souk Vongsak was Minister of Education. Sithon Khommadam and Faydang, serving as Ministers without Portfolio, represented for the first time in any Lao government the two great tribal minority groups of Laos, the Kha and the Meo.[6] According to a former PL official (A-14) who attended this congress, two important Vietnamese advisers, Hung and Chanh, actively guided the Lao leaders at the meetings as the new resistance government proclaimed its internal and external policy.[7]

In February 1951, a national congress in the DRV announced the founding of a specifically Vietnamese Communist party to be known as the Lao Dong (Workers) Party. This national party was proclaimed to replace the Indochinese Communist Party (ICP) founded in 1930, which had been "officially" dissolved in 1945 with the arrival of Chinese Nationalist troops in Vietnam, although, in Ho Chi Minh's words, "in reality it went underground." [8] The fact that a number of Cambodian and Lao leaders attended the 1951 congress in Vietnam adds significance to the passage in the official manifesto regarding Vietnam's relationship to its brother countries in Indochina:

The people of Vietnam must unite closely with the peoples of the Pathet Lao and Khmer country and give their every assistance in the common struggle against imperialist aggression, for the complete liberation of Indochina, and for the defense of world peace.

In the common interests of the three peoples, the people of Vietnam are willing to enter into long-term cooperation with the peoples of Laos and Cambodia with a view to bringing about an independent, free, strong, and prosperous federation of the states of Vietnam, Laos, and Cambodia if the three peoples so desire.[9]

Immediately following this Lao Dong Party congress, and perhaps at the very same location, the Viet Minh convoked a meet-

ing of Vietnamese, Lao, and Cambodian leaders, including Ton
Duc Thang (now, after Ho Chi Minh's death, President of the
DRV), Sieu Heng (head of the Khmer Liberation Committee),
and Souphanouvong. On this occasion they announced the creation of a Vietnamese-Khmer-Lao alliance committed to struggling jointly against both French colonial power and the "American interventionists." According to Burchett, this "alliance of the
Pathet Lao with the Viet Minh paved the way for Vietnamese
volunteers. They were strongly reinforced by Vietnamese already
living in the country." [10]

The Viet Minh were important in helping the Lao revolutionary leadership mobilize a modest military force.[11] While the Vietnamese insurgents welcomed any military effort that contributed
to making trouble for the French, the Lao troops were never a significant factor in the Viet Minh's ultimate success. (Estimates of
their troop strength ranged from 1500 to 3000 troops at the time
of the 1954 Geneva Conference.) Most of the Lao units, supplied
by the Viet Minh with rice, arms, and money, were used merely
for support activities. In those few cases where the Lao did operate independently of the Viet Minh, they proved much less vigorous in pursuit of the enemy than did their Vietnamese allies.

One former Lao commander (A-24) of such a Lao unit told us
of the accommodation which his officers had worked out with
their compatriots in the Royal Lao Government (RLG) forces,
then still under the control of the French: "We agreed that as
long as we didn't meet any French, if Lao met Lao, we would not
do anything." Relations were so relaxed that the children of PL
and RLG officers played together. As our informant explained, it
was not a severe war for the troops, since they seldom encountered
any French.

The case of one of our interviewees (A-18) illustrates the Viet
Minh's role in training and employing Lao units prior to the Geneva Conference of 1954. Recruited from his father's opium business in Vientiane in 1945, he was sent with twenty-four other Lao
to North Vietnam for a month's training by Vietnamese who
spoke Lao and was then assigned to northern Laos. There he be-

came the leader of the twenty-five Lao recruits, who were attached to a Viet Minh battalion to serve mainly as guides, interpreters, and propagandists. When the battalion approached a village, his unit would be sent as an advance party, usually to engage in propaganda among the local people.

We Lao knew the local habits and customs. The Viet Minh didn't and, therefore, feared incidents if they had direct contact with the population.

When this Viet Minh battalion was pushed back into North Vietnam by the French two years later, he and about thirty others (twenty ethnic Lao and ten Lao Theung) were given further training by the Viet Minh and then assigned to a unit of some two hundred Vietnamese operating in Sam Neua Province. This time the task of the Lao was not only to conduct propaganda but to engage in guerrilla tactics. As our informant explained,

We could reach the Meo and the Lao Theung in the mountains, where the French didn't go. We set ambushes against the French near the Na Ma River. The Meo and Lao Theung lacked salt — we brought it. They lacked needles and buttons and things like that. We brought these too.

In describing his relationship with the Viet Minh, the interviewee made it clear that the Lao functioned as ancillary elements of the Viet Minh military. Significantly, his description did not reveal resentment at this subordinate role, but rather left the impression that the Lao then looked upon the Viet Minh as mentors whom they respected because they were strong and competent. He pointed out that the Viet Minh, recognizing the Lao sensitivities, sought to promote the myth that Lao and Vietnamese units were fighting alongside each other. For example, his own unit was given arms by the Viet Minh prior to entering a village as a way of demonstrating to the population that the Lao revolutionary movement possessed some military strength independent of the Vietnamese.

The Viet Minh's decisive contribution to the Pathet Lao's claim to power at the Geneva Conference of 1954 was the situation created in Laos by the major military offensive of 1953/1954 in which the Viet Minh plunged through northeastern, central, and southern Laos. This campaign "liberated" the Lao provinces of Phong Saly and Sam Neua as well as other areas on the frontier of Vietnam. Partly to honor the French treaty commitment to defend Laos and partly because General Henri-Eugène Navarre, the French Commander-in-Chief in Vietnam, thought he could trick the Viet Minh who were overrunning Laos into attacking an invulnerable fort, the French blundered by concentrating a powerful force at Dien Bien Phu, near the border of northern Laos. The disaster inflicted by the Viet Minh on the French forces there is well known. At the Geneva Conference, which opened with the French defeat at Dien Bien Phu, the Viet Minh, in an attempt to further Pathet Lao interests, claimed that the 1953 offensive against the French in eastern Laos had been unleashed by Lao forces with only limited support from the Viet Minh. Our interviews clearly show that the reverse was true: The Viet Minh provided the bulk of the troops and were assisted by a small number of Lao guerrillas. After the elimination of the French outposts, the Lao "resistance government," still under close Vietnamese guidance, was transferred from Vietnam to Lao soil in Sam Neua.

Although we have no doubt about the fact that the Vietnamese Communists played a critical role in the development of the Pathet Lao movement from 1950 to 1954, there are gaps in our knowledge of the methods they used in working with the Lao. Even today, little is known about the decision-making process of Lao Communist leaders in the early years, and even less about their Vietnamese advisers. Though we succeeded in identifying some of the advisers, it was more difficult to obtain biographical details or to uncover information about their personal relationships with the principal Lao figures. Nor was it easy to learn what role Vietnamese residents of Laos played in the Lao Communist movement.

An indication of the extent to which some Vietnamese became

involved in the Lao nationalist struggle at an early date is contained in the account of a one-time chief of the Viet Minh security unit, Tran Van Dinh. He had been assigned by Ho Chi Minh to accompany Prince Souphanouvong back to Laos in September 1945 to help him build an independence movement. Dinh, who described himself as Chief of Staff of the Viet Minh forces in Laos in 1945, claimed that, in addition to recruiting Lao to serve as partisans with Souphanouvong, he and his Vietnamese officers were using the Prince as a front while they recruited Vietnamese residents of Laos and Thailand for the insurgent movement.[12] The Royal Lao Government, suspecting the Vietnamese residents of Laos of collaborating with Viet Minh and Pathet Lao organizations, expressed those suspicions at the Geneva Conference of 1954.

The Geneva Conference of 1954 [13]

When the Geneva Conference met in May 1954, the absorbing concern of the delegates was to produce a settlement of the conflict between the French and the Viet Minh. The future of Laos was treated as a secondary issue. Of the Pathet Lao's Communist allies, the USSR and China were obviously the dominant powers at the Conference. Communist China's immediate aim in regard to Laos was to eliminate the presence and influence of the Western powers from its southern flank. The Soviet Union had little direct interest in Laos at the time and supported the demands of its Chinese and Vietnamese Communist colleagues within the context of its world power position, particularly its goals in Europe. The DRV's primary interest was in obtaining as favorable a solution as possible in Vietnam, and the decisions about Laos were important to its security. DRV spokesmen wanted the French troops withdrawn not only from Vietnam but from all of Indochina, and they sought guarantees that other foreign troops — particularly American — could not be introduced in the future. Like Communist China to the north, the DRV also wanted the provinces of Laos adjoining its own borders to be under the control of the Lao faction friendly to the DRV. It is even possible (though it can be neither proved nor disproved) that the DRV had aspirations to replace the French as the dominant power in all of Indochina.

In keeping with its active role in Laos, the DRV acted as the principal advocate for the Pathet Lao at the Geneva Conference and advanced bold claims on their behalf. The DRV delegation included the Lao Communist leader Nouhak Phomsavan, who reportedly was traveling on a Vietnamese passport.[14] In the course of the bargaining, however, the DRV proved willing to modify its demands with respect to Laos in return for concessions in Vietnam.

As regards the Pathet Lao leaders at the Geneva Conference, it is difficult to get an accurate sense of their expectations. (Since they were not officially represented, there is no public record on the bargaining, and their private views can only be surmised.) They must have realized that the advantages they could derive from the negotiations depended less upon their own feeble assets than upon the vigor of their diplomatic sponsors. The goals of the Royal Lao Government, which was represented at the Conference, are clear. They included withdrawal of the Viet Minh "invaders," an end to Viet Minh military support of the "rebel" groups so that the Royal Government might establish control throughout the country, and an international guarantee of the territorial integrity and sovereignty of Laos.

The first issue debated at Geneva was the demand of all three Communist powers for representation at the Conference of the "Pathet Lao resistance government" as well as the Cambodian "Khmer resistance government." With the support of Molotov, speaking for the USSR, and Chou En-lai, representing the Chinese Communists, chief DRV delegate Pham Van Dong claimed that "the resistance government of Pathet Lao" had liberated half the country and that in the "liberated areas" it had "carried out democratic reforms and all the measures necessary to raise the people's standard of living." [15] He further contended that the Lao and Cambodian resistance governments "enjoy the support and warm affection of the population in liberated areas, and they enjoy great prestige and influence among the population of both countries. These governments represent the great majority of the people of Khmer and Lao, the aspirations of whom they symbolize." [16] The French delegate, in reply, labeled these governments "phantoms." And the chief RLG delegate, Phoui Sananikone, vigorously disputed the DRV claims, pointing out that there were no more than 125 Lao with the Viet Minh before the Vietnamese aggression in the spring of 1953.[17] He said that "the government and people of Laos learned with great surprise of this so-called government of Pathet Lao under the leadership of Prince Souphanouvong . . . This so-called Pathet Lao represents absolutely nothing." [18] For the Royal Government, "there is no civil war in Laos; rather, there has been a characterized [sic] foreign invasion . . . these foreigners who are foreigners to Laos by race, by ideology and by tradition, apply their efforts to establish in the future conditions which would be propitious to a civil war." [19]

The Western powers supported the Royal Government in rejecting Pathet Lao representation, pointing out that the Berlin Conference, which had established the terms of reference for Geneva, had called for attendance only of interested "states"; in the words of the American delegate, the "nonexistent so-called government of the Pathet Lao" had not been recognized even by its Communist sponsors. The Communist nations· finally gave up their claim, but not until mid-June, having meanwhile exacted from their adversaries a number of compromises in regard to Vietnam. The decision not to seat the representatives of the Pathet Lao at the Geneva Conference seems to have sprung from a realistic appraisal of the Pathet Lao's weak claim to legitimacy as a government. Nevertheless, since the Pathet Lao and their Communist allies had pressed for recognition as official participants, this denial represented a defeat for them.

The substantive discussions at the Conference regarding the future of the Pathet Lao revolved around their political and territorial claims. The Communist powers advanced the position that elections should be held simultaneously in Laos, Cambodia, and Vietnam six months after the cease-fire and, furthermore, that an electoral commission should be set up in each country to prepare and supervise the national elections. In Laos the Pathet Lao and the Royal Government would be equally represented on such a commission. The Communists persisted in their demands until the closing days of the Conference, when they finally accepted the government's stipulation that elections be held in accordance with the Constitution of Laos, "in the course of the year 1955, by secret ballot and in conditions of respect for fundamental freedom," as the Final Declaration of the Conference put it.

Communist China and North Vietnam, for obvious reasons of self-interest, concentrated upon securing for their Lao allies military and administrative control of as much territory as possible in the northeastern provinces bordering on China and North Vietnam. This issue was focused on the number, size, and location of "provisional assembly areas" into which the Viet Minh and the Pathet Lao would be required to move their forces. The Communists opened with the exorbitant demand for almost half of Laos, but in the final hours of the Conference settled for an arrangement which gave the Viet Minh five provincial assembly areas and the Pathet Lao twelve areas (one in each province of Laos). Within 120 days after the cease-fire, all Viet Minh forces were to be withdrawn to North Vietnam, and all Pathet Lao forces that did not choose to be demobilized on the spot were to be moved out of ten of the twelve provinces of Laos and concentrated in the two provinces of Sam Neua and Phong Saly, "pending a political settlement." Although the Western powers and the Royal Government understood the agreement to mean that an area *within* each of the two provinces was to be designated for regroupment, the article was not specifically worded. Thus, the Pathet Lao were able to claim subsequently that the agreement authorized them to occupy Sam Neua and Phong Saly in their entirety, as indeed they did.

Another important issue concerned the future of those Vietnamese who had settled in Laos before the hostilities but had joined the Viet Minh invading forces. The RLG considered them disloyal foreign residents and demanded that they withdraw with the Viet Minh forces. The Communists contended that they were simply dissident but legitimate residents of Laos who should not be expelled. No agreement was reached on this controversy, and its solution was put off for later negotiation between the parties and conclusion of a special convention, which was, in fact, never concluded.

During the Conference and immediately following it, there were reports that the Pathet Lao, assisted by the Viet Minh, were engaged in a vigorous recruiting campaign designed to increase the strength of the troops before they were moved into the assigned regroupment areas. Our interviews tend to confirm these reports. According to one source, the Pathet Lao forces grew from 1,500 in July to 3,000 in August 1954 and were up to 4,000 by the time the Communist forces finally moved into their regroupment areas. The Viet Minh informed the International Control Commission (ICC) — the supervisory agency established by the Conference and composed of Canada, Poland, and India (as chairman) — that they planned to withdraw 5,000 troops from Laos, including all Vietnamese/Lao "volunteers" whom the Royal Government had sought to expel. There was no way for the ICC to know whether this figure represented all the Viet Minh forces in Laos, nor could the ICC control their actual departure. Our interviews suggest, as the next chapter will show, that the bulk of the Viet Minh troops departed, but that political and military advisers were left behind in Sam Neua and Phong Saly to give technical assistance and advice to the Pathet Lao.

The settlement at Geneva, when considered in the light of the Pathet Lao's purely indigenous strength (as distinct from their DRV support), served their interests well. In its implementation the Lao Communists secured a base area in the two provinces from which, with DRV assistance, they could build up their political and military strength. By the time of the second round at Geneva, in 1962, the Pathet Lao had become powerful enough to win recognition as a Conference participant, gain admission in a coalition government, and achieve de facto control of a much larger area.

V

North Vietnam and the Lao Communists' Bid for Power, 1954–1962

As Laos gained independence after the Geneva Conference of 1954, it soon became evident that the Pathet Lao had no intention of limiting their struggle for power to mere participation in Vientiane politics, that is to say, to competing with other political groups within the framework of the existing political system. While engaging in cautious negotiations with the Royal Lao Government, they sought to consolidate their control over the two provinces of Sam Neua and Phong Saly, which had been designated by the Conference as regroupment zones for their military forces prior to integration into the national army. At the same time, the Lao Communists began to build their own political and administrative institutions in the two northeastern provinces so as to have a permanent base for future advances into other areas.

Hanoi meanwhile was busy repairing wartime destruction at home, consolidating its political power, and converting army and party to peacetime functions. The first two years after the Geneva Conference were filled with internal turbulence for North Vietnam. Almost three quarters of a million refugees, mostly Catholics, had fled to the South. The revolutionary agrarian program, modeled on the Chinese Communist experiment, had gone badly, caused great discontent, and culminated in a peasant uprising in Nghe An Province in 1956.[1] In view of these conditions, the North

Vietnamese were all the more interested in ensuring that the Lao provinces adjacent to the DRV border remained in "friendly" hands, and therefore they encouraged and assisted the PL leaders in consolidating their control over Sam Neua and Phong Saly. Although they seem to have been skeptical about the Pathet Lao's participation in politics in Vientiane, they apparently made no attempt to interfere with these efforts. Indeed, North Vietnam's role in Laos between 1954 and 1959 was low-keyed, especially as compared with its active military engagements there immediately preceding and following this period.

Pathet Lao Activities and North Vietnamese Support, 1954–1959

Consolidating their political domination in the two northeastern provinces, the Pathet Lao set up as their "government" base the wartime headquarters that they had established, with Viet Minh assistance, in Sam Neua Province in 1953. They directed their attention to constructing an administrative apparatus with which to govern those areas under their control and to selecting and training village, district, and province officials. They established schools and published a newspaper, the *Lao Hak Sat*. In January 1956 they created a political party, the Neo Lao Hak Sat (Lao Patriotic Front), commonly shortened to NLHS.[2] This party was not formed merely to obtain popular support. The Pathet Lao, in line with the Geneva Agreements, had agreed to merge their armed forces with the national army. But there was nothing in the Agreements to prohibit them from establishing their own separate party organization against the eventuality that their military forces might be integrated and thus removed from their control.

This new body, which replaced the Neo Lao Issara, was meant to constitute a mass organization that would attract various strata of both the Lao and the non-Lao population. Prince Souphanouvong was elected its chairman, a position he continues to hold to this day, and Nouhak, Kaysone, Sithon Khommadam, Faydang, and virtually all the leading NLHS figures of today appeared prominently on its roster from the beginning. NLHS cadres went out into the villages to mobilize the local populace in such constituent organizations as peasant, women's, young men's, and young women's federations. And during the same 1954–1959 period there also emerged the real instrument of political control of the Pathet Lao movement—as contrasted with the open NLHS political party—the Phak Pasason Lao (PPL), the People's Party of Laos, a semisecret Communist party, whose role will be discussed more fully later.[3]

While the Communists were consolidating their military control in the two provinces of Sam Neua and Phong Saly and continuing vigorously to recruit new soldiers after the signing of the Geneva Agreements,[4] the Royal Lao Government, eager to return the two provinces to its domination, dispatched military missions there from time to time. Frequent skirmishes resulted between PL and RLG troops, because the Communists were determined not only to protect their investment but actually to expand it.

To judge by the testimony of those we interviewed, the bulk of the Viet Minh troops who had fought in Laos against the French before 1954 were withdrawn to the Vietnamese side of the border after the Geneva Conference. But the Vietnamese military and political cadres who were left in Phong Saly and Sam Neua to serve as advisers to their Lao allies and to fill certain technical posts made a significant impact upon the Pathet Lao during this period, particularly in the training of the military.

Pathet Lao soldiers were sent to schools in North Vietnam where they were taught both political and military subjects, sometimes by Lao with Vietnamese advisers, sometimes by Lao-speaking Vietnamese, and sometimes by Vietnamese using Lao interpreters. One important training center was at Son Tay (in the northwest sector of Vietnam), where military and political instruction was given to cycles of as many as two hundred students at a time, the length of a course varying from three to six months.

Among our interviewees were several men who had received technical training in Vietnam at, for example, a mechanics school, and one man, a former PL captain, who had been selected from his group of thirty recruits to study medicine in Ha Dong, North Vietnam. Two months after the Geneva Conference, the North Vietnamese helped transfer the principal Pathet Lao officer candidate school, the Khommadam School,[5] from Phu Quy in Nghe An Province, North Vietnam, to Sam Neua Province. Most of the PL officer corps has passed through this school. According to the man who was its director in 1954 and 1955 (A-18), the institution had a Vietnamese advisory component of twenty men who helped with the operation of six-month training cycles for three hundred to four hundred cadets and a Lao instructional staff of twelve — six for military and six for political subjects.

It appears that the principal control mechanism used by the North Vietnamese in Laos during this period was a command headquarters known as Doan (Group) 100. The above-mentioned director of the Khommadam School, who later served in the Pathet Lao military high command, gave an account of Doan 100 from personal experience. About two months after the Geneva Agreements, Doan 100 was moved from an unknown location in Vietnam to Ban Na Meo, directly on the Lao border. It was only a short walk from there to the headquarters of Souphanouvong and Kaysone in Sam Neua Province. Our source estimated that three hundred Vietnamese were assigned to Doan 100; two hundred had military advisory functions and one hundred did political tasks. Those performing political tasks were the more important, and were all members of the Lao Dong Party. The organization of Doan 100, which our informant reconstructed from memory, is shown on Chart I.

Attempts at Integration

While they were building up their forces in the years immediately following the Geneva Conference, the Pathet Lao were reluctant to negotiate with the Royal Lao Government on any diminution of their power in the two provinces where they had

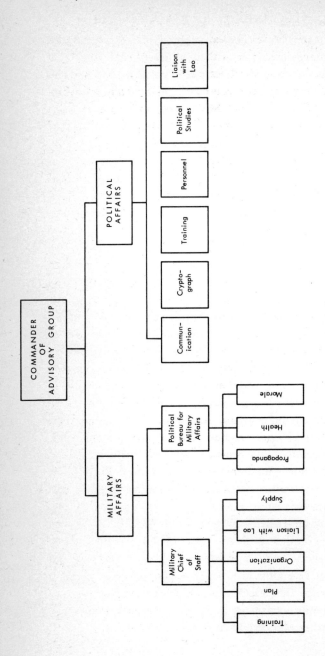

The commander of the Advisory Group was reported to be Colonel Chu Huy Man; the head of Political Affairs, Mr. Hung, probably Colonel Dai Viet Hung. There were approximately 200 men in the Military Affairs section and 100 in the Political Affairs section. The Military Affairs section directed the Vietnamese advisory functions to the L.P.L.A. The Political Affairs section, whose staff were all members of the Lao Dong Party, carried out the more important political advisory tasks.

CHART I.   Vietnamese Advisory Group, Doan 100, for Laos, 1954–1957 established themselves. They refused, for example, to take part in the elections for the National Assembly, scheduled for 1955 under the Geneva Agreements, unless their administrative control of those provinces was recognized. In the spring of 1956, Souvanna Phouma, occupying a position between the rightist and leftist factions, resumed office as Prime Minister in Vientiane and appealed for integration of the Pathet Lao into the national political process, thereby creating a new political climate in Vientiane. By the fall of 1957, Souvanna Phouma and his half-brother Souphanouvong had finally arrived at a plan for national reconciliation. Souphanouvong and another prominent Pathet Lao, Phoumi Vongvichit, would be admitted to the Vientiane government as ministers, the NLHS would contest the partial elections for the National Assembly scheduled for 1958, the two northeastern provinces would be absorbed into the national government with the NLHS sharing in the appointment of its administrative chiefs, and fifteen hundred Pathet Lao soldiers (about one-fourth their total number) would be integrated into the Royal Army in two battalions.

As we pointed out earlier, the North Vietnamese did not attempt to sabotage the efforts at integration; neither were they strongly in support of them. They seem to have been willing to wait and see if the NLHS could gain political advantage by entry into the government in Vientiane, while continuing through their advisers to help the Pathet Lao build military strength and solidify Communist control of the provinces adjacent to the DRV. Testimony that the North Vietnamese were retaining a PL military hedge against the failure of negotiations for integration came to us from an interviewee (A-20) who had been sent to Dien Bien Phu in 1957 for officer training. While there, he and other Lao trainees learned on the Vientiane radio that agreement had been reached to integrate two PL battalions into the RLG army and that the Pathet Lao were to join the national government and community. When their Vietnamese training officers gave no sign of any plan to send them back to Laos, he and his friends asked for an explanation and were told:

We know that there has been an announcement that the Lao people have been united. This does not mean that the war in Laos is over. It is only a temporary cease fire — but the struggle continues. You know that Souphanouvong has no hand in the government. He is just considered a representative of the NLHS. Many members of his party have not been admitted into the government.

We are training you here so that you will replace the two battalions — the only force of the NLHS — in case they are destroyed by the Americans. All of you must remain here and continue your training.

In 1958, however, the prospects for integration dimmed. On the political side, the Royal Lao Government had entered the two northeastern provinces, and nationwide supplementary elections had been held, as agreed, in May 1958. To the dismay of their RLG opponents, the NLHS won 9 seats contested, and their allies, the Santiphab Party, won 4 seats; the NLHS had benefited from the infighting among their adversaries, who had run 85 candidates for the 21 seats contested. The elected NLHS deputies, who included several of the most prominent men in the NLHS organization,[6] took their seats in Vientiane, but they were constantly harassed by close police surveillance.

On the military side, even though men from the two PL battalions had been selected for integration with the Royal Army, the actual implementation was stymied by differences between the NLHS and the Royal Government over the ranks to be assigned to certain PL officers. The pro-integration forces suffered a political defeat in August 1958 with the coming into power of a right-wing government under Phoui Sananikone and the rise of a new political party, Comité pour la Défense des Intérêts Nationaux (CDNI), the Committee for the Defense of National Interests. Both were vigorously hostile to the Communists. The NLHS leaders who had gone to the capital as negotiators or as newly elected deputies found the atmosphere in Vientiane increasingly unsympathetic. They viewed with distrust the growing American influence that accompanied the huge flow of American aid, the arrival of American and Filipino military advisers, and the developing links to SEATO. They were appalled by the burgeoning of an American-supported RLG military apparatus that took an increasingly active role in politics and by the flagrant corruption in the army, the bureaucracy and the political leadership.

In the new anti-Communist climate of Vientiane, two important incidents marked the end of efforts to bring the Communists and the Royal Lao Government together. First, in May 1959 the Royal Army troops surrounded the two battalions and attempted to disarm them. Any possibility of integrating the forces was thus destroyed. A part of one battalion was captured, but the remainder escaped, as did the entire second battalion, and subsequently fled to North Vietnam. Second, RLG police arrested sixteen NLHS leaders, including the seven prominent deputies who had been elected to the National Assembly.[7] The NLHS leaders were held in prison in Vientiane for approximately a year; they succeeded in escaping to their home base in May 1960.[8]

The Communist Offensive: Summer 1959

The mounting hostility between the government in Vientiane and the Pathet Lao erupted in July 1959 in a series of Communist military actions against Royal Army posts in northeastern Laos.[9] As they had done on numerous earlier occasions, the RLG leaders sounded the alarm over what they described as another North Vietnamese "invasion." On September 4, 1959, they appealed to the United Nations for assistance. The Security Council appointed a three-nation subcommittee on Laos, with the Tunisian delegate as chairman, to investigate these complaints. The fighting, which included an intensive attack from July 28 to 31 and which continued through early September, abated with the arrival of the UN commission. After listening to witnesses presented by the Royal Lao Government, the commission reported that "hostile elements received support from the territory of the DRV consisting mainly of equipment, arms, ammunition, supplies, and the help of political cadres." As to the presence of

North Vietnamese troops, the subcommittee reported that the "ensemble of information submitted to the subcommittee did not clearly establish whether there were crossings of the frontier by regular troops of the DRV." [10] This report has frequently been viewed as evidence that Vietnamese troops were not involved in the fighting in a major way.[11]

Our study sheds a somewhat different light on the DRV's role in this military campaign. The UN subcommittee, with only a few weeks to work and a small staff, was not equipped to conduct an independent investigation of the activities of the North Vietnamese. Because the Communists did not permit subcommittee members to travel in the areas they controlled or to interview any Pathet Lao or North Vietnamese, the committee was compelled to rely entirely upon evidence supplied by the Royal Lao Government. The RLG assigned two officials to present the Lao government's views; these two men and their small staff were overwhelmed by the importance and urgency of the task. We interviewed the key man on the RLG staff, an intelligence officer,[12] and through him we came to appreciate the enormous problems they faced. They were given very little time to prepare evidence of North Vietnamese involvement — at most a few weeks — and there were neither captured documents nor prisoners to show incontrovertibly the North Vietnamese role in the attacks.[13] In the end, the UN committee's report did not state that there were no North Vietnamese troops in Laos; it said only that the documentation examined did not prove their presence.

In subsequent interrogations of Pathet Lao prisoners and defectors who had participated in this campaign, the intelligence officer cited above was able to reconstruct a more specific account of the North Vietnamese role in this summer offensive than had been reported to the UN commission. In essence his account shows that the following North Vietnamese units, with central headquarters in the DRV, were engaged in this campaign: the 174th Regiment and the 176th Regiment of the 316th North Vietnamese Division; battalions from the 280th Regiment and the 673rd Regiment of the 335th Division (these units attacked

RLG posts in Sam Neua Province); the 910th Battalion, the 920th Battalion, and the 930th Battalion of the 148th Independent Regiment; Battalion 263 of the 270th Regiment (attacked in a region of Central Laos just north of the 17th parallel); the 120th Independent Regiment (attacked in Khammouane Province).

The pattern of engagement by North Vietnamese units in this campaign has been followed more recently, both before and since the 1962 Geneva Accords. The North Vietnamese would throw first-line troops against predetermined RLG objectives, complete their mission, and thereupon withdraw to the DRV, leaving Lao forces that had accompanied them as support elements to secure the gains. In the event of a counterattack, the North Vietnamese could be called in again from their bivouac areas across the border.

Although we do not have enough corroborative evidence to prove that in 1959 North Vietnamese units were involved in precisely this way, our other interviews confirm that it was the general pattern of North Vietnamese participation in the campaign. Lending weight to this interpretation is the fact that the military organization was in disarray at the time. The two PL battalions which were to have been integrated into the Royal Army had fled to North Vietnam only a few months before the attack and would hardly have had time to regroup or prepare for such an offensive. Though the Pathet Lao may have had several thousand men, in addition to the fifteen hundred who had been designated to fill the ranks of the two battalions, they were not organized in well-trained units likely to achieve such striking successes. In fact, the summer of 1959 was probably the low point of PL military strength.

The interests of both the PL and the DRV were advanced by this successful, if limited, military campaign. Regions of Sam Neua and Phong Saly that had been reoccupied by government forces after the 1957 agreements on integration were returned once again to Communist control, permitting the further development of the PL base area. From the Communist point of view, the attacks were a response to the Royal Government for alleged duplicity in violating the integration agreement and, particularly, in surrounding the two PL battalions and arresting the NLHS leaders. The attacks served as a warning to the RLG that the Pathet Lao commanded powerful outside support that could swiftly be brought to bear in case of future threats.

Moreover, the DRV through this offensive was signaling to the Royal Government its displeasure at the growing US involvement in Laos, reflected in the appearance of US technicians in civilian clothes who had been dispatched to train and outfit the expanding Royal Lao Army. The Vietnamese also objected to Laos' increasing ties with the SEATO powers.[14] In an editorial of August 1, 1959, the official DRV newspaper *Nhan Dan* charged the "U.S. imperialists" with being "the chief promoters of the tensions in the relations between Laos and the DRV." It further claimed that the United States had drawn Laos into a military alliance with Thailand and South Vietnam with the aim of inducing Laos to call for SEATO help. This accusation was clearly aimed at discouraging Vientiane from tying itself too closely to the anti-Communist bloc. Even as it was signaling this message to the Royal Government, however, Hanoi denied any direct involvement in this campaign and masterfully camouflaged its true role. The difficulty of proving its military participation and the limited nature of the engagement in Laos served to reduce the risk of retaliation from the United States or other SEATO powers.

The Period of Turbulence, 1959–1962

The failure of efforts at national reconciliation in Laos may not have been unwelcome to Hanoi, and the resumption of fighting between the Royal Government and the Pathet Lao in 1959 came at a fortuitous time, for it coincided with a new turn in the DRV's policy.

At the Plenum of the Central Committee of the Lao Dong Party, held in May 1959, Hanoi had decided to step up its contribution to the insurgency in South Vietmam. At the September 1960 Third Party Congress, this decision was formalized and officially marked a new phase with the call for a national Liberation Front. It therefore became particularly important for the North Vietnamese to secure and control the territory in the southern panhandle of Laos through which their personnel and matériel had to pass on their way to the south, those infiltration routes that are commonly known as the Ho Chi Minh Trail. Regular infiltration over these routes began in 1959.

The period of renewed political turbulence in Laos, which started in 1959 and only ended — temporarily — with the Geneva Accords of 1962 and the establishment of a tripartite government including the NLHS, offered the DRV an excellent opportunity to advance its own objectives at the same time that it was helping its Lao Communist allies. During these years of coups and countercoups, the Communists made significant territorial gains, extending their control into new areas of Laos. They benefited particularly from the confusion which followed the coup of the paratroop commander Kong Le in the summer of 1960. The young captain, son of a Lao Theung tribesman, with little formal education, but a vigorous combat officer and charismatic leader, had pledged that he would put an end to corruption in Laos and to the internecine struggle among Lao; he had returned the leader of the Neutralist faction, Prince Souvanna Phouma — half-brother of Souphanouvong — to power as Prime Minister.

From the beginning, however, Souvanna faced serious difficulties in re-establishing peace among the contending parties. Met with bitter hostility not only from right-wing elements in Laos but also from the United States, which cut off its aid to the Royal Government, Souvanna Phouma turned to the USSR for assistance. Beginning in December 1960, therefore, a massive Soviet aid program was mounted on an emergency basis.[15] This Soviet aid was transported through the DRV, and the North Vietnamese had a key role in its distribution. As a result — so we were told by Neutralist officers who during this period had served in Hanoi and on the Plain of Jars (where Neutralist and Pathet Lao headquarters were established side by side) — these supplies were directed first to the North Vietnamese in Laos, second to the Pathet

Lao, and last — and least — to the Kong Le Neutralist military forces. As Soviet aid began to pour in through North Vietnamese channels, the PL forces were substantially reinforced in equipment and supplies. With active North Vietnamese guidance, the two battalions which had fled from Laos to North Vietnam in 1959 provided cadres for the organization of new PL units. In addition to the Soviet supplies, the PL forces had received a windfall of arms and supplies which their ally, Kong Le, had seized from the Royal Army stocks. With these added assets, they were able to expand their hold over the province of Sam Neua, capturing Sam Neua city in September 1960. In November they seized the strategic town of Ban Ban, at the juncture of Routes 6 and 7, which led into North Vietnam.

The countercoup, on December 8, 1960, by the "Revolutionary Committee" of right-wing General Phoumi Nosavan made another major contribution to political chaos in Laos from which the Lao Communists and the DRV ultimately profited. As a result of the coup, Prime Minister Souvanna Phouma fled first to Phnom Penh, Cambodia; later, he set up headquarters at Khang Khay, on the Plain of Jars, to which Kong Le's troops had retreated from Vientiane. Three separate headquarters were established at Khang Khay: one by Souvanna Phouma's Neutralists, another by the Pathet Lao, and still another by the North Vietnamese.[16]

Between mid-December 1960 and May 1961 there was active fighting as a result of which the PL forces, thanks largely to the support of the North Vietnamese, consolidated their control of significant new territory. The hostilities had begun with an attack on Route 13 by Phoumi Nosavan's forces, including tanks, followed by a counterattack from the Communist forces, which were composed mainly of North Vietnamese troops from the 925th North Vietnamese Battalion and other unidentified North Vietnamese units plus the 6th PL Battalion and other unidentified PL units. In a major engagement at Pha Tang, north of Vang Vieng on Route 13 (the country's chief north-south artery, which links Vientiane with Luang Prabang), the Communists succeeded in pushing the RLG troops as far south as Hin Heup, some sixty miles north of Vientiane. At the same time, battalions of the 325th North Vietnamese Division directed minor attacks against Tha Vieng and Tha Thom, north of the Mekong River town of Paksane. In the now familiar pattern, the North Vietnamese forces acted as spearheads and were followed by PL troops and sometimes by Kong Le Neutralists, who consolidated the gains and provided camouflage for the earlier presence of the North Vietnamese.[17]

The Geneva Conference on Laos, 1961–1962

When President Kennedy took office, in January 1961, he was confronted with a serious situation in Laos. The Communist military offensive was making steady headway, and the West had reason to be concerned about its ultimate objectives. As the United States and the Soviet Union were actively backing contending forces in Laos, they were on a collision course that threatened to lead them toward an unwanted military confrontation. Late in April 1961, therefore, the two powers agreed to defuse the situation. A cease-fire was to be arranged among the forces fighting in Laos and an international conference called, in an effort to find a way of taking Laos out of the East-West conflict.[18] The chances for convening such a conference were good, as Communist China, too, seemed interested in a political solution that would eliminate any possibility that US ground forces would one day enter Laos and appear on China's southern borders.

As the prospects for an international conference on Laos brightened, the Communists hastened — as they had done on the eve of the 1954 Geneva Conference — to seize as much ground in Laos as possible before a cease-fire stabilized the situation. It was during those months that such key points of access to Vietnam as Mahaxay and Tchepone fell to the Communists. The Pathet Lao displayed little interest in concluding a cease-fire agreement even after it became clear that the convening of a conference at Geneva hinged on whether some arrangements could be worked out to suspend the fighting while negotiations were under way; no

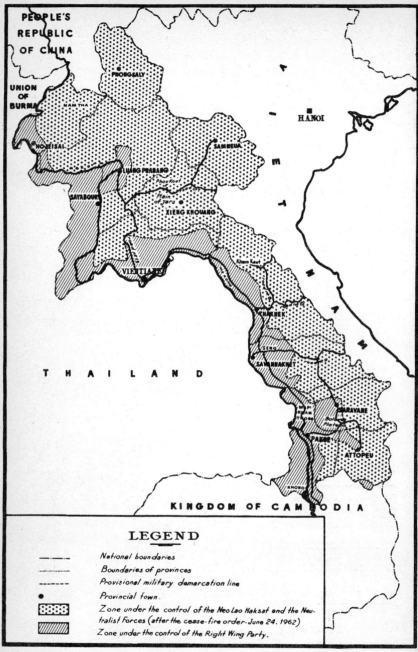

MAP IV. Political Control in Laos at the Time of the Signing of the 1962 Geneva Accords—the Communist Version (from *Twelve Years of American Intervention and Aggression in Laos*, Neo Lao Haksat Publications, 1966)

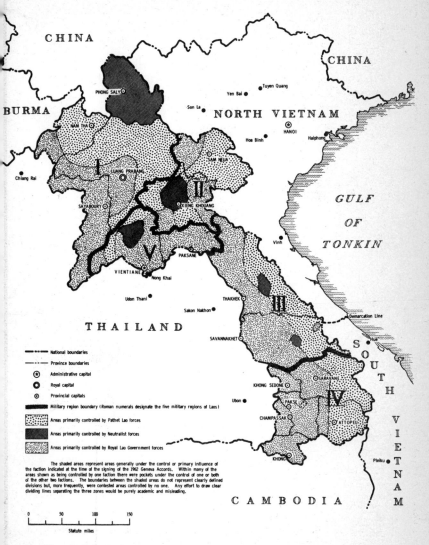

CHINA

CHINA

BURMA

NORTH VIETNAM

PHONG SALY

Yen Bai   Tuyen Quang

NAM THA

Son La

HANOI

Hoa Binh   Haiphong

Chiang Rai

I

LUANG PRABANG

SAM NEUA

GULF

OF

TONKIN

SAYABOURY

II

XIENG KHOUANG

Vinh

PAKSANE

VIENTIANE   Nong Khai

Udon Thani

THAKHEK

THAILAND

Sakon Nakhon

III

Demarcation Line

SAVANNAKHET

Hue

S
O
U
T
H

KHONG SEDONE

SARAVANE

Ubon

PAKSE

IV

CHAMPASSAK

ATTOPEU

V
I
E
T
N
A
M

KHONG

Pleiku

- - - - National boundaries

- - - - Province boundaries

⊛ Administrative capital

◉ Royal capital

◎ Provincial capitals

▬ Military region boundary (Roman numerals designate the five military regions of Laos)

▒ Areas primarily controlled by Pathet Lao forces

█ Areas primarily controlled by Neutralist forces

░ Areas primarily controlled by Royal Lao Government forces

The shaded areas represent areas generally under the control or primary influence of
the faction indicated at the time of the signing of the 1962 Geneva Accords. Within many of the
areas shown as being controlled by one faction there were pockets under the control of one or both
of the other two factions.   The boundaries between the shaded areas do not represent clearly defined
divisions but, more frequently, were contested areas controlled by no one.   Any effort to draw clear
dividing lines separating the three zones would be purely academic and misleading.

CAMBODIA

0   50   100   150

Statute miles

MAP V.   Political Control in Laos at the Time of the Signing of the
1962 Geneva Accords—the Non-Communist Version

doubt, they were hoping to improve their territorial holdings while taking part in protracted talks about a final settlement for Laos. The United States, on the other hand, insisted on an end to the fighting as a prerequisite for diplomatic talks. Eventually, a compromise was reached,[19] and in mid-May the International Control Commission announced itself satisfied that "a general *de facto* cease-fire" had been achieved, thus clearing the way for the opening of the conference. Throughout the following months, however, frequent violations of the cease-fire were reported from Laos. The situation there was further complicated by the absence of any official territorial demarcation line separating the three rival factions and by the fact that the ICC lacked the capabilities for an effective enforcement of the cease-fire.

The Geneva Conference on Laos opened on May 16, 1961, and held its last session some fourteen months later, on July 21, 1962. The length of the negotiations was due primarily to the complexity of the internal situation in Laos, but the large number of Conference participants — fourteen[20] — also proved rather cumbersome. While the discussions were going on in Geneva, representatives of the three Lao factions fought and negotiated for a political formula that would satisfy their conflicting claims. The Laos settlement of 1962 thus grew out of two separate sets of negotiations.

In the seven years that had elapsed since the Geneva Conference of 1954, the Pathet Lao's position had visibly increased in strength. Militarily, their forces, aided by the North Vietnamese and allied to the Kong Le Neutralists, had overrun half the country and seemed capable of sustaining their momentum. Politically, they were allied with the Neutralists of Prince Souvanna Phouma, whom the Communist powers as well as some of the non-Communist nations recognized as the legitimate chief of the Lao government. The enhanced status of the Pathet Lao was reflected in the role they played at the 1962 Conference. In 1954, their top representative, Nouhak, traveling on a Vietnamese passport, had had to be satisfied with the status of an observer. In 1961, the Pathet Lao delegation,[21] unlike the Rightists and the

Neutralists, did not claim to represent a government. Nevertheless, it was recognized as one of three coequal delegations intended to be superseded by a single delegation after the establishment of a national-union tripartite government.

Prodded by the major powers, the titular leaders of the three Lao factions (Prince Boun Oum na Champassak for the Rightists, Prince Souvanna Phouma for the Neutralists, and Prince Souphanouvong for the NLHS) finally met in Zurich on June 19, 1961, and agreed in principle to form a government of national union that would include the three parties. It took another three months for the rival factions to agree on Souvanna as the leader of such a coalition government. Meanwhile fighting had once more flared up, and thereafter virtually no progress was made in translating the Zurich Agreements into specific terms acceptable to all three parties. The Pathet Lao and the Neutralists, enjoying military superiority, were extremely reluctant to slow the momentum of their drive and to make any concessions at all for the sake of national unity. Just as reluctant — and, as the months went by, more so — was the Rightist faction, for it hoped still to redress the military balance by enlisting outside support; in the meantime, it preferred to stall rather than pay the political price of military inferiority.

By December, the Geneva Conference had finally approved the provisional drafts for a Declaration on the Neutrality of Laos, but as long as the situation in Laos remained unsettled, and in the absence of a Lao government recognized by all the major powers, the Conference participants could not place their signature on the agreement. The resistance of the Lao contestants was such that even a meeting of the three princes in Geneva under the watchful eyes of the Conference powers brought no resolution of the rival claims for ministerial portfolios and positions of influence. The deadlock was finally broken when Communist forces, in early 1962, scored a convincing military victory routing Phoumi Nosavan's troops at Nam Tha in northern Laos.

A large portion of General Phoumi's troops had been stationed in that locality, only a few miles from the borders of Communist

China, when a Communist counterattack sent them in disarray to the Mekong River and thence to safety on the Thai side of the border. There is some difference of opinion as to whether the majority of the troops on the Communist side were Lao or North Vietnamese. Arthur Schlesinger states that Nam Tha was seized by the Pathet Lao, though with North Vietnamese support.[22] Our interviews, however, indicate that the North Vietnamese were the major force at Nam Tha, with the Pathet Lao forces serving, in the familiar pattern, as support troops.

As a result of this rout and of the pressure that the United States put on the Rightists to accept a compromise settlement, the three princes were able to meet once more for a serious attempt at implementing the agreed-upon principle for reconciling their differences. It is a testimony to the deterioration of the Boun Oum government's position that this final meeting of the princes, in June 1962, took place at Khang Khay on the Plain of Jars at the Neutralist/Pathet Lao headquarters rather than in the capital of Laos or at a neutral site.

At the June conference, the three factions announced agreement on the details of a coalition government to be headed by Prince Souvanna Phouma, with Prince Souphanouvong serving as Deputy Prime Minister and Minister of Economic Planning, and Rightist leader Phoumi Nosavan as another Deputy Prime Minister and as Minister of Finance.[23] On June 23, 1962, the King of Laos formally approved the new government, which thereupon dispatched its representative to the Geneva Conference. On July 23, the Conference participants signed the Declaration on the Neutrality of Laos and a related Protocol outlining the provisions for the neutralization of Laos. This was to have been the first step toward a complete withdrawal of foreign forces from Laos and the beginning of an era of national reconciliation among the contending Lao factions.

Why were the Pathet Lao and the North Vietnamese Communists willing to accept a political settlement short of all-out control over Laos after they had convincingly demonstrated at Nam Tha that the military balance of forces was in their favor? One explanation is that at least the North Vietnamese may have been afraid that further advances in Laos would provoke a US response and endanger their earlier gains. Soviet policy, no doubt, also exerted a moderating influence, and so did the American reaction to the events in Laos. Though the United States had made clear its willingness to accept an uncommitted Laos under a government headed by the Neutralist Prince Souvanna Phouma, this did not mean that it would permit a direct military takeover of Laos by the Communists. In fact, in response to the critical situation caused by the Communist attack against Nam Tha and as a signal to Hanoi and Moscow, President Kennedy had dispatched some 500 US troops to northeast Thailand, where they would be able to cross the Mekong into Laos on short notice.

The opportunities presented by the looseness of the arrangements made at Geneva and among the three factions in Laos also facilitated the Communists' acceptance of a troika coalition government and of the agreement for the removal of foreign forces from Laos. In compliance with the Geneva Accords, US and Filipino personnel who had been fighting on the side of the Royal Lao Government were withdrawn from the country.[24] The same could not be said of the North Vietnamese forces (estimated at 10,000 men) who had been the backbone of Pathet Lao military strength. The North Vietnamese never admitted the presence of their fighting units, and only forty of their personnel passed through the ICC checkpoints after the signing of the Geneva Accords. This concealment of the Vietnamese role in Laos was possible only because the International Control Commission remained ineffective[25] as a result of its inadequate authority and enforcement capability; in addition its Communist member (Poland) was able to veto or obstruct any investigative action that might reveal the continued Vietnamese presence in Laos or otherwise embarrass the Communist side.

The negative attitude of the North Vietnamese and of the Pathet Lao with regard to international inspection and enforcement of the neutralization of Laos was clearly stated by their representatives at the Geneva Conference. The DRV delegation insisted that "the neutrality of Laos should be mainly safeguarded by the Laotians themselves"; the Pathet Lao expressed their view in these brutally frank terms: "We should like to add that we will not tolerate guarantee or control by an international body, however constituted, of our country's sovereignty and neutrality." [26] North Vietnamese forces thus remained free to cross over into the Communist zone of Laos at will. Meanwhile, as long as the military and administrative integration of the three factions remained to be carried out, the NLHS, now enjoying the status of a legitimate political party and constituent element of the national union government, retained full possession of the large zone that it occupied thanks to massive assistance from North Vietnam.

By the time of the Geneva Accords of 1962, the territory which the DRV and PL forces controlled was roughly the same as the territory the Viet Minh had held at the close of the war against the French in July 1954. This meant the bulk of the highlands of Laos, or about half the territory, although the population in these areas was only 20 to 30 percent of the country's total.

The evidence is strong, therefore, that the Communist military success at the end of the 1961–1962 offensive in Laos was due primarily to the troop commitment from North Vietnam.[27] From their own point of view, the North Vietnamese had made substantial gains: Not only was the area of the Ho Chi Minh Trail now securely in Communist hands, but the northern provinces bordering on Vietnam were also clearly within Communist control, thereby providing a buffer between Vietnam and a potential enemy. In the future, this buffer zone could serve as a staging area for further advances into other parts of the country. Laos was now divided, and it seemed unlikely that peaceful reunification could be achieved without North Vietnamese consent.

The role of the North Vietnamese had made possible substantial gains for the Pathet Lao forces too.[28] In 1959 the two PL battalions of seven hundred and fifty men each had been dispersed. Only two years later, at the time of the cease-fire of May 31, 1961, PL troops were estimated at 16,000, and by the conclusion of the Geneva negotiations, in July 1962, they had further increased their strength to an estimated 19,500. Pathet Lao control of approximately half the territory of Laos was in effect legitimized by the 1962 Geneva Accords, as conditions at the cease-fire resulted in the drawing of an unofficial dividing line between the NLHS- and RLG-controlled areas. It must be stressed, however, that the Royal Government never accepted the contention that the cease-fire line constituted a de facto recognition of a partition of Laos. And, indeed, no official demarcation line was ever agreed upon. But in the circumstances created by the cease-fire, both sides now had time to regroup their forces, consolidate political control, and work at building their strength.

Part Two: The Present

VI

The Context of the Current Struggle

In June 1962 Prince Souvanna Phouma, with the support of the major interested nations and the consent of the three domestic factions contending for power — the Rightists, the Neutralists,[1] and the Neo Lao Hak Sat — established his troika government. From the beginning it seemed doubtful whether the difficult balancing act attempted by the Prince could bring about a reunification of the country and a return to conditions of peaceful political competition. Less than a year after the signing of the 1962 Geneva Accords, the two most prominent NLHS representatives in the coalition government, Prince Souphanouvong and Phoumi Vongvichit, left Vientiane to return to the Neo Lao Hak Sat stronghold of Sam Neua, contending, not entirely without justification, that their security was threatened in the capital. They were soon followed by the two other NLHS representatives in the cabinet. They left behind in Vientiane only a small military contingent under the veteran Pathet Lao Colonel Sot Phetrasy, who to this day maintains liaison with the Royal Government, but must operate from a position of isolation in a hostile environment.

From the very inception of the coalition regime, it became evident that none of the three contracting parties, particularly not the NLHS, was prepared to make concessions for the sake of national reunification. Each faction held onto the military power it had developed earlier, and each, in accordance with the Zurich Agreements,[2] sought to continue administering the areas under its physical control. The lines between the three zones were never

85

neatly drawn because there had been no official cease-fire line and small-scale fighting had continued even at the height of the coalition period. The Pathet Lao thus maintained their hold over the regions along the Vietnam borders which they had been ruling for a decade with the active assistance of the Vietnamese Communists.

To judge by the available documentary evidence, corroborated by our interviews, the focus of the Communists' attention was on the areas they held rather than on the Vientiane experiment in political integration. (One indication of this is the fact that Kaysone Phomvihan, who by the 1960s had become the ranking member of the Lao Communist hierarchy, stayed away from Vientiane, dividing his time between the NLHS zone along the Vietnamese border and frequent visits or prolonged stays in North Vietnam itself.) The mission of maintaining, and if possible expanding, the Communist foothold in the hostile territory of right-wing-dominated Vientiane was assigned to Prince Souphanouvong and Phoumi Vongvichit, who were the chairman and secretary-general, respectively, of the NLHS. Phoumi Vongvichit, a former high official in the Lao government, was particularly suited to this task. Souphanouvong, although nominally the leader of the NLHS, by 1962 apparently was no longer free to make important decisions on the spot, according to interviews with men who worked with him, but required the consent of (or perhaps had to defer to) his colleagues in NLHS territory and, directly or indirectly, the North Vietnamese. As we shall show later, there is also ample evidence that the Vietnamese Communist forces were never completely withdrawn from Laos, that their advisers remained to stiffen the NLHS administration and military apparatus, and that the top figures in the Lao Communist movement continued to look to the Vietnamese for political guidance and inspiration.

The period of coalition in Vientiane lasted less than a year, from the fall of 1962 to the following April. It was thus too short to allow Souphanouvong and his associates to leave a mark on the national government's policies and programs, especially since the careful balancing of the three factions' influences tended to militate against any drastic departure from the status quo. We know from our interviews with government officials who worked under Souphanouvong that the Prince, while competent and hard-working, was careful not to reveal his inner thoughts on such issues as the future of the coalition or his functions in the Communist apparatus. It is fair to say that the brief episode of the NLHS' participation in the national government left no substantive legacy that would clarify their social and economic policies. For such information one must look at the experience of the border provinces which have formed the base of the NLHS administration. Here a virtual government apparatus has emerged over the years, with its own administrative structure, its armed forces, and a set of social and economic policies that have been formulated without reference to the programs of the national tripartite government in Vientiane.

On the basis of the slender evidence available it is impossible to say to what extent — if at all — the North Vietnamese mentors of the Pathet Lao were directly responsible for breaking up the coalition of the three power groups in Laos and for provoking, in 1963, open warfare by the Communists against their one-time Neutralist allies under Kong Le. It seems probable, however, that Souphanouvong's decision, in the spring of 1963, to abandon his cabinet post in Vientiane and to resume the civil war could not have been taken without the consent and the cooperation of the Vietnamese Communists, on whom the Pathet Lao were dependent in all respects.

Trouble between the Neo Lao Hak Sat and its Neutralist allies developed almost immediately upon the official cessation of the fighting in 1962. The Neutralists and the Pathet Lao maintained headquarters adjacent to each other in the Khang Khay area on the Plain of Jars, where they also shared the airfield. Both parties were dependent upon Soviet supplies, which arrived via North Vietnam and were distributed by the Vietnamese. Given the ambitions of the NLHS to gain control over all of Laos, it is not surprising that friction developed between the two factions that eventually turned into open military conflict. Though it appears that the North Vietnamese encouraged the NLHS to break with the Neutralists, there is no unequivocal evidence that Vietnamese forces in Laos directly assisted the Pathet Lao forces in their operations against Kong Le.

In the spring of 1963, the Pathet Lao forced Kong Le out of his headquarters at Khang Khay, and within a year he had been compelled to retreat toward Vientiane, leaving the strategic Plain of Jars region to the nominal control of a few self-styled Neutralists who were opposed to him. By thus evicting the principal Neutralist military leader, the Lao Communists had achieved two things: They were now able to consolidate their position in an important area of Laos in preparation for further advances, and they had effectively destroyed the power base which would have permitted Souvanna Phouma to speak from a position of strength as a Neutralist. Souvanna's influence was thus greatly reduced, since it had been understood that each faction would have a voice commensurate with the strength of the military forces under its command.

As a consequence of these events, the Plain of Jars became the headquarters of new and different Neutralists, utterly dependent on their Communist "allies," who had virtually created them and have continued to provide their encadrement. This small splinter group of Neutralists still in the Communist camp is commanded by Colonel Deuane Sounarath, an enemy and rival of Kong Le. It consists probably of not much more than a thousand men (although the figure of two thousand is sometimes mentioned[3]). These have been described by the Communists as "true" or "genuine" Neutralists and, more recently, as "Patriotic Neutralists."

If the Communists choose to maintain a nominally separate identity for the Neutralists they created in 1963 rather than to absorb them, it may be partly because, in the familiar pattern of Communist movements, it strengthens their claim during the initial phase that their administration is not a Communist monolith but represents a broad range of political views. But there may be the additional reason that in any future political settlement for the re-establishment of a national union government that would comprise the three Geneva factions — Rightists, Neutralists, and NLHS — the "Patriotic Neutralists" could constitute an important asset. For the Communists could assert, that only Colonel Deuane and his men deserve to be called Neutralists, whereas Souvanna Phouma had forfeited his claim by virtue of his cooperation with the United States.[4] If the Pathet Lao succeeded in gaining for the Patriotic Neutralists recognition as representatives of the Neutralist faction, the Communists and their sympathizers would form a majority in a future national union government, whereas under the arrangements worked out by the Lao factions at the time of the Geneva Accords of 1962 they constitute a minority.

Kong Le, having been evicted from the Plain of Jars, was forced into a relationship of dependence on the powers in Vientiane. He was no longer able to draw on Soviet supplies arriving via Vietnam, and Souvanna's request to the Soviet Union that it supply Kong Le directly had met with refusal. As a result, Kong Le's forces, like those of the Rightists, became dependent on support from the United States.

By 1964, the process of polarization which had been briefly interrupted by the implementation of the Geneva formula had once more reached a critical stage in Laos. The NLHS was proceeding all but in name to the establishment of a separate government while seeking to wrest new territories from Vientiane. In April 1964, Prince Souvanna Phouma survived a Rightist military coup, but the course of events in Laos increasingly pointed toward a confrontation between the Communist forces on the one hand and a combination of non-Communist conservatives and Neutralists on the other. By the spring of 1964, a serious military struggle had developed, in which the Vietnamese Communists were playing a major role. The major stages of this struggle are discussed later.

Distribution of Power

Though the NLHS representatives abandoned their cabinet posts in 1963, these chairs have been kept vacant, formally awaiting the return of the incumbents to Vientiane while their colleagues have temporarily assumed their duties. Prince Souvanna

Phouma continues to head the coalition government, but the line between Neutralists and Rightists is more blurred today than it was several years ago. In the National Assembly the NLHS lacks representation, having refused to participate in elections. The symbol of the country's unity remains the King of Laos. He resides in Luang Prabang, and all three factions continue to swear formal allegiance to him.

Although the NLHS and the Royal Lao Government are at war with each other, contacts between them have not entirely ceased: The two princes have exchanged diplomatic notes and even personal communications,[5] and at a number of low-level meetings their representatives have discussed the prospects for political integration.[6] The contending parties frequently issue claims (always conflicting) as to the size of the territory and population they control. Under prevailing circumstances it is impossible, or at best not very meaningful, for either side to confirm or deny such claims. Much of Laos is sporadically or sparsely populated, and the discontinuous, fluctuating front characteristic of guerrilla warfare and small-scale military engagements constantly shifts the boundaries of control between the two main areas involved, not to mention the many enclaves in enemy territory. Moreover, population figures in government-held territory are known to be highly unreliable, and this is probably just as true of those regions where the Communists have the upper hand. Any statistical assessment is further complicated by the mass movement of refugees from Communist and contested zones.

While the Communists after their reconquest of the Plain of Jars in early 1970 now hold almost two thirds of the land area of Laos, the government controls a much larger portion of the total population, perhaps more than two thirds. The government's influence reaches into only a few of the mountainous and sparsely populated regions along the border of the two Vietnams, but it is paramount in the more densely populated Mekong Valley, where all the country's larger towns are situated. Some provinces, such as the old Communist strongholds of Sam Neua and Phong Saly — both bordering on North Vietnam — are firmly in the hands of the NLHS. In others the Communists have only a small toehold, as in Sayaboury Province, on the right bank of the Mekong, where their influence until the intensification of their activity in 1969 was estimated to reach no more than five percent of the population. On the whole, until 1969 there had been remarkably few changes in the geographic distribution of political control since 1962, an indication that neither side wished to risk upsetting the precarious balance lest any major change in the situation provoke even greater foreign military intervention and large-scale internationalization of the conflict. Each side, however, continued to nibble at the other's position. Since 1969 and especially since the new conditions created by the overthrow of Prince Sihanouk in Cambodia, the military situation also in Laos has become more unstable. Thus, late in April 1970, the Communists seized for the first time a provincial capital — Attopeu in southern Laos — hitherto held by the RLG. Soon thereafter Communist forces took another provincial capital, Saravane, in southern Laos. This departure from the past practice of not seriously upsetting the territorial status quo came significantly immediately after the Indochinese Summit meeting at which the revolutionary movements of North and South Vietnam, Cambodia, and Laos forged a united anti-US front. The available evidence suggests that the Communist offensive in southern Laos was closely geared to the North Vietnamese efforts to consolidate a new route into South Vietnam through western Cambodia in reaction to the joint US-South Vietnamese intervention in Cambodia.

Communist Instruments of Policy Control in Laos

The Neo Lao Hak Sat regions of Laos are controlled by three indigenous and interrelated instrumentalities: the Communist Party and its political front organization; the administrative apparatus; and the military organization. As will be shown, these internal control mechanisms are in turn inspired, stiffened, and guided by an external force — North Vietnamese Communism.

Laos' own Communist apparatus is rather feebly developed and not highly centralized, if we apply the standards of other Communist organizations, particularly the Vietnamese. But the physical, economic, and political conditions of Laos are not the same as those in Vietnam. If the Lao Communists appear far inferior to the Vietnamese Communists in organization, sophistication, and drive, we must remind ourselves that their adversary, the Royal Lao Government, suffers from similar inadequacies and handicaps that are inherent in the Lao scene, including the difficult topography, the paucity of natural and human resources, and the underdeveloped state of both the economy and the cultural life of Laos. It is these conditions which have made all contenders for political power in that country so dependent on foreign assistance, encouraging, on one side, the Pathet Lao's symbiotic relationship with the Vietnamese Communists and, in turn, forcing the Royal Government to rely heavily on the United States for economic and military assistance.

There has been some controversy over the years as to whether or not there is a separate Communist party in Laos, apart from the mass organization known as the Neo Lao Hak Sat (NLHS). Those who believe that there is, disagree among themselves on the exact name of the party. Our interviews, the documents we have collected, and a study of the existing literature on the subject have enabled us to throw some light on this issue. We are satisfied that a Communist party does indeed exist in Laos, and that it is recognized as such by other Communist parties. It is the Phak Pasason Lao (PPL), the People's Party of Laos, to this day a semisecret organization. Because of the clandestine nature of its operations, little was known about this Communist party until recently, and even now it is not possible to piece together a full picture of its history, organization, and activities.

A captured document intended for the training of Party members states that the Phak Pasason Lao was officially proclaimed on March 22, 1955, although, it is pointed out, the organization already existed before then. The document emphasizes that the PPL was to continue the thought and spirit of the Indochinese Communist Party, which, founded in January 1930, had provided leadership in the struggle against the French in the three Indochinese countries of Vietnam, Cambodia, and Laos. (It must be recalled that in 1945, to camouflage its identification with Communism and present a more effective nationalist appeal, the ICP had formally dissolved itself and been replaced publicly by a broadly based political association, though there is little doubt that the former ICP continued to furnish leadership for another six years.)

In 1951, according to the training document, the Second Congress of the Indochinese Communist Party decided to break up the ICP into three separate parties. As for the Lao party, the manual states that "though it had been organized and expanded sometime before, the People's Party of Laos was proclaimed on March 22, 1955," identified in the document as the official birthdate of the People's Party of Laos.

Such evidence as we have been able to find confirms that the establishment of the PPL was indeed officially proclaimed on March 22, 1955. But our sources differ as to the when and how of the party's actual origins. One source (A-14), who was with the Pathet Lao until 1957 and subsequently studied the organization of the Lao Communist movement, claims to have attended a founding session of the PPL in 1954, some time after the Geneva Conference. He was then serving as a propagandist at Mahaxay, in the eastern part of Khammouane Province in South Laos. The meeting, presided over by Prince Souphanouvong, was held in the jungle somewhere in Sam Neua Province, and was attended by some twenty leading members of the Pathet Lao, including Kaysone, Nouhak, Phoumi Vongvichit, Faydang, Prince Souk Vongsak, Ma, Khamtay Siphandone, Phoun Sipaseuth, Sisavath, and Sisana Sisane. It was during this meeting, according to our source, that Nouhak proposed that they set up a "leading party," a recommendation supported by Kaysone, Khamtay, and Sisavath. Souphanouvong, Phoumi, and Faydang apparently agreed that such a party might be useful but expressed certain reservations (which our informant did not make clear). Sisana Sisane led the faction that strongly opposed the idea of a new party. After three days of discussion, the meeting ended without having reached a decision. Some time later in 1954, however, the Party was formed, and, according to our source, it had begun to plant its cadres in key positions in the administration and the military before being proclaimed in March of 1955. We have not been able to verify this account, but its author has been a useful and reliable informant on other subjects.

Still another source (A-9), who had rallied to the Royal Government in 1955 and currently holds a leading position in the Special Branch of the Lao police in southern Laos, claimed to have been a member of the People's Party of Laos as early as 1950 (or, more likely, 1951), when he had the responsibility for issuing PPL membership cards. According to him, it had been decided after the dissolution of the ICP that new parties with new names would be established in each of the three countries, and this had led, in Vietnam, to the forming of the Lao Dong Party; in Laos, the Phak Pasason Pativat (literally, the Revolutionary People's Party); and a party of a similar name in Cambodia. The informant contended that Phak Pasason Pativat was an earlier name for Phak Pasason Lao, but gave no precise indication of when the name changed. Although again we could not verify this account of the PPL's origin, the interviewee did provide details about its recruiting activities and its method of control within the civil and military hierarchy, all of which correspond to information we have from other sources.

At any rate, in the light of these accounts and other, corroborating evidence, we have no doubt that for the last fifteen years the PPL has been the controlling instrument in the Neo Lao Hak Sat areas, making the key policy decisions to be carried out by the administration and the military.

The People's Party of Laos subscribes to the principle of Marxism-Leninism. Its exact position on the Peking-Moscow spectrum is not easily determined, because, like the Vietnamese Lao Dong Party whose orientation it follows closely, it must seek to maintain amicable relations with both of the great Communist powers and therefore has, on the whole, refrained from taking positions that would identify it with either. The sympathies of several of the PPL's leading figures appear to lean toward Peking, but the overriding influence on its international position is without doubt that of its sponsors, the Vietnamese Communists.

In the past, when the PPL appeared at foreign Communist Party congresses and international Communist functions, it kept its existence secret. Its recent public acknowledgment[7] may be a sign of growing strength and confidence and may also indicate that the PPL is ready to assume openly the directing role in Lao affairs, superseding its front organization, the NLHS, in this function.

From interviews with former Pathet Lao members, the study of Lao reports, and other source materials we conclude that the PPL, in its upper echelon, is organized like most Communist parties, with a Central Committee (composed of some twenty members) and a Secretary General (Kaysone). Among its Central Committee members, Nouhak — an early associate of the Vietnamese Communists — appears to be the most influential. We know that membership in the organization is small. It may be only a few hundred for all of Laos,[8] but the meagerness of available data makes this at best an educated guess.

Because of the secrecy surrounding it, we have only scant information about the PPL's operating principles and activities. We know that, like the Lao Dong in North Vietnam, it seeks to practice democratic centralism, and that it directs the open political party, the NLHS. Communist Party cells permeate the key institutions of society, that is, the administration and the armed forces, at least at their upper levels. Virtually all prominent figures of the movement who are mentioned in public reports as governmental or military leaders also appear on various rosters of PPL members we have examined. An important exception may be Prince Souphanouvong, whose Party membership is not clearly established, despite the high position he occupies in the public eye and the historic role he has played in strengthening the Pathet Lao-North Vietnamese alliance.[9]

Although there is no doubt that from the inception of the Pathet Lao movement its leaders have worked most intimately with the Vietnamese Communists, the precise relationship between the Lao Dong Party of North Vietnam and the Communist Party in Laos remains unclear. According to one widely held theory, North Vietnam keeps control of the Lao Communist movement by having certain Lao Communists maintain dual membership in the PPL and the Lao Dong Party.

In December 1958 an informant contended that there had been seventeen Lao members[10] in the Lao Dong Party when it was formed in 1950,[11] but that "the strict subordination of the Lao to the Vietnamese dissatisfied the Lao, and in 1952 the Lao section was made independent of the Lao Dong under the name of the Workers Party (Phak Khon Ngan)." This informant further asserted that "all the directives passed through the Lao Dong to the members of the Lao Communist Party, who were also members of the Lao Dong." Principally on the basis of this report, the thesis has gained currency that there are four concentric circles of control, the innermost of which consists of the seventeen Lao Communists who have joint membership in the Lao Dong Party, and the next, of members of the PPL, with members of the NLHS and, finally, the population at large occupying the farther circles.

Though we cannot disprove this thesis, we have searched unsuccessfully for evidence to support it; instead, we find that it contains a number of clear-cut mistakes. For example, it appears that there never was a Lao Party known as the Phak Khon Ngan. (This term is simply a translation into Lao of the Vietnamese words Dang Lao Dong, meaning Workers Party.) According to a number of knowledgeable persons interviewed, the PPL has been the leading Party in Laos from the outset. Our investigation suggests that the thesis of joint membership came from a single source, whose motivation at the time the information was recorded was judged as dubious. The story seems to have been picked up in subsequent reporting and found its way into the literature on the subject.[12] At this point, there is insufficient evidence to prove or disprove the existence today of a dual-membership arrangement by which certain Lao Communists also are Lao Dong members.[13]

If the PPL is the guiding instrument of policy and control in the Pathet Lao regions, the transmission belt and mass mobilization mechanism is provided by the Neo Lao Hak Sat, or Lao Patriotic Front. The NLHS, as we have already mentioned, constitutes a broad political organization, which has functioned (and been recognized by the RLG) as a legitimate political party since its creation in 1956. It admits freely "all progressive people," as is clear from the documents we have studied and from the accounts of eyewitnesses. Since the PPL does not normally make its existence known even to most of the inhabitants of the Communist-controlled zone, we have a situation wherein a true Communist party organization, the PPL, operates but is very rarely mentioned, while an open political party, the NLHS, appears on the surface to be the only political organization of that zone. This impression is reinforced by the official foreign Communist press, such as *Pravda,* and in Soviet writings on Laos, which avoid mention of the PPL and tend to talk only of the NLHS.

The Neo Lao Hak Sat corresponds to the National Liberation Front in South Vietnam. Prince Souphanouvong, who has been the chairman of its Central Committee from the beginning, also serves as the international spokesman for the Pathet Lao and is acclaimed in the literature coming out of the Communist zone, as in the book *Worthy Daughters and Sons of the Lao People* (issued in 1966 by the official Neo Lao Haksat Publications), which calls him "the respected leader of the Lao people" (p. 31). Yet there is ample internal evidence to suggest that Souphanouvong, despite his worldwide reputation and official rank, occupies a lower position of influence than PPL Secretary General Kaysone and some of his less-known associates. The NLHS reaches down to the villages, where it commands a variety of constituent organizations, including those for farmers, young men, and young women.

On the administrative level, the Pathet Lao have modified the traditional system, which operates through the provincial, district, and canton level down to the villages by adding a parallel chain of command whose function it is to provide the political supervision. At each level in the chain of command this political component adds the label "Neo" (meaning "front," and referring to the NLHS) to the administrative designation. Thus, a province will have a Chao Khoueng, a provincial governor, and in addition a

Neo Khoueng, whose responsibilities are primarily political ones, such as the implementation of PPL policy (via the NLHS channels) and the supervision and control of personnel. Informants have told us that the Neo officials look over the shoulders of their colleagues on the administrative side to make sure that the instructions emanating from "the Center" are followed throughout the chain of command.

In comparing the rosters of high administration officials in the Communist zone with those of the NLHS Central Committee and the various lists of PPL members, we find, not surprisingly, that there is considerable overlap, for Laos suffers from a dearth of qualified administrative and technically competent personnel and must make the most of available talent. Moreover, the combination of the underdevelopment of their region and the destruction brought about by the war has greatly complicated the administrative task of the Lao Communists, who have been forced to operate from makeshift headquarters (often in caves) and from primitive "offices" that are moved around the jungle areas.

The Lao People's Liberation Army (LPLA) has improved in size and quality over the years as a result of continuing battle experience, Vietnamese assistance and instruction, and the allocation of substantial resources to the military buildup. Figures regarding its military strength vary substantially, partly because of the difficulty of obtaining information in conditions of guerrilla warfare but also because one must distinguish among regular forces, regional troops, and the village militia. The regular forces probably number about 25,000. To these must be added the regional troops and village militia and, most important, more than 40,000 North Vietnamese forces estimated to be stationed in 1970 in Laos.[14] Some NLHS publications describe the active role that women play in both military and political capacities.[15] As documents from LPLA military forces make clear, the People's Party of Laos has firm control over the armed forces. One document puts it this way:

The military are under the leadership of our Party [the PPL] . . . they must act in accordance with its policy.

Our sources lead us to conclude that little fundamental revamping of the social and economic life of those under NLHS rule has yet been attempted. No doubt, this moderation is the result of the severe physical difficulties encountered in modernizing Laos, the limited availability from abroad of resources for civilian purposes, and the desire to avoid adverse political repercussions during wartime. Thus, there has been no collectivization of agriculture, but only a slow trend toward mutual-aid teams and cooperative management; no large-scale expropriation of "capitalists," but restrictions on trade and distribution of goods. While class origin is increasingly a factor in the selection for responsible positions, a "bourgeois" or aristocratic background (as in the case of Prince Souphanouvong, Prince Souk Vongsak, and Singkapo Chounramany) is in itself apparently no serious obstacle to success.[16] However, obligatory self-criticism and study sessions, in addition to more severe disciplinary measures, are widely used to eradicate what are considered failings springing from "capitalist" or "reactionary feudalist" tendencies, and to inspire dedication to the ideal of an "anti-imperialist, antifeudalist, and progressive, democratic Laos." There is no question but that the Communists have made a determined effort to raise the level of social consciousness and to instill ambition in the people. Despite wartime conditions, programs for adult education are under way throughout much of the Communist zone.

Probably the most drastic changes have taken place in ethnic policy. The Pathet Lao have from the outset stressed the need for equality of opportunity and close cooperation among all ethnic groups. This is reflected to some extent in the leadership structure, where the tribal leaders Faydang and Sithon Khommadam have risen to positions of at least nominal prominence.[17] Pathet Lao textbooks, newspapers, and other literature constantly hammer away at this theme, and, to judge by the accounts of defectors, Communist practice appears to live up to these principles.

The Pathet Lao and the Communist Powers

The North Vietnamese remain the single most important outside influence affecting the character and orientation of the Lao revolutionary movement, as will be demonstrated in some detail later. Because of the strategic location of Laos in Southeast Asia, however, the great powers are strongly interested in its fate and have become involved, directly and indirectly, in the domestic struggle. It was to prevent a dangerous confrontation of outside powers over Laos that fourteen nations met in Geneva in 1962 and agreed to refrain from intervening in that country's internal affairs.

The policies of the USSR and Communist China toward the Lao Communist movement are of special interest here because of the role of North Vietnam, whose operations in Laos are, in a substantial manner, dependent upon those two powers. For example, without Soviet or Chinese aid, or both, North Vietnam would be obliged to cut its deliveries of weapons to the LPLA; indeed, Hanoi would be unable to carry on its operations in South Vietnam on the present scale, and this in turn would affect the situation in Laos.

Soviet interests in Laos can hardly be considered of great significance in themselves. Nevertheless, the Soviet Union is in an awkward position from which to conduct a consistent policy toward Laos: on one hand, its interests do not warrant the risk of provoking a hostile reaction from the United States; on the other hand, as a Communist power increasingly in competition with Communist China, the Soviet Union can ill afford to ignore North Vietnam's interests in Laos but must provide at least limited support to a fraternal Communist "liberation movement."

Prior to the Geneva Conference of 1962, the Soviet advisory role to the Pathet Lao had been very brief, and no organic relations had developed between Moscow and the Lao revolutionaries. Since then, Soviet policy toward the Lao Communists may appear contradictory at first glance, for Moscow officially supports Souvanna Phouma and his government while paying at least lip service to the cause of the NLHS. Thus, the USSR maintains its Embassy in Vientiane and receives Souvanna Phouma in Moscow despite NLHS criticism of him as an "American tool." It listens patiently to the Royal Government's objections to North

Vietnamese interference in Laos, but, although the Soviet government continues as Co-chairman of the Geneva Conference powers, it refrains from fulfilling its responsibilities with regard to the Vietnamese role. At the same time, Soviet newspapers and broadcasts give propaganda support to the NLHS, and the Soviet Union is certainly aware that some of its aid to North Vietnam flows on into the Communist areas of Laos.[18]

This seeming inconsistency of Soviet policy is merely one more reflection of the anomaly of the situation in Laos. As we have seen, although Laos has a tripartite government, the country is in fact divided. While international agreements have in theory removed Laos from the international power struggle, in practice various nations, directly or indirectly, have intervened to maintain a balance of power. Vientiane, the capital of the tripartite government, thus provides an unusual setting for international diplomacy: Not only does it shelter an NLHS mission — in the midst of a civil war pitting the Royal Lao Government against the Neo Lao Hak Sat — but it can boast of accommodating the South and North Vietnamese embassies as well as the Embassy of Communist China, although the last two also maintain Economic and Cultural Missions at Khang Khay in the NLHS zone.

The Lao Communists must recognize that Soviet aid to North Vietnam benefits them, but the ambivalence of the official Soviet policy toward them makes for rather tenuous relations. The Soviet Union does not, like the DRV and Communist China, maintain an Economic and Cultural Mission in the NLHS zone; its journalists, and other Soviet and East European visitors, reportedly have not been as free in the past to move within that zone as have the Vietnamese and Chinese, although recently more and more such visitors have entered the zone from Hanoi and their reports have received considerable publicity in the Soviet and East European press.

In view of the Soviet-Chinese competition in Asia one might expect Peking to play a particularly active role in the Communist-controlled zone of Laos. In fact, the Chinese have made vigorous efforts to propagate the Chinese line within the Lao Communist movement. But they have refrained, it seems, from interfering in the organizational sphere. Although there are indications (such as the extension of the Chinese road network into adjacent areas of northern Laos) that Peking may wish to establish more direct influence over the PPL, for the moment at least it continues to respect North Vietnam's vested interests in Laos. Peking's sponsorship of the Summit Conference of the Indochinese revolutionary movements, in April 1970, does not seem to have affected its Laos policy. So long as relations between Peking and Hanoi do not seriously deteriorate, their present division of labor in the Laos area is likely to continue.

Meanwhile, the Chinese Communists maintain their Economic and Cultural Mission in Khang Khay, run a Sino-Lao Friendship School in NLHS territory, provide their Lao friends with a profusion of Chinese cultural exports (such as films, propaganda literature, and theatrical and opera troupes), and offer scholarships to Lao students for study in Mainland China. In exchange for this Chinese support (and also reflecting, no doubt, their own anti-American sentiments), the Lao Communists have not hesitated to congratulate Peking on its nuclear testing and on the "accomplishments of the Cultural Revolution"; otherwise, however, they have gone to great lengths to avoid involvement in the Sino-Soviet conflict. With respect to the Paris talks, they have followed the Hanoi line, which had the support of the Soviets, but, initially at least, was opposed by Peking.

The Nature of the War

If the war in Laos until 1970 seldom made the headlines, it was not only because it was overshadowed by the more important events in Vietnam but also because the fighting in Laos rarely produced the dramatic engagements that attract journalistic attention. In this relatively large but sparsely populated territory, operations are conducted mostly by small units, rarely bigger than company or at most battalion size. Such units frequently move undisturbed through isolated villages in a no-man's-land where neither side is permanently in control. The fighting consists largely of attacks on isolated positions, combat over road control points and tactical mountain top sites in sparsely populated highland areas.

Because forces on each side hold enclaves within the area of the other, from time to time they venture forth on reconnaissance, ambushes, or hit-and-run operations. Curiously enough, terrorism is rare in urban areas, and the LPLA generally refrains from attacking the towns under government control. Until the escalation of the fighting in 1969, the nibbling operations of the two opponents hardly changed the outline of the political map, as the alternation of dry and wet seasons offered certain advantages and opportunities to each side in turn. The wet season, as a rule favors the armed forces of the Royal Lao Government (commonly known as the FAR, the Forces Armées Royales), whose small air fleet (C-47s and helicopters as well as light planes) and powerful US air support[19] provide mobility and allows it to strike at Communist outposts immobilized by the rains. During the dry season, the North Vietnamese and the LPLA normally turn the tables on their opponent and end up retaking the territory lost during the wet part of the year.[20]

A change in this pattern appears to have begun with the Communist dry season campaign of the fall of 1968. This campaign did not abate, as it had in previous years, with the onset of the rainy season, and the Communist gains were substantial, if not decisive. They also attacked certain Mekong Valley areas which previously had been seldom molested. At the outset of the dry season, the Government forces launched an attack against the enemy positions on the Plain of Jars and, with US air support, succeeded in temporarily dislodging the Communist forces. During the following wet season, in June 1969, two battalions of NVA, with Russian tanks and accompanied by LPLA units, retook the positions they had lost earlier. In September of that year, following intensive bombing, the RLG launched a major operation against the enemy and succeeded in occupying the entire Plain of Jars. In these almost continuous and escalating engagements both sides suffered substantial losses. At the beginning of 1970, NVA forces with LPLA support again seized the initiative. They not only recaptured their former positions on the Plain, but moved beyond against the government's key positions of Sam Thong (where the dependents of many Meo tribal people fighting with their leader General Vang Pao reside) and of Long Cheng which serves as Vang Pao's headquarters. Thus, by early 1970, the military situation in Laos was more fluid than it had been in a long time. In the spring, the ouster of Prince Sihanouk in neighboring Cambodia and the subsequent fighting there further stimulated NVA/PL action in southern Laos, resulting in the seizure of the important provincial capitals of Attopeu and Saravane which had for many years been controlled by the government.

Although the fighting in Laos has not quite reached the grim proportions of the war in Vietnam, it has disrupted the lives of a significant segment of the population, particularly in the Communist and contested areas. In neighboring government-controlled regions one can see this reflected in the makeshift refugee settlements strung out along the roads, which testify to the painful dislocation suffered by these refugees. Many are tribal people who once inhabited the highlands and mountain valleys of eastern Laos and who have been forced out by the pressures of war — primarily the intensified bombing. Their number over the past few years has been placed at 250,000; in 1969, an official Lao report mentioned the astounding (aggregate) figure of "nearly 700,000." [21] The evacuation by the RLG of the Plain of Jars region has further swelled this flow of refugees.

The effect of the war on the country's economy, too, is far from negligible. The RLG maintains an army whose real strength is between 55,000 and 75,000 men, or probably as much as 3 percent of the total population. This number, which would correspond to a six-million-man army in the United States, constitutes a heavy burden on a country that is particularly dependent on its labor force because of its primitive, largely agricultural economy. The manpower problem is even more severe in the Communist areas, which lack a sufficient pool of labor, yet must maintain armed forces capable of holding their own against the FAR. Their attempt to fill the gaps through forcible conscription has intensified popular resistance and increased the flow of refugees and defectors to government-held areas. Another consequence has been the Communists' continuing need for Vietnamese military support.

VII

North Vietnamese Advice and Support

The North Vietnamese continue to play a substantial role in supporting the Communist cause in Laos. Their political and military advisory staffs are placed at key points throughout the Lao Communist political, administrative, and military system, Vietnamese domestic and foreign policies shape those of their Lao allies whom they also provide with training (both in Laos and in Vietnam), logistic support, medical and technical aid, and communications.

The picture of the North Vietnamese advisory effort presented in the following pages is a composite of various sources. Much of the information is drawn from interviews with and written memoirs of two former North Vietnamese military advisers in the NLHS province of Nam Tha (northern Laos), Mai Dai Hap and Ngo Van Dam. Many of these points are illustrated by the personal account of Captain Hap in Chapter 8. More recent reports from Xieng Khouang province have served as a useful corrective and strongly suggest that conditions in the Communist zone may vary rather widely as a result of the underdeveloped nature of the country and the existing difficulty of communications.

The Political and Administrative Advisers: Organization and Role

Doan 959

The Vietnamese Doan 959 (Group 959) is the key instrument through which North Vietnam furnishes advice to the Lao leadership. Doan 959, we discovered, had its historical precedent in the earlier, similar advisory organization labeled Doan 100.[1] In addition to these principal channels for guiding their Lao comrades, the North Vietnamese have no doubt influenced the PPL through their constant and close contacts with Lao Communists in Hanoi. We know, for example, that the most prominent leader of the PPL, Kaysone, spent long periods in Hanoi and that he has returned there frequently. The same is true, if to a lesser degree, of most leading figures in the Lao Communist organization, and particularly of Nouhak, whose close ties to the Vietnamese Communists go back to the 1940s and whose influence is considered second only to that of Kaysone. There are thus ample opportunities for the North Vietnamese to exert influence over the PPL leadership even without their having to resort to such a formal disciplinary mechanism as the institution of dual party membership (although, as stated earlier, the existence of such a mechanism cannot be ruled out). Also, at the present level of military pressures from the FAR, the Lao Communists are heavily dependent on Vietnamese assistance of every kind.

Doan 959, located at Gia-Lam (some four kilometers from Hanoi), serves as the mechanism through which the North Vietnamese direct their political guidance and administrative support to the Pathet Lao. Its headquarters, which Mai Dai Hap visited in 1964, was then staffed by some fifty persons, headed by Nguyen Van Vinh, a member of the Committee of National Defense in the DRV Ministry of Defense. Doan 959 receives its instructions from the Central Committee of the Lao Dong Party and from the Commander-in-Chief of the North Vietnamese military forces. It maintains a forward command post in Sam Neua Province, where the Pathet Lao have their central headquarters. Very likely, this North Vietnamese forward command in Laos performs an advisory mission with the Central Committee of the People's Party of Laos.

Most of our interviewees' information about the advisory and

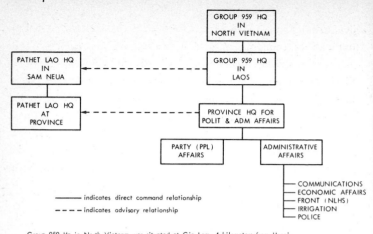

Group 959 Hq in North Vietnam was situated at Gia Lam, 4 kilometers from Hanoi. In 1964 it was commanded by Nguyen Van Vinh. Group 959 Hq in Laos was set up in Sam Neua, where it interacted with the NLHS Administration and Party as well as with the PPL. A Vietnamese advisory team headquarters was located at each of the NLHS provinces (*khoueng*). Ten to fifteen cadres were assigned to each province.

CHART II. Vietnamese Advisory Group, Doan 959

support operations that Doan 959 directs concerns the province (*khoueng*) and district (*muong*) levels. Permanent advisory posts do not normally extend below the level of the province, though province advisers are responsible for the districts in their regions and visit them periodically.[2] The NLHS administrative hierarchy is composed of dual echelons at every level. At the province level, for example, we find the regular administrative channel (*Pok Khong Khoueng*)[3] and a numerically smaller, but more important political channel (*Neo Khoueng*). Vietnamese advisers are assigned principally at the NLHS level, where the important Lao cadres are members of the ruling party, the PPL. Among the important tasks of the Vietnamese advisers, almost all of whom are members of the Lao Dong Party, is the guidance they provide to PPL members in their decision-making roles. It is not surprising therefore that the political program of the NLHS (adopted in 1968) bears a striking resemblance to the political program of the Hanoi-sponsored NFLSV adopted the previous year. Administrative advisers give technical assistance in such fields as policy formulation, communications, economic affairs, irrigation, and education.

A former NLHS district chief (A-16), or *Chao Muong*, in an NLHS-controlled region of Luang Prabang Province told us of the work of four Vietnamese advisers who were stationed at the Neo Khoueng office there. He pointed out that when difficult problems arose the Lao cadres asked their advisers for opinions, which were invariably accepted because of the stature of the Vietnamese. To make the point, he recounted the following incident:

For instance, there was an order from the Center that one ton of rice had to be conscripted from the people in a certain village. Before the conscription was made, members of the Pok Khong Khoueng and the Neo Khoueng held a meeting to discuss the matter. The Chao Khoueng, who realized that the village was small and the people could not afford to give that much rice, objected to the order. A long discussion followed. During the discussion, the Vietnamese advisers generally kept quiet. They did not say anything until they were called upon. Then, the Vietnamese advisers suggested that the Chao Khoueng reduce the amount of rice to the quantity he believed the people could afford to give and told both the Chao Khoueng and the Neo Khoueng to submit a report of this decision to the Center. Decisions of the Vietnamese advisers were, as a rule, approved by the Center, even if they did not conform to previous orders.

In the mid-1960s, ten to fifteen Vietnamese advisers were reported to be working on the civilian side in Houa Khong (NLHS Nam Tha) Province. The triple function of these cadres was frequently designated by the slogan "Dan Chinh Dang." "Dan" (Vietnamese for "people," meaning mass organization) referred to the advisers' role in helping organize the population into groups of young men, young women, farmers, older people, and other mass organizations as members of the NLHS. "Chinh" (government) referred to technical assistance to the NLHS administration. "Dang" (Party) meant the advisory effort to the People's Party of Laos (PPL).

Unfortunately, we have little firsthand information about the Vietnamese advisory process at the Center. However, from the data that we have assembled it seems certain that Vietnamese advisers work closely with the policy-making officials of the PPL, and, undoubtedly, there are advisers at the political level at headquarters in Sam Neua, just as there are in the provinces, as well as advisers assigned to the key administrative posts. Throughout the system — at least to the province level and in some cases down to the district level — the Vietnamese provide experienced, disciplined personnel who add competence to the operations of their Lao associates. We have found that these Vietnamese advisers are widely respected by the Lao for their dedication to duty. By their example, by on-the-job training, and by guidance, generally tactful, they goad the less vigorous Lao into better performance. They frequently act as arbiters of internal disputes within the Lao organization. And they are particularly important in directing essential resources from the DRV to the proper channels in Laos.

The Military Advisory Effort

The military advisory effort is handled through a separate North Vietnamese hierarchy. The Northwest Military Region, at Son La in North Vietnam, directs all North Vietnamese military operations in the northern provinces of Laos, including the advisers; and the Fourth Military Region, at Vinh, has charge of operations in the central and southern provinces. Each NLHS province has its Vietnamese military mission, whose chief is located at the LPLA province headquarters. He is responsible for commanding the Vietnamese military advisers assigned to LPLA units within the province, for advising the Lao provincial authorities on military matters, and for advising the Vietnamese military units assigned to the province. These units normally consist of two or three companies of one hundred to one hundred and twenty-five men each (they are called "volunteer forces" for reasons of morale) and of mobile forces assigned from North Vietnam and transferred throughout Laos, as required.

Normally, each LPLA battalion is assigned one military and one political adviser. The two have a staff of from three to five men, all of whom serve at the battalion headquarters. Formerly,

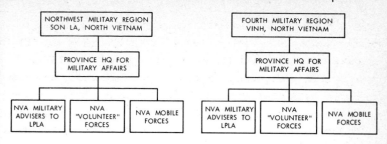

The Northwest Military Region (commanded by Colonel Vu-Lap, who replaced Brig. General Bong-Giang in 1964) controlled NVA activities in the 6 (NLHS) provinces of northern Laos, and the Fourth Military Region controlled NVA activities in the 6 (NLHS) provinces of central and southern Laos. Each province headquarters for military affairs normally commanded the three components shown above: (1) advisers to LPLA; (2) "volunteer" forces, 2 or 3 companies of 100 to 125 men; (3) mobile forces sent from North Vietnam, as required.

CHART III. NVA Command Structure for Military Activities in Laos

organized battalions also had advisers at the company level, but these were discontinued in 1966 for reasons that are not entirely clear. Very likely, the DRV, under growing pressure for trained military personnel, did not wish to use the experienced officers necessary for advisory duty in Laos at the company level and relied upon the battalion advisers, as one of the latter told us, to exert their influence on the subordinate companies. However, advisers to LPLA "independent" (*ekalat*) companies (that is, companies operating at the district level which are not part of an organized battalion) have been continued.

At least once a month, the key Vietnamese officers at all levels of the LPLA hierarchy report to the Military Region Headquarters in North Vietnam on the military situation in their province, usually by 15-watt radio. Every three months, they send a broader summary of general conditions. In unusual circumstances, they may ignore this schedule and consult headquarters immediately for advice or action. The Military Region Headquarters also sends officers into Laos to inspect the work of its representatives. In addition, the advisers are called back from time to time, generally once yearly, for a conference to exchange views and to receive instructions about future plans.

Such a convocation, participated in by Mai Dai Hap, took place at Son La in September 1966. It was presided over by Colonel Vu Lap, then commander of Northwest Military Region, and attended by Deputy Political Commissar Colonel Le Hien, Chief of Staff Senior Colonel Thang Binh, and about two hundred other officers. During the five-day meeting there was a discussion of the strengths and weaknesses of the past advisory performance in Laos, and the superior officers of the Military Region on this occasion unfolded a plan of activity for the dry season of 1966–1967, described as follows by Captain Hap:

> The goals for the Vietnamese and Lao were laid out. We were to hold on to the zones already liberated, maintain control of the population there . . . organize and consolidate the popular guerrilla forces; develop secret political and military bases; and improve the strength of existing military units . . . The aim of the meeting was to assess our past aid operations in Laos and project future plans for 1966–1967.

As Hap learned in discussions with the advisers he met at the Son La conference, his own advisory team to the 408th PL Battalion in NLHS Nam Tha Province was characteristic of North Vietnamese advisory operations throughout the provinces. His five-man team, which advised a battalion made up of 147 Lao Theung (highlanders) and 6 Lao Loum (lowlanders), was composed of the military adviser (himself), a political adviser, a logistics officer, a coder and decoder, and a radio operator. The advisers had received no special training for Laos prior to their assignment, but the two chief advisers, military and political, were captains, that is to say, experienced officers, who had served since Viet Minh days and, as devoted Lao Dong Party members, were expected to adapt themselves to their new situation.

Hap maintained that the command made no special effort to send Vietnamese of minority groups as advisers to Laos. Although he pointed out that two officers on the province advisory staff were of the Tho minority, he attributed their presence, and that of some thirty-five Vietnamese Black Tai in the NVA transport company operating in the region, to the large minority population in the Northwest Military Region in Vietnam, some of whom would normally be assigned to Laos. Hap's description of both the North Vietnamese and the LPLA organization and advisory structure in Nam Tha Province is reproduced in Chart IV.

North Vietnamese policy in Nam Tha Province was discussed informally when the military and political cadres met from time to time, but a formal mechanism called a "command" committee and composed of three military officers and three political cadres coordinated the Vietnamese political and military effort in the province. Chart V shows the organization of these committees.

The principal aim of the Vietnamese advisory effort in Laos, both military and political, is to improve the effectiveness of Lao operations. Although the Vietnamese try to respect Lao sensibilities, they are directed not simply to make friends for the DRV but to get the job done. The differences in the two cultures make it improbable that the North Vietnamese will ever be satisfied with the performance of their Lao allies. The easygoing Lao and the diverse highland-tribal minorities are unlikely to adopt the rigorous habits of their Vietnamese neighbors. They look upon the puritanism of the Vietnamese cadres with respectful amazement, but our Lao interviewees note that it would be difficult for Lao soldiers to emulate. Most of the control mechanisms used by the Vietnamese have been introduced into the Lao system, but they function differently there. For example, the self-criticism sessions of the Lao Communists seem slovenly and lackadaisical to the Vietnamese. Even though the Lao do not meet the Vietnamese standards of performance, there is no doubt that they operate a good deal more effectively than they would without the Vietnamese presence.

The Vietnamese military adviser plays an important role in the planning of LPLA operations. After making intelligence estimates, assessing logistic needs, and coordinating his projections

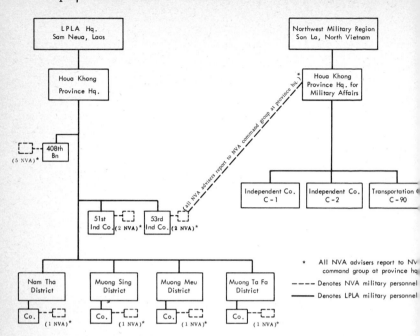

The Northwest Military Region Hq (on right side of Chart), at Son La, North Vietnam, commanded all NVA military activities in the six northern (NLHS) provinces of Laos, including Houa Khong (NLHS Nam Tha) Province. There was an NVA province command post, located in a forest in Nam Tha town, with 30 to 35 men. The headquarters consisted of a command group, directed by a military officer and a political officer, a security section, and a communications unit which had a 15 watt Chinese radio. Three NVA companies were under the command of this group: C-1 and C-2, "independent" companies of "volunteers" of 125 men each; and C-90, a transport company of 47 men (3/4 Black Thai Vietnamese and 1/4 lowland Vietnamese). The province command group also gave instructions to the NVA military personnel assigned to LPLA units.

The LPLA headquarters at Sam Neua, Laos, commanded military activities in all twelve (NLHS) provinces, including Houa Khong (NLHS Nam Tha) Province. Assigned to the 408th Battalion (147 Lao Theung, 6 Lao Loum) was a Vietnamese advisory team of 5 men (including Capt. Mai Dai Hap, source for Chart). Also under provincial military command were two "independent" (ekalat) companies, the 51st, with 70 men (all Lao Theung), and the 53rd, with 50 men (all Lao Theung). Both independent companies were assigned 2 NVA advisers, one military and one political, who were lieutenants. Each of the four districts had a company whose strength varied from 20 to 80 men, and was composed of the local ethnic group (Black Thai, Lu, Ko), each with one NVA adviser. All NVA advisers to LPLA units were responsible to the NVA command group at province headquarters.

CHART IV. LPLA and NVA Military Command Structure in Houa Khong (NLHS Nam Tha) Province

with Vietnamese units in the area, he initiates campaign plans for his Lao unit. He then discusses these plans with the Lao officers — careful to avoid offending their sense of authority — and the officers in turn communicate the decisions to lower echelons. Political and administrative advisers, too, provide inspiration for program plans that are later "ratified" by their Lao counterparts.

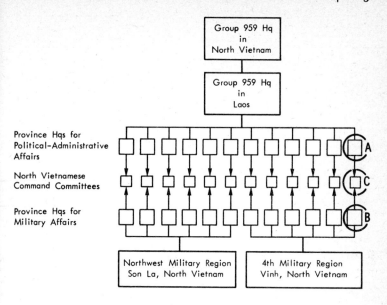

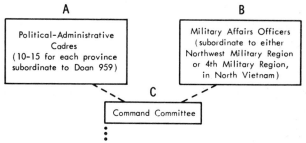

Normally composed of three military officers at province-level assignment, and three province-level political-administrative cadres. Met intermittently, between once monthly and tri-monthly, though more frequently in extraordinary circumstances. A military officer generally presided. The Committee coordinated all Vietnamese activity in the province and determined overall policy. There was a command committee in each of the twelve (NLHS) provinces of Laos.

CHART V. North Vietnamese Command Committees at Province Level

It has been charged that the DRV is more interested in ultimately absorbing the territory of its Lao allies than in simply strengthening the viability of their operations. We shall touch on this important question in the final section of this study. Suffice it to point out here that, whatever the future aims of the DRV in regard to Laos, the maintenance of its advisory system, with access to and influence in all key posts, certainly helps to keep Vietnamese Communist options open for a variety of choices.

Training

To provide training, both in North Vietnam and by advisers in Laos, has been an important contribution of the DRV to the strength of the Lao Communist movement. Its long-range effect is likely to make itself felt increasingly in the policies, organization, and personnel of the Communist zone in Laos.

Before 1954, the Viet Minh helped recruit and train the "seed" cadres — that is, the older generation of the Lao Communist movement, who are now in the important civil and military posts — and the Vietnamese style of the Lao Communist organization and operations reveals the significant impact of that training. A second generation was trained from 1954 to 1962 at such schools as Son Tay and Dong Hoi in North Vietnam, and with the help of Vietnamese advisers at the Khommadam School for officers and at other training facilities in Laos. The Vietnamese advisory staff of the Khommadam School developed the curriculum and provided the basic lesson plans in both military and political subjects for that institution, which has produced the majority of the LPLA officers.

From 1959 to 1962, the DRV reorganized and trained the two battalions that had fled Laos after the failure of integration, and it subsequently moved them back into Laos to serve as encadrement for the Communist forces there, which were expanding as a result of active recruiting by the Lao Communists and their Vietnamese advisers. Since the 1962 Geneva Accords, the North Vietnamese have continued to provide in their own country military, political, and technical-specialist training in a variety of fields to selected Lao candidates, particularly young officers, teaching them skills for which Lao Communist schools do not have adequate resources.

Among those we interviewed, for example, was a former second lieutenant (A-31), who had been recruited by the Communists in 1961 from his home in Pakse, one of a group of three hundred Lao to be sent to Dong Hoi, North Vietnam, for a month and a half of political and military training; he was then selected with sixteen others from his group, to attend the Thai Nguyen Technical School. There, from November 1961 to November 1963, a class of one hundred and sixty-five students, including Meo, Kha, and lowland Lao from fourteen Lao provinces, were taught auto mechanics, weapons repair, and electrical generator maintenance. (Another such cycle began as soon as this group was graduated.) The instructors were Vietnamese, and they used as interpreters two Vietnamese from northeast Thailand, where a Thai dialect almost identical with Lao is spoken. Another of our informants, the medical chief of the NLHS Province of Attopeu (A-10), had received five years of medical training (1959–1964) at Ha Dong, about seven miles from Hanoi, together with eighty other Lao and thirty Vietnamese. One of the instructors was a Vietnamese who had lived in Northeast Thailand and spoke Lao, and there were also some Russian and Chinese faculty. Lectures were translated into Lao during the first six months, after which the students were expected to understand Vietnamese.

Training schools in Vietnam had a great impact both in shaping the attitudes and in developing the military skills of young Lao recruits. This was perceptible, for instance, in our discussion with a former LPLA captain (A-20), who had gone through three cycles of training in North Vietnam. In 1954, he was with a group of two hundred youths aged 13 to 20, and including both lowland and highland Lao from Sam Neua, Phong Saly, and Luang Prabang provinces, who attended a six-month basic training program at Dien Bien Phu. He told us that, before this training, he and sixty other youths in his unit had grown homesick and discontent with the harsh life they had already endured for six months, and they had threatened to quit the army. However, "after the training, I was no longer lonely and I didn't want to go back home any more." Having proved himself a good soldier during the next couple of years, he was selected for training at a school for military cadets near Dien Bien Phu, along with a group of fewer than a hundred, ranging in age from 15 to 19. The training included political indoctrination, combat tactics and other military subjects, and a course in leadership. As in his earlier course, the instructors were Lao who gave lessons prepared by their Vietnamese advisers. In December 1961, the informant was sent to North Vietnam once again, this time to attend an advanced military course at Son Tay. The class was composed of two hundred officers up to the rank of captain, and the five instructors, all Vietnamese, used three interpreters.

In each of these three training cycles, the informant's instructors, in keeping with Vietnamese Communist practice, placed great emphasis upon political indoctrination. To judge by his and the experience of other Vietnam-trained Lao we interviewed, the indoctrination provided by the Vietnamese is well suited to Lao conditions: It is unsophisticated and appeals primarily to the emotions of the Lao youth. Its political orientation is toward Maoism rather than a Soviet-style Marxism or "revisionism." The former LPLA captain recounted the lessons he learned, reiterating the theme we had heard from many others:

I was repeatedly told that I was the owner of Laos. Laos is a beautiful country, with an abundance of rivers and streams and natural resources. The Lao people could not do anything to use these resources because of the aggression and oppression of foreign countries. The French, for instance, had ruled Laos for more than sixty years. As the owner of the country and a member of the Issara, I should fight for freedom. Members of the Issara should never surrender.

They told us that now the principal enemy of the Lao people is the American imperialists. They said that the French had already withdrawn from Laos and that the Americans seized the opportunity to dominate Laos by using Katay Sasorith as their tool. At that time there were no American troops in Laos — but later on the Lao troops would be commanded by Americans. From squad and platoon leader up to the commander-in-chief would be Americans. And so the country would be under the rule of the American imperialists.

Almost unanimously, interviewees who had received training in North Vietnam stated that they had found these political lessons credible and impressive. Since a large percentage of the Lao who attend schools in North Vietnam are or will become officers in the LPLA, the Vietnamese mark on their thinking is all the more significant.[4] Also, the determined efforts of experienced NVA advisers raise the level of training in Laos and thereby contribute to the improvement of military skills, discipline, and "revolutionary consciousness."

The support given to the Lao Communists through North Vietnamese training points to the larger issue of education in general. We did not gather conclusive data on the Lao studying in North Vietnam — except for the military trainees — or on the Vietnamese impact upon the educational system in Laos. On the basis of information gleaned from interviews and documents, however, we are certain that a very small number of students receive scholarships to study in Communist China and the Soviet Union, and even fewer in the East European countries. The major educational opportunities for the promising young Lao Communists continue to be primarily in North Vietnam.

It is too early to judge the effect of this Vietnamese education on the men who one day will constitute the Communist Lao elite. Vietnam-trained Lao to whom we have talked clearly appreciate their own opportunity for gaining an education. Though some secondary schools have recently been established in the Communist part of Laos — there are at this point no institutions of higher learning — it seems likely that for some time to come the young Lao in that zone will continue to depend on the North Vietnamese for much secondary and most technical training. This arrangement is facilitated by the widespread teaching of the Vietnamese language in the zone. As for who will be chosen, we have not thus far learned much about the role of the North Vietnamese in selecting Lao youths for education. Nor do we know the ethnic distribution of those selected, an important question for the future leadership of Laos.

Medical and Other Technical Aid

From interviews with former residents of the Communist zone of Laos and a variety of eyewitness reports that have appeared in the Soviet, French, East European, and Japanese press, we know that a beginning has been made in developing indigenous technical skills. Some spinneries and other simple production facilities have been established in recent years (several of them in caves, to avoid bomb damage). These modest facilities are apparently staffed largely, perhaps even wholly, by Lao, some of whom have undergone training in North Vietnam. But there remains a serious shortage of many essentials of civilian life, and most of these still come in by road from North Vietnam.

Particularly valuable is the North Vietnamese contribution to Communist Laos in the field of medicine. As mentioned earlier, a few able Lao students are regularly chosen to study medicine in the DRV. Medical supplies, largely of Soviet and Chinese manufacture, are provided by North Vietnam to the medical installations in Laos.[5] The North Vietnamese have been instrumental in setting up a simple medical training school in Sam Neua Province, for which they furnish the key training staff. Other Vietnamese medical personnel not only care for the Vietnamese troops and advisers in Laos and treat some Lao, but they also teach Lao nurses.

A Vietnamese medical technician (B-10), who had served in (NLHS) Nam Tha Province, told us that in March 1967 he helped to set up a course that would graduate twenty-five Lao nurses every three months, and a more advanced program designed to turn out forty nurses in six months. The teaching staff for these training programs was Lao, but the materials and methods were prepared by Vietnamese. At the more sophisticated medical installation at Muong Sai, the instructors are all Vietnamese; they teach in Lao, using Vietnamese only for technical terms. A male nurse (A-2), who from 1963 to 1966 worked in the hospital at Khang Khay that served the Neutralist faction of Colonel Deuane, told us that the medical personnel there, too, included Vietnamese.

Logistic Support

The Communist areas of Laos are dependent upon the DRV for many of the supplies which their own primitive economy does not produce, and they rely heavily upon the North Vietnamese for management of their logistic apparatus. It appears that the North Vietnamese have assumed responsibility for supplying the sector east of a line that might be drawn from the Nam Ou River to Muong Sai, through the middle of Luang Prabang Province. The Communist Chinese supply the western sector, but their logistical support is administered through North Vietnamese channels. Our sources unraveled for us the complicated procedure by which this logistical operation is apparently conducted in NLHS Nam Tha Province in the Chinese supply sector, and this process is likely to be much the same in Phong Saly and in the northern, Communist-held sector of Luang Prabang Province that Lao Communist broadcasts often refer to as Udomsay.

In other parts of the Communist zone of Laos, the logistic operations involve directly only the DRV and the Lao. The authorities of both in each province are required yearly to submit, through their own channels, a list of their supply needs to the appropriate headquarters. Vietnamese requisitions go to the Northwest Military Region at Son La, North Vietnam, from where they are forwarded to the central government. The Lao send their requisitions to the Center, in Sam Neua, where the requests are combined in a total supply list, which is then transmitted to the DRV central government. Having thus received both sets of requisitions, Hanoi then presents the Chinese government with a request for supplies for the western sector of Laos. Once the Chinese have determined the kinds and quantities of supplies they are willing to provide, they inform Hanoi, which in turn notifies the headquarters at Son La and Sam Neua.

Next, Vietnamese and Lao representatives are ordered to Kunming, Yunnan Province (China), to receive the supplies and establish a schedule for transporting them to Laos. To handle the North Vietnamese portion, NVA Company 90, assisted by civilian labor, will go to the Sino-Lao border near Muong Sing to transport the supplies to depots in the town of Nam Tha, from which further distribution is then made to Vietnamese units in the province. Then supplies will include arms and ammunition, basic staples (such as salt, canned meat and fish, fish sauce, sugar, milk, cigarettes, soap, and toothpaste), as well as rainproof clothing, kitchenware, sandals and shoes, blankets, and mosquito nets.

NLHS agents receive their goods at the Chinese frontier and store them in warehouses on the Lao side of the border, from where Lao civilians later transport them to other points. Besides the kind of items furnished to the Vietnamese, the Lao also receive groceries, agricultural tools, cloth, and other merchandise, to be sold by the NLHS authorities to the civilian population. Proceeds from these sales, according to Hap, are used to defray NLHS administrative expenses in the province.

Propaganda

The DRV provides important support to Communist propaganda efforts in Laos. North Vietnamese advisers, whose doctrine places great emphasis on winning over the population, help train Lao propaganda agents and guide the NLHS authorities in developing propaganda activities. Occasionally, they even assign Vietnamese — especially members of ethnic minority groups that are similar to those in Laos — directly to propaganda duty on behalf of the Lao Communists. One such example was a Vietnamese Meo, a defector (B-19), who had been trained in propaganda for two months and assigned in early 1966 to work among the Meo in northeastern Laos. In his interview with us he described the activities of the soldiers who had trained with him:

The Meo would propagandize in the Meo villages and the Vietnamese in the Lao villages. Some of the Vietnamese could speak Lao since they came from areas near the Lao-Vietnam border, and some who were Black Tai or White Tai could speak Lao.

Of his own duties he said:

I seldom met NLHS officials in the villages where I was. When I finished with my mission, I would report to the battalion commander, who would take care of everything. I guess he had contacts with the civilian officials. Our battalion worked under the authority of the LPLA forces. Individually, we had no contact with them. But when, say, they needed some propaganda in a village, my battalion commander would receive orders from LPLA headquarters; then he would assign us to carry out some propaganda.

Other Support Activities

There are a great many Vietnamese support activities, in addition to those already discussed, that will not be treated in detail here. Some derive from the presence of Vietnamese troop units and include the maintenance of roads by Vietnamese engineers, transportation assistance by Vietnamese military vehicles, and artillery and antiaircraft support from NVA units. A variety of technical assistance, both civilian and military, is provided by Vietnamese specialists. Some of this is furnished by the advisory teams. Mai Dai Hap reported, for example, that the Lao commander in his military unit used the Vietnamese communication channels to maintain contact with his superior headquarters, because the Lao communications were unreliable. In short, the Vietnamese make an effort to give, within the limits of their resources, whatever assistance is required to keep the Lao Communist system operating.

How Lao and Vietnamese See Each Other

It is not possible to study the role of the North Vietnamese in Laos without being impressed by their effective influence on the Lao. In view of Lao nationalist sensibilities about domination by

North Vietnam, considerable tension between the Lao and their Vietnamese mentors might be expected. And our interviews did indeed turn up some cases of resentment, which we shall describe; but we were struck by how successful the Vietnamese were in keeping such resentment at a minimum.

Even Lao defectors who denounced the political role of the Vietnamese in Laos admitted that the Vietnamese advisers got on well with their Lao counterparts. Most informants agreed that the Vietnamese were diplomatic in their dealings, making suggestions rather than demands, keeping their presence and their role discreet, and paying attention to the particular sensitivities of the local authorities they advised. Vietnamese cadres were always careful to work through the proper Lao or Vietnamese channels. For example, a Vietnamese adviser who wished to pursue a certain policy but who found it impolitic to approach his Lao counterpart directly might communicate through Vietnamese channels to his own superior, requesting that the appropriate Lao commander order his subordinate to carry out the desired policy.

Vietnamese military advisers live at the same level as the Lao personnel they advise, wear the same clothes, eat the same food, and share their hardships. A former LPLA junior officer (A-31) spoke frankly about the respect that the Vietnamese advisers had gained among the Lao troops:

> The troops in Laos very much respected the Vietnamese advisers. They tried to give them good food, but the Vietnamese advisers wouldn't accept the food. They ate the same food as the soldiers and stayed with them. The Lao officers, and some soldiers, seemed to be very grateful for their assistance.

In regard to the Vietnamese troops in Laos (to be discussed in the next chapter), our interviews suggest that there is almost unanimous respect in the LPLA ranks for their fighting ability. They are thought to be well trained, unusually well disciplined, militarily competent, and possessed of high morale. One former Lao officer (A-21), who had served in southern Laos where he had

had frequent contact with Vietnamese troops commented on their quality:

> During our fighting together, I can say that the Vietnamese troops had higher morale than the Lao. The Vietnamese were prepared to sacrifice their lives for their duty. They often said that they preferred to die rather than stay alive, since death would be the end of their fighting duties. They have higher morale because the Vietnamese officers are well trained. They fight with greater devotion, never complaining about their problems.

Another former LPLA officer (A-20), who also had been engaged in joint operations with the Vietnamese over a period of several years, was questioned about his reaction to the entry of the Vietnamese into an engagement in Sam Neua, in 1961. He said:

> We fought together — shoulder to shoulder. I didn't have anything more than a feeling of relief that the Vietnamese had come to our assistance during this attack [in Sam Neua]. Once the Vietnamese were able to capture their objective, the Lao would not have to fight for that position.

As regards the relations of the Vietnamese with local civilians, our research indicates that the Lao concerned find them generally satisfactory. Vietnamese troops are kept clear of the Lao population centers, generally bivouacking in sparsely settled areas. In the rare case when the troops do have contact with the local people, they appear to be well behaved. One former Lao soldier (A-4), who had grown up in Vietnam and had served with the Vietnamese forces in Laos before joining an LPLA unit, made the following observations:

> The Vietnamese military dealt with the Lao civilian population in a very nice way. They never took anything free of charge. If they wanted something, they bartered.
> They don't drink, and women are against regulations. With Lao soldiers, it's different.

Several other Lao defectors confirmed the observation that the North Vietnamese generally behaved better toward the local inhabitants than did the Lao soldiers. LPLA troops were less disciplined than the rigidly controlled Vietnamese and frequently helped themselves to local products (such as chickens and fruit) as well as girls. Punishment is severe for any Vietnamese soldier who chases the local girls, whereas for the Lao troops, though the rules are similar, the enforcement of discipline is much more lax.

The only ones to express resentment toward the Vietnamese were defectors who had disliked their interference in Lao matters. Even some of those who were grateful to the Vietnamese for supporting Lao independence found the continuing Vietnamese involvement in local Lao affairs intolerable. A former district chief (chao muong) (A-16) told us that, in 1953, he had been convinced that the Vietnamese were only helping the Lao in their struggle and that "once the Lao were free, the Vietnamese would return to Vietnam." He changed his mind, however, in 1963, when he became Chao Muong and could observe that they were still interfering. "There were Vietnamese advisers in the province, and every decision was made by them," he complained. The Lao physician mentioned earlier (A-10), even though he was indebted to the Vietnamese for his medical education, expressed animosity toward the interfering Vietnamese major who had been his adviser. The officer (A-21) whom we quoted as admiring Vietnamese troop morale said that he defected because of his opposition to the pervasive Vietnamese domination of Lao affairs, and particularly because he resented the Vietnamese attempt to influence his own decisions. Still another defector (A-17), who was appreciative of his training in North Vietnam, intensely disliked the surveillance by his Vietnamese adviser to which he was subjected in his post as chief of an LPLA quartermaster unit. We do not have sufficient data to judge how widespread and intense this discontent with the Vietnamese presence is. We suspect that, despite some resentment among the Lao, the problem is not as yet a serious threat to the relationship of the two allies.

Captain Mai Dai Hap gave us an insight into how at least one

Vietnamese adviser saw the Lao ally, and the problems he encountered were reminiscent of those often described by American military advisers in South Vietnam. Many of his observations, moreover, were confirmed by the Vietnamese medical technician (B-10) who had served as adviser to the Lao medical services in the same province. Hap complained that the LPLA leadership was poor, troop discipline shamefully inadequate, and morale low. Whenever Lao and Vietnamese went into battle together, the burden of the assault always fell upon the Vietnamese. In Hap's comparisons the Vietnamese military forces invariably were far superior to the Lao, as in the following characteristic judgment:

The Vietnamese are disciplined and well organized. The Lao are not. Sometimes the Lao troops will say frankly that they want to defect or that they don't want to work. Their chiefs will often just listen and smile. If that happened in a Vietnamese unit — watch out. If there were a Vietnamese unit operating in Laos, and someone said he wanted to defect, a meeting would be called immediately. The person who said this would have to explain himself. It would be dealt with either at the platoon, or company, or battalion level, as the case demanded. It might even call for the person being repatriated to NVN and appearing before a military tribunal. But in the Pathet Lao, a cadre who would discipline such a man would have to fear being shot, either by the man or by another soldier in the unit. At best, the cadre would fear upsetting the men in his unit if he tried to enforce such discipline. If you sent a soldier back to his home village in Laos, the people would rejoice. They would say that it's just fine; he has been liberated from the army. In North Vietnam, by contrast, the family would lose face.

Captain Hap recalled that, when the Soviet and Communist Chinese advisers had assisted the Viet Minh in their struggle against the French, they had provided only "general advice" while "we, the Viet Minh soldiers, devised the plans and programs. The Vietnamese are intelligent, and we handled our own decisions. But with the Lao, you must tell them everything . . . even what to do about rusty cartridges." Hap believed that the

Lao troops depended on their Vietnamese advisers for their continued operation. "If the Vietnamese went home," he contended, "the Lao wouldn't know what to do." He disclosed that Vietnamese officers were disdainful of the Lao officers, though they hid their disdain. "They mocked the Lao officers, who often carried their pistols in a holster far down on their hips, with a swaggering walk." Hap believed that the LPLA soldiers respected the Vietnamese advisers more than they did their own officers. This was indirectly confirmed by some of our interviews with defectors from the LPLA, who stated that Lao officers at times used this respect for the Vietnamese advisers to tighten discipline among their Lao subordinates.

There are some indications, however, that the young Vietnam-trained Lao, who are returning to Laos in increasing numbers, are a tougher, "Vietnamized" breed. As they begin to replace the more typical Lao throughout the military, political, and administrative structure of the Communist zone of Laos, the character of its regime is likely to undergo a change, particularly at the upper levels of the hierarchy.

VIII

The North Vietnamese Military
Adviser in Laos: A First-Hand Account

Important insights into the North Vietnamese role in Laos are afforded by the testimony of North Vietnamese Captain Mai Dai Hap, a member of the Communist Lao Dong Party who served as military adviser to a Pathet Lao battalion in Nam Tha province in northern Laos from February 1964 until his defection in December 1966. The substance of his account is borne out by documentary evidence as well as by the testimony of Pathet Lao defectors and of other Vietnamese military who deserted their posts in Laos. The picture presented by Mai Dai Hap reinforces the conclusion that North Vietnamese support for the Pathet Lao forces plays a vital role in their ability to maintain the insurgency against the Royal Lao Government.

The Adviser, Mai Dai Hap

Mai Dai Hap was born in 1930 in a village of Thanh-Hoa Province in the coastal lowlands of North Vietnam. Like the great majority of rural Vietnamese, his family engaged in rice-farming. They were slightly better off than their neighbors, being classified as "middle" farmers by Viet Minh standards. Prior to his military service, Hap had only five years of formal education. He entered school in his native district when he was seven, but had to drop

129

out at the age of twelve when his father died and he was needed in the rice paddies to help support his widowed mother and four brothers. In 1950, when the Viet Minh was expanding its military organization in the struggle against the French, the then twenty-year-old Hap joined the Viet Minh forces. Two years later he became a member of the Lao Dong Party.

Hap's army history shows steady promotion within the infantry up to the grade of senior captain, which he was awarded in October 1966, shortly before his defection. Most of his army service before his assignment to Laos was in the Northwest Military Region of North Vietnam, the highland area adjacent to Laos. In the 1953 Viet Minh offensive in Laos, his unit fought in an area near Dien Bien Phu (although he was not engaged directly in the major battle at that fort in 1954). From 1953 to 1958, he served with the 159th Independent Regiment in the same region, and from August 1958 to February 1960 he attended an infantry officer school at nearby Sontay. Graduated with the rank of lieutenant, he was assigned as commander of the 5th Company, 1st Battalion, of the 316th Brigade, which was stationed in the Dien Bien Phu sector. In December 1963, two months before his assignment to Laos, he was promoted to Captain 2nd Class.

From February 1964 until his defection in December 1966, Captain Hap served in Laos as military adviser to the 408th Pathet Lao Battalion in the Nam Tha region on the Laos-China border. During this period he only once went back to North Vietnam, leaving Laos in July 1966 for the long journey through southern China to attend a week-long meeting for North Vietnamese advisers to Pathet Lao units. It was held at Son La, the headquarters of the Northwest Military Region in North Vietnam, which directs the North Vietnamese military operations in Laos. Before reporting for the meeting itself, he was granted home leave, which permitted him to visit his mother, his second wife, and his three children. (The children were by his first marriage. Their mother having died in 1960, he had married his second wife that same year.) He returned to Laos in October 1966.

We interviewed Mai Dai Hap in Vientiane, with the aid of an

interpreter, in April and May 1967. Some ten sessions of three to four hours each produced a transcript of approximately a hundred pages. At our request, Hap also supplied written answers to a set of questions and, in addition, wrote a seventy-page memoir in which he related his experiences as a military adviser to a Pathet Lao battalion.

From this wealth of information we have selected a few portions that tell Hap's personal history and reveal some of his attitudes. But our main interest has been in presenting material to show how a North Vietnamese adviser to a Pathet Lao battalion sees the problems he faces and how he copes with them. In grouping related statements under individual topics, we have added explanatory notes wherever Mai Dai Hap's observations might confuse the reader, and we have deleted repetitious passages. In general, however, we have allowed Hap to speak for himself.

Our long conversations with Mai Dai Hap left us in no doubt about his intelligence. He was alert and articulate. Our interpreters and translators described his Vietnamese as quite literate, and his spoken Lao as exceptionally good for someone without previous language training. He was particularly competent in military analysis and, in keeping with his Party training, sensitive to the political dimensions. His good mind and twenty-two months of service in Laos combined to give him a sound grasp of both Vietnamese and Pathet Lao operations.

Certainly, Mai Dai Hap's attitudes must be interpreted in the light of his defection. We are satisfied, however, that the information he gave is substantially true. Our other interviews with both Pathet Lao and Vietnamese sources, as well as documentary evidence, support his account.

To preserve as much as possible of the original flavor of the story as Mai Dai Hap told it, we shall quote him directly in the pages to follow. Brief paraphrases and comments appear in brackets.

His Account

Reassignment

One day in December 1963, I was vacationing at Cua Ong, a coal-exporting harbor in North Vietnam. I was enjoying life, that peaceful

MAP VI. Background Map for the Account of Captain Mai Dai Hap

life which reigned in our prosperous country, when suddenly I received a telegram to report to the Headquarters of the 316th Brigade in Dien Bien Phu to accept a new assignment. I confess that I was half happy and half apprehensive. We had been taught to accept responsibilities, to be ready to assume any new duties assigned to us by the Party.[1] It was our task to save the country from the American invaders. The telegram led me to think that my new assignment might send me either to the South [i.e., South Vietnam] or to Laos. I was happy at the news because I felt that I had gained the confidence of the Party, but at the same time I was troubled because I knew that I would be separated from my beloved family and my beloved country. I knew that I would be facing war, and I confess that I did not like to fight or to be separated from my native land.

In January 1964, I called at Brigade Headquarters and met Lt. Col. Chu Phuong Doi, the Brigade Commander, who told me: "Comrade, procure the necessary papers and proceed to Headquarters to receive your new assignment."

Before our departure, the Brigade gave a banquet for the thirty cadres, from senior captain down, who were departing. In his address to us the Brigade Commander said, "No matter what role you play, no matter what duties you assume, whether you are assigned to the South, to Laos, or to duty in the North, always maintain and develop the prestige of our troops, particularly the prestige of our Brigade." He then proposed a toast to our health. Our representative stood up to assure the Brigade Commander of our determination to fulfill the duties assigned to us by the Party.

We left the 316th Brigade at Dien Bien Phu in late January for leave to visit our families, our native place, our fertile land. I felt very enthusiastic about going back to the lowlands[2] for a rest and a visit with my parents, my wife and children, and my close friends, from whom I had been separated for so many years. I also thought that I might be leaving these northwestern highlands forever.

I had just reached my home on February 1, when a telegram called me back again on February 5: I was to report to the Commander's Headquarters immediately to accept my assignment. The message cut short my joys and filled my family with sorrow. After my years of separation from them, my month's leave had ended after only five days. I tried to comfort my family, and in the evening of the day I had received the cable, I boarded a train headed for Hanoi. Promptly on February 6, I reported for duty at Headquarters, where a major met me and gave me the Commander's order. I learned then that I was to go to Laos as a military adviser to the 408th Pathet Lao Battalion. Simultaneously I was given the status of a Battalion Commander, although I was still officially ranked as a Captain 2nd Class.

Preparation for Service in Laos

The major took me in his jeep to Group 959 at Gia-Lam [on the outskirts of Hanoi], which commanded all [political and administrative] operations in Laos. I was apprehensive about my future role of adviser to the Pathet Lao: I did not know any foreign language, and I knew that living with the Pathet Lao troops would be miserable and that my life would be in danger. I assumed that their fighting capabilities were poor and that in case of danger they would leave me. These were the reasons that tempted me to refuse the assignment. But I confess that I did not dare speak up because I was afraid of the negative effect this refusal could have on my future.

When I arrived at Doan 959 Headquarters, I met Senior Captain Tho, a cadre on permanent duty there, who gave me instructions on how to prepare for my Laos assignment. I was to leave behind anything that would identify me as a North Vietnamese officer, to take off all insignia, and to draw new uniforms and the equipment necessary to a cadre assigned to Laos. I received warm clothing and long-sleeved shirts, underwear similar to that worn by a Pathet Lao soldier, a blanket, a mosquito net, two pairs of shoes, three meters of "ni long" (nylon) waterproof raincoat material, one hammock, an individual first-aid kit, one pistol, and fifty cartridges. [I was told that] Doan 959 Headquarters would be responsible for sending my monthly salary to my family. In case of sickness, my family would be entitled to free medical care in any military hospital; in case of material need, they would receive assistance from regional cooperatives; in any popular gatherings, they were entitled to occupy seats of honor. I was introduced to several company-level cadres who had been assigned as advisers to various companies of the 408th Pathet Lao Battalion.

It took three days for all the preparations. Then we were given money and allowed a few days' rest. We received sugar, milk, cigarettes, cakes, and candies. On the evening of February 9, Doan 959 organized a farewell banquet in our honor. Mr. Nguyen Van Vinh, an important member of the Party, addressed us with comforting words and encouraged us to develop the prestige of our troops and whole-heartedly to fulfill our duties. He also told us about the characteristics of the Pathet Lao cadres and troops, the customs and ways of the Lao people, the international situation at the time, the actual situation of our country, and the enemy's strategy in Laos.

Deployment to Laos via China

On the morning of February 10, ten of us went by train from Gia-Lam to Yen-Bai, where we rested overnight. Then, in the afternoon [of February 11], we took the train from Yen-Bai to Lao-Kay [Lao Cai],[3] on the Chinese border, where we arrived at 3 AM of February 12. There we met the 1st Battalion of the 316th NVA Brigade,[4] also headed for Laos. With them were two Lao officers on the way back to their country after a period of training in Hanoi. They were Khamseng, the 408th Battalion Commander, and Khamphoui, his executive officer. Both knew Vietnamese. I was feeling much better by then, because I was meeting people who were going my way, particularly the two cadres of the battalion with whom I was to work. Their knowledge of Vietnamese was going to help me considerably in solving the problems I would soon face.

At Lao-Kay the train crossed into China. This was the first time I had set foot on the immense land of our ally. The train sped past cities and towns, rice paddies, and plants of our Chinese friends. I was filled with great joy, and determined to fulfill my duties. We were on the train all day, until 6 PM of February 12, when it finally stopped at Bang-Khe,[5] in the province of Yunnan. There we joined a regiment of the Chinese People's Liberation Army for food and rest. On the morning of February 13 we went on by truck and drove continuously for five days, past Mong-Tu, Xi-Mao, and Muong-La [Men-la]. In the evening of February 17, we arrived at Muong-Mang, only two kilometers from the Lao border. We washed up, did our laundry, and rested for the night. The next morning, all cadres from company level up gathered at a meeting at which a cadre from the Chinese regiment gave us an intelligence report[6] on the enemy's situation [across the border] in the Muong Sing[7] [region of Laos].

[Thereafter Captain Hap and his group crossed the border from China into Laos to report to their duty post with the 408th Pathet Lao Battalion, which operated throughout northern Nam Tha, along the borders of Communist China.]

The Adviser's Mission

All North Vietnamese cadres and advisers, when helping the Pathet Lao, must act as if those duties were their own. For instance, the provincial advisers of Nam Tha must consider Nam Tha their own province. I, as adviser of the 408th Battalion, must regard the 408th as [I would] my own unit. A North Vietnamese adviser to a Pathet Lao military or administrative unit is like a helmsman who must guide the boat to its port. The Pathet Lao are like the crew, under the guidance of the helmsman. That is the objective laid down by the [Vietnamese] Lao Dong Party and the People's Party of Laos. If anything happens that could damage the friendship and solidarity between Laos and Vietnam, the North Vietnamese advisers must bear the major responsibility, no matter who is right or wrong.

To take an example of a military adviser at work, suppose he had to prepare the battalion for a certain battle. He must possess a thorough knowledge of the Pathet Lao organization. He must get all the information about the enemy's situation, the population, the state of the unit's equipment, food supplies, arms, and ammunition. Then he must devise his military plan. It is up to the political adviser then to consider the objectives of the battle, examine the difficulties, and propose measures. Afterward the military and political advisers would communicate their plan to the Pathet Lao cadres, who would discuss it and present their own ideas. Then, the Pathet Lao battalion cadres would convoke the cadres of their companies and platoons and inform them of the battle plan. The advisers are allowed to attend the meetings and to present any additional comments and suggestions.

As an example of a political adviser at work, let us suppose that a district adviser wanted the Pathet Lao district cadres to carry out a tax reform. After receiving and studying the documents sent down by the provincial advisers, the district adviser would invite the Pathet Lao district cadre to get acquainted with the regulations and with ways of implementing them at the canton or village level. After the district cadres thoroughly understood the program, they would form teams to go and work in every canton and village. Each team would be accompanied by one adviser, who was constantly at the side of the Pathet Lao cadres to help them correct any mistake and guide them at every step.

Generally speaking, everything is initiated by the North Vietnamese advisers, be it important or unimportant. If the North Vietnamese advisory machinery were to get stuck, the Pathet Lao machinery would be paralyzed. The Pathet Lao leadership relies upon the North Vietnamese advisers; it seldom gives instructions to the lower echelons or tries to find out what is going on among them. The subordinates themselves seldom report to their superiors and show no respect for them. That is the reason why advisers finally have to go into the individual unit to watch over everyone's ideological development, study the results, and make plans.

Training

[Hap describes a period when he and other Vietnamese advisers organized a training program for the Pathet Lao units to which they were assigned.]

We prepared for the Pathet Lao units to go into training. At first we gave them one month in which to work on stabilizing the situation among the population. In that time we set up exercise fields and classrooms and developed instructional materials. The Pathet Lao battalion cadres were entrusted with the responsibility of controlling and supervising the programs. We advisers divided up the task of preparing the teaching materials. We had to base our political and military instruction on the guiding principles handed us from above. For example, our program included [the following topics]:

Political
    Objectives and tasks of the Lao revolution.
    The land of Laos is beautiful and rich, the population of Laos is
        industrious; why the Lao people are suffering.
    The enemy of the Lao people.
    The tasks and nature of the Lao Liberation Army.

Military

The education of discipline and self-awakening in the revolutionary army.

The methods of troop management by a revolutionary cadre.

The capacity and use of various weapons.

Instructions on the five great techniques: the use of the bayonet, the use of grenades, shooting a rifle, digging fortifications, and creeping and crawling.

Instructions on tactics, operations, attacks, ambushes, hand-to-hand combat, breaching of defense perimeters, etc. . . .

After preparing the instructional materials, we had to teach the Pathet Lao cadres first, so that they in turn could teach the lower levels. We did not teach the Pathet Lao classes directly because we were not fluent in their language.

After we had finished preparing the materials, I, as military adviser to the battalion, had to arrange the programs for every month, week, and day for the whole battalion and then suggest ways for the Pathet Lao battalion cadres to work. Captain Chinh, the political adviser of the battalion, had to make preparations for such political matters as setting forth the objectives of the training programs and encouraging competition within the battalion so that the troops would study effectively. The training period was divided into three months of political training and two months of military training.

The task of setting up the training program for the Pathet Lao was a great deal more demanding than that of training a North Vietnamese battalion. For the most part, the Pathet Lao lacked discipline. They attended training sessions as their mood prompted them; they would stay away when they didn't feel like coming. The lower cadres were usually of a low cultural level. This was true even of many battalion-level cadres. Their vision was narrow, and they were not used to planning but were prone to handle problems as they came up.

Morale and Discipline

[Hap described a period when the Royal Lao Government forces that his unit faced increased their strength, which discouraged the local population from helping the Pathet Lao forces and seriously reduced their supplies. In the face of such hardship, the desertion rate increased. Hap discusses problems of troop morale.]

The men of the 408th showed discouragement, wishing that another unit would replace them. They still accepted their share of duties, since the enemy forces were not numerous in this region. Though we had some encounters with them, they were not fierce. But our men had witnessed many of their friends being wounded and left without proper care. While the cadres and the healthy troops had helped themselves to war booty, the wounded men sometimes did not have anything to wear. I interceded for them, but the battalion commander would not do anything.

Moreover, whenever we won a victory, or whenever the enemy eased his pressure, the Pathet Lao troops became careless. If we met with defeat or faced a difficult situation, they lost their fighting spirit and were discouraged and confused. Their cadres were stirred into action only when there was an operation; otherwise they cared very little about their units. The cadres worked when they liked; when they were depressed, they would do nothing. If their pride was hurt, they would refuse to listen to the adviser.

[Describing another period, when enemy pressure had let up, Hap discusses the problems of discipline he confronted in his Pathet Lao unit.]

The Pathet Lao troops did not equal the North Vietnamese troops — they felt free to do as they liked. They had little sense of responsibility and, of ten planned items, carried out at the most only five or six. In transport duty, for instance, they were to make two trips a day, each time carrying twenty kilograms. Sometimes they gave up after one trip, or carried only ten to fifteen kilograms.

When they saw that the enemy was relatively peaceful, they became "subjective" and neglectful. From time to time, they would shoot into the air for no reason at all. Little groups of three to five men would go to the woods to shoot birds or hunt bear. Soldiers showed little respect for discipline; they would get drunk and play around with girls. In fact, the battalion commander himself would take out his gun to fire it in front of girls. Once I criticized him so severely that he became angry and didn't do a thing for a whole day.

Whenever an incident occurred, cadres of the North Vietnamese military unit would whisper to one another, "What are those advisers doing over there? They let their soldiers be so disorderly." One would say, "If I were a Pathet Lao adviser, I would not let them act that way." We advisers were very vexed by this attitude. Some of us replied, "If you wish to be advisers, we will gladly cede our positions. This matter should be brought up before the Military Region Advisers for review, you know."

The Military Region Advisory Group [Ban Co-Van Quan Khu] decided to organize "Ten Days of Vietnamese-Lao Solidarity" [Doan-Ket Viet-Lao]. Each Vietnamese company was to team up with a Lao company, with Vietnamese and Lao of the same rank instructing one another on how to deal with troops, work from practical experience, and bring about mutual understanding. Unfortunately, these days of Vietnamese-Lao solidarity were just "painful" days for us in the advisory unit.

Counterpart Relations and Control

[Hap describes several incidents which reveal some of the problems he and his colleague, the political adviser of the 408th Battalion, faced in dealing with the Lao battalion commander.]

One day I had a quarrel with the battalion commander. The enemy had sent a company to a location controlled by us where we had only one platoon. The platoon requested reinforcement, but we had no reserve troops, since our forces had been spread out. We could not withdraw any unit without leaving several important points unprotected. Finally, we managed to send one platoon to the threatened areas. I suggested that the battalion commander send his deputy along with the platoon, but the commander himself wanted to go also. Since the two platoons already had one company commander, I objected. The reason I had suggested that the deputy commander of the battalion should go was that I wanted him to assess the general situation (not to assume the command of the platoons). If both men were to go, nobody would be left behind to command the unit. They would not listen to me. Finally, over my strong objection, they cancelled the order to send the reinforcement, and no one went. I was enraged. I told them that it was their duty, and if they refused to fight, they would have to account for that to their superiors.

Another time, during a criticism session, the battalion commander asked the political adviser pointblank: "Who is the boss here: we Lao or you Vietnamese?" This occurred at a time when he was drunk and didn't want to listen to the report of his unit's activities for the day. The political adviser had grown impatient, and his insistence had made the commander angry. After the fit of drunkenness, the Lao recovered his calm and soon settled matters with the advisers.

[From time to time, both Lao authorities and the Vietnamese advisers at the province level would visit the 408th. Hap describes one of these visits, at a time when the battalion was facing heavy enemy pressure in the region of Muong Sing.]

In early 1966, a delegation of provincial advisers and cadres arrived at our unit. It included the [Vietnamese] provincial senior adviser, Major Canh, and the Pathet Lao provincial delegate (whose name I forget). When the delegation arrived, everyone in the unit, Vietnamese advisers and Pathet Lao cadres, was very much encouraged, because we were about to get help from the higher echelon. The provincial adviser gathered the battalion advisers together to give them encouragement and listen to their reports. He recognized our difficulties, but he encouraged us to persevere and told us: "You must strive to help our friends to hold the unit together. Do not let it disintegrate. Do not let them withdraw from their position without orders from above. Although the population has departed, it is a strategic location, and if the enemy occupies it, Muong Sing will be threatened."

The Pathet Lao provincial cadres assembled the [lower] cadres to review the situation. They then convened the Party members to examine the reasons why the unit had regressed and to review the role of all Party members. Thereafter, the provincial delegate personally went to encourage each company, and the provincial authorities gave the battalion two cows as well as cigarettes as material tokens of their encouragement. After this drive, the unit's condition improved noticeably, and the elements entrusted with patrol, search, and ambush duties proved more eager.

Hap's Personal Life

Both administrative and military advisers at the province and district levels live in special quarters, next to the Pathet Lao provincial headquarters. They eat separately from the Pathet Lao. Each adviser is allowed 50 kip of spending money per day and also raises poultry and grows vegetables to improve his diet. He is issued two uniforms and can buy one additional uniform from the supply service. Such items as sugar, milk, cigarettes, soap, and toothpaste can be bought from the North Vietnamese quartermaster unit in Nam Tha. The adviser can buy items on credit by signing a receipt. The quartermaster sends the receipt to the central office, where the amount is deducted from the man's salary [to be paid out] at home. Each North Vietnamese adviser sent to Laos receives a special pay supplement equal to 50 percent of his base pay.

Advisers attached to battalions and independent companies in the field are in the same situation, but because they must live with the Pathet Lao they must eat like them. Moreover, they are assigned to remote places where it is difficult to send supplies, so that they are somewhat at a disadvantage [compared to those at province and district headquarters]. However, they can save more money.

One just couldn't compare Lao and Vietnamese standards. A Lao was given only 8 kip a day. Moreover, the Vietnamese food was cheaper because it came from Vietnamese aid and was priced according to Vietnamese standards. The Lao had nothing and depended on the villagers for their food purchases, and, if the village population fled, they had nowhere to buy food. At times they even shot some of the villagers' buffaloes, but they could not do so if the Vietnamese adviser was at their side. As for our advisory unit, since we lived with the Lao and it was wartime, we did not feel right eating separately, and we therefore put in a contribution of 8 kip each and ate with the Lao. This was a hard thing for us to do, but we just closed our eyes and ate the way the Lao did.

[Hap describes a relatively peaceful period for his unit in Muong Sing, from January to September 1965. During that time, his living conditions were adequate.]

The place looked prosperous, with a large population, animated market activities, a clear communications line to China, an adequate supply of food and commodities, and rather low market prices. A chicken cost 150 kip, a fat duck 150 kip, one kilogram of pork 50 kip, and beef 30 kip per kilogram. As there was ample food, my group of Vietnamese advisers could organize their own mess, with each of us contributing only 30 kip per day. From time to time, there was a large festival and we were invited here and there; at the time, the life of a battalion adviser was quite "high class." I had no thought other than to fulfill my task.

[In December 1965, Hap's unit was engaged in dangerous operations. In one battle, his battalion had attacked the enemy, who was firmly emplaced on high ground. The attack failed, and when retreat was ordered, Hap's forces fled in confusion, leaving behind eight dead. The battalion was demoralized, and Hap was in low spirits.]

I was very much discouraged and pessimistic. I had to endure much hardship: sleeping in the forest, on the ground, in the open, exposed to inclement weather, and eating poor food. I had also failed in my leadership; I had to bear the responsibility for the decline of the battalion. I told myself that it was much too difficult to lead the Pathet Lao — that they were really poor troops. [Moreover], I was not their direct commander: I had to go through their own cadres for everything, but those cadres were not competent; yet, if anything went wrong, I would be reprimanded by my superior in the advisory mission. In effect, I had great responsibility but no power. The prospect was gloomy indeed. I felt very depressed, and I wished very much that someone would be sent to replace me so that I could return to my country and there go to school or assume other less demanding duties.

The enemy's strength was developing rapidly, his troops were numerous, and the population was now on his side. On our side, there was no substance in our propaganda, only empty words. We said that we were fighting for a just cause, that we had the support of the people. In our unit we had only Lao Theung [highlanders]; no Lao Loum [lowland Lao] were joining the Pathet Lao. How could we say that the people supported us? How could we defeat the enemy? His cannon pounded Muong Nang at regular intervals. His airplanes were constantly flying over our heads. We had to move our camp every two or three days to escape the bombing. It was really miserable. I could not sleep at night and was obsessed by all kinds of thoughts.

[In January 1966, the military pressure on Hap's unit continued, and his morale was still low.]

It has been a long time since I received a letter from my people, and I did not know why. Tet [the Vietnamese New Year] was drawing near, and all families must be getting ready to welcome the return of spring. My loved ones were surely talking about me; it had been two years since I left them. When would I be allowed to go home? In the present situation, if the enemy attacked, our unit would only flee in disorder. They [the Pathet Lao] might abandon me in their flight, and in that case I would surely die.

Combat Experiences

[In the early months of Hap's service in Laos in 1964, the 408th Pathet Lao Battalion, together with elements of the North Vietnamese 1st Battalion of the 316th Brigade, attacked a Royal Lao Government position. Though Hap was not fully satisfied with their performance, the friendly forces were victorious. Here are some of his recollections.]

As the month of August began, our military unit entered a period of relaxation. We made a general review of what we had learned and prepared ourselves for the Muong Nang operation.

From the period of our recent activities I learned that both Vietnamese and Lao units were inexperienced in fighting regional forces. Since these were local people, they knew all the routes very well. As soon as both sides entered combat, it did not take [the regional forces] long to disperse, and they were able to regroup immediately. If they were not encircled right away, it was impossible to destroy them. As for the Pathet Lao soldiers, their morale was low; they were poor fighters and poor shots. Sometimes they still fired when there was no enemy present at all. Their cadres were unable to control the soldiers during combat. They could not keep operations secret. All these deficiencies were brought up to educate our troops.

One point had to be noted: The alliance between Lao and Vietnamese troops was very difficult. The Vietnamese did not trust the Lao, and the Lao relied on the Vietnamese, so that coordination in battle was not tight enough to defeat the enemy. The Pathet Lao forces were weak. If they were sent somewhere, a Vietnamese unit had to be sent with them. For example, if one Lao battalion was sent, one Vietnamese company had to go along; if one Lao company was going, one Vietnamese platoon had to accompany it.

[In late 1965, Hap was informed by his superiors at province headquarters that the 408th would soon face attacks by the Royal Lao Government forces. The Vietnamese units which had formerly been stationed nearby had been sent elsewhere, and now the Vietnamese advisers at the company level of the 408th were also to be withdrawn.]

I myself felt very apprehensive, because fighting this time would involve a great deal more hardship than in 1964. The battalion would be fighting by itself, without the support of the Vietnamese troops, without even the close guidance of the upper echelons. Moreover, the battalion political advisers had just received orders to transfer to another place and were to be replaced. Since the Vietnamese advisers at the company level were also to be withdrawn, this left a single adviser in the whole unit — myself. Despite the fact that the 408th had undergone a training period and had matured somewhat, I still did not have full confidence in them. Moreover, in the fighting I would have to forget all my sentimental ties [a reference to his future Lao wife]; I would have to start a new life in the open air, in the woods, which, to tell the truth, I did not relish. But then, to whom could I relinquish my responsibility? I had to go, outwardly seeming enthusiastic and courageous to set an example for everyone.

[Hap continues his account of the engagements in late 1965. Though once again Pathet Lao units were successful in pushing out the Royal Lao Government forces in his sector, he was still dissatisfied with the fighting effectiveness of his battalion.]

From all this, I drew the following conclusions: This situation has resulted from the fact that the 408th did not have enough fighting experience and had had few encounters with enemy planes and artillery. Until recently, they had always been supported by Vietnamese forces. But now that they were by themselves, they did not have the capability to accomplish their mission, and, because their fighting spirit was low, their reconnaissance party was afraid to get close to the enemy. As a result, they were like a blind man walking on a strange road, stumbling and getting hurt at every step, becoming more and more confused, and every now and then losing the will to go on.

I was pessimistic and discouraged myself and very much wanted higher echelons to reinforce us with a Vietnamese company. But this request was in vain. The telegrams sent by the provincial advisory mission offering us their advice were not much help. They only told us that, if we were not in a position to destroy the enemy, we should send reconnaissance parties to find out any weak points in the enemy's defense and then strike at them; even a small victory would lift the morale of our troops. The provincial advisory mission did send one battalion political adviser and two company political advisers to help me improve the unit's condition. With that reinforcement, the leadership went to each company to work individually with the cadres, and the morale of the troops in general was raised somewhat. We noted fewer absences under pretense of illness.

[In this final selection, Hap describes an engagement that took place in February 1966. The main part of the 408th Pathet Lao Battalion was moved to Muong Long, where the enemy had concentrated its forces to destroy the Pathet Lao base in the Co (a highland tribal minority) area. Hap explains that in this region the Vietnamese and Pathet Lao had built resistance bases against the French, so that the Co people welcomed them heartily, especially after seeing the Vietnamese with the unit. The unit's target was Phieng Luong, the weakest of the enemy's positions although protected with fortifications. With the help of local informants who had access to the post, the Pathet Lao attack succeeded. Hap tells of the plan he devised.]

I discussed the following plan with the Pathet Lao battalion commander:

Contact the Phieng Luong population and ask them for information about the enemy's position and the terrain;

send reconnaissance parties and ask the Phieng Luong people to
guide them;

ask the villagers to get food supplies for us; allow the troops to
rest and to get ready for the attack;

within the battalion, convene all members of Party and youth organizations, the cadres of all echelons, and the well-seasoned
elements among the troops to acquaint them with the plans
and to seek their opinion and ideas;

encourage the people's organizations to visit with the unit;

build a sand table reproducing exactly the enemy's post, to fa-
miliarize the unit with our attack plan.

After assessing the situation, I devised the following plan. We
would use one company of infantrymen. The company would divide
into two groups: one would advance to the main gate, while the other
would follow to support it. After the battalion cadres had agreed to
the plan, the troops were notified. The preparations took about three
days. On February 18, 1966, we launched our operation against the
Phieng Luong outpost. Our unit was in high spirits and determined to
vanquish the enemy.

[Following is the account of the battle.] At 3 AM of the 19th, the
first group advanced toward the post's gate, and close to the bunker
met the sentry. When the sentry flashed his light on us, he was killed
instantly by the advance squad, which took possession of the bunker.
A second squad followed and stormed into the post, using a B.40 gun
to burn a number of buildings. At this moment, the second group
joined with the first one. The enemy was caught by surprise. Nevertheless, it took more than two hours of fighting in the trenches and
blockhouses to complete occupation of the post, at 5 AM of February
19, 1966. The enemy lost 4 dead, 10 wounded, 2 prisoners; the rest
fled. Our side suffered 4 dead and 3 wounded. We captured one 60
mm mortar, one DK 57 gun, one bazooka 90, 2 submachine guns,
a number of rifles, and a quantity of military uniforms and equipment. With this victory, the morale of the battalion got a big lift.
Although we had suffered some casualties, this was an exemplary
victory.

Defection

[Hap went back to Vietnam in July 1966 for a meeting of Vietnamese advisers to Pathet Lao units held at the headquarters of the Northwest Military Region at Son La. On that occasion, he was given home leave. Though he requested reassignment to service in North Vietnam, Hap's orders called for him to return to his post in Nam Tha. As he stated earlier, Hap had by then become quite gloomy about his life in Laos.]

I had to find a way out of this situation. I hated to be sent indefinitely to serve as adviser to the Pathet Lao. In October 1966, therefore, when I returned to Laos, I decided to defect with my present wife, whom I had met in Muong Sing in June 1965 while my unit in Laos was spread out to avoid the enemy bombardment. Our forces were then stationed two or three kilometers from Muong Sing, and [the members of] our battalion lived with the population in Xieng Le, Tai Xieng Vieng, and Muong Sing. For a whole year before that, we had gone from one operation to another and bivouacked far from the populated areas, and consequently we had had little personal life. When we began living with the population, I felt as if my heart had been warmed. At the time, I was living right next to my future wife's house. Her father was a member of the village council. Therefore, during my spare time, I would visit their house, and during the village council meetings I would contribute opinions as a way of helping local cadres in their work.

Those were the circumstances that brought my wife and me together. From mere acquaintances we soon became secret lovers. Why secret? Because, as a Vietnamese on a mission in Laos, I was not allowed to marry a Lao or chase after women. I was a Vietnamese officer and, if such conduct became known to my superior, I would have to face disciplinary measures.

Earlier, in 1963, my [present] wife had given in to pressure from her family and married a Burmese who had come to Muong Sing to trade. He was quite a lady's man and gambler, and my wife felt no love for him. They lived together for a time, but after she became pregnant he left her for good and took other wives. Also, the Pathet Lao had suspected him of espionage activities. [In the end], the authorities arrested him and handed him over to the Burmese government, and for the next three years there was no news of him. My wife had the right to marry again, but she was reticent about making our love known. For my part, I loved her at the beginning just to have someone to love, to change my arid personal life, so that I would not have to face cold loneliness. As the months went by, our love became stronger. I started to realize that time was fleeting and that my return home to North Vietnam was still very much undecided. Moreover, in October 1965 I received orders to go to the front. What would living under the open sky and braving [the enemy's] guns bring me? I thought that, if this went on, I might not see my family [in Vietnam] for a long time.

To add to this, the 408th Pathet Lao Battalion which I was advising was then in bad shape. Its strength was diminishing daily, though the plan for the province called for an increase in force strength. The population was joining the enemy, and they could now attack us from every direction. Besides, we learned that in South Vietnam the war was expanding and nobody could guess when it would end.

While I was back from the front for a mission in Muong Sing for a couple of days, I thought about making the final decision to defect. I shared my sentiment with my future wife, but she dared not decide at that time, for since childhood she had never yet left her family. However, after I had gone back to North Vietnam in July 1966, had been refused reassignment, and had witnessed the ravages of war on that land, it became necessary for me to make a decision. Out of love and pity for my mother and my young children, I did not have the heart to do so at once. Circumstances, however, forced my hand and, unhappy as I was about it, I had to abandon that part of my life. Consequently, while I was in Vietnam, I collected my salary for my Laos service, which amounted to 2,000 Dong, and bought various things for my mother and children to make it easier for them after I was gone.

By the time I got back to Muong Sing in October 1966, the situation there had changed a great deal. The roads leading to the Chinese frontier, to Muong Nang and Nam Tha, had been ambushed three or four times, including even Xieng Le, the village of my wife's family, where a North Vietnamese platoon was stationed. Nine or ten Vietnamese comrades had been killed or wounded. The people of Muong Sing were quite confused. The North Vietnamese in Muong

Sing had only one company left, Company 90 (a transport unit), with about sixty men, and would thus be vulnerable if we tried to defend our Muong Sing position. The Pathet Lao had a little over one platoon, but these were troops of low quality. The enemy's strength started me thinking.

At the time, there was no one in Muong Sing from the Vietnamese provincial advisory committee. Only the commanders of Company 90 were there, and as I was a battalion officer, they had absolutely no authority over me. At 8 AM after breakfast, when the unit went into the woods to hide from the planes, I would go to my wife's home. Circumstances allowed us to discuss our plans carefully. At first, my wife was suspicious. She was afraid I might trick her into defecting and then send other cadres after her. She was afraid that the Pathet Lao might ambush and kill us. She was afraid that I might try to kill her on the way.

I did my best to make her understand my views. I told her that I had intimate knowledge of all the plans of the Pathet Lao and the North Vietnamese, and that above all the two of us should in no way let a third person in on our plans. Once I had her full agreement, I told her to get in touch with the government forces. Unfortunately, she was too innocent and did not know how to go about it. The result was that we contacted no one. But I decided we should go just the same. We waited until there was a big fair in Muong Sing, when a great many people would be coming into town from the mountains. We could then follow them [unnoticed] when they went back home. When the time came to leave, my wife informed her mother, who agreed readily and said: "You go ahead and find some place to settle. Once you have a place, you can come back and take us with you." We started our escape at 9 AM on December 9, 1966.

IX

The North Vietnamese
Military Presence

An estimated 67,000 North Vietnamese military personnel now serve in Laos.[1] In 1968, when only 40,000 NVA were reported in Laos, some 25,000 of these were thought to operate the infiltration system over the Ho Chi Minh Trail, which runs through the southern panhandle of Laos to South Vietnam. This figure included service units such as engineers who maintain the Trail, labor battalions who perform coolie functions, and security forces; it did not include the thousands of military personnel who regularly hike through the Trail on their way from North to South Vietnam. The remaining 15,000 fell into three categories: the advisers to the LPLA forces (approximately 700 men); mobile units, as required; and NVA troop units assigned to the several provinces.[2]

NVA units assigned to a province often undertake joint operations with the area's LPLA forces.[3] While there is interaction between the Lao and the Vietnamese officers at the command level in such cases, the troops serve in their own units, obey their own officers, and sleep, eat, and fight separately. Technically, therefore, the Lao do not serve within Vietnamese units, nor do the Vietnamese serve as "encadrement" for the LPLA except when they are temporarily called upon to act as guides and local support personnel. But because Vietnamese advisory personnel are assigned as low as at company level (in the so-called "independent companies"), their influence goes well beyond that of ordinary "military advisers." Moreover, they possess superior military (and political) training and educational background and are closer than are the Lao commanders to the source of real power—the DRV. Thus, even though the LPLA units operate under their own Lao commanders, the Vietnamese advisers, while not formally part of the LPLA command structure, are in fact the decision-makers.

Operating the Trail

As part of their task of operating the infiltration system to South Vietnam, the North Vietnamese run the Ho Chi Minh Trail as if it were a strategic rear area of South Vietnam. Vietnamese engineer units maintain existing roads and build new ones for intermittent motor vehicle, bicycle, animal, and human transportation. Vietnamese labor battalions, which include women units, keep the roads and paths in good repair. They construct bridges over the streams and install wooden planks on those segments of the road where trucks might otherwise be mired in the mud.

In earlier years, the Vietnamese used local hill people in the Trail area as laborers, porters, and guides. More recently, although some of the local employees may have been retained, most of this work has been done by Vietnamese. However, Vietnamese commanders operating in the Trail area sometimes enlist assistance from the nearby Lao authorities. For example, a Lao mechanic (A-31), whom we interviewed, normally was employed at repairing Lao trucks in an NLHS-controlled area of Savannakhet Province. Since his repair shop was only half a mile from a segment of the Trail, he was called upon from time to time to repair Vietnamese trucks. Before he could begin to work on such a truck, however, the Vietnamese driver was required to show the written approval of the local LPLA commander.

At suitable protected areas near the Trail, the Vietnamese have established storage points for the distribution of equipment and supplies. Trained Vietnamese medical personnel staff infirmaries in the corridor; they treat both infiltrators and locally assigned Vietnamese and distribute drugs and other medical supplies to the passing infiltrating groups. To provide some distraction in the arduous life of the Vietnamese stationed in the Trail area, entertainment troupes pass through from time to time with presentations of patriotic plays and songs. During the Christmas 1966 bombing pause, the North Vietnamese showed moving pictures in the Mu Gia Pass region, just across the border from Laos, to the hundreds of road maintenance personnel in the area.

Traffic for the Trail starts from various points in North Vietnam and enters Laos mostly through the Bannakai and Mu Gia mountain passes. The Vietnamese infiltrators, who are trucked through North Vietnam late at night, continue their difficult journey on foot once they are in Laos, marching mostly by day along well-camouflaged trails. The infiltrating groups, which may range from small squads of a few men to units of over five hundred troops, are led by local guides, who take them one day's march southward. An infiltrator who falls ill — and large numbers suffer from malaria — may be treated immediately and continue with his group, or he may be detained for treatment in a rest camp until he can join a later infiltrating group. All the infiltrators interviewed who have described their journey recall the strenuous mountain climbs, great fatigue, chilly nights, and general hardships of their one- to three-month trek through Laos. The strains of this long march have been a contributing motive in some defections.[4]

Even prior to the intense Vietnamese activity in the southern panhandle of Laos, the area was only sparsely populated by mountain-tribal groups. In the past few years, as the infiltration has been stepped up, bombing and military engagements in the area have increased, causing many of the hill people to flee. Most infiltrators nevertheless report having caught a fleeting glimpse of local people in Laos, but they had been ordered not to speak to them; indeed, they do not know their language. Here is a typical account by a Vietnamese soldier:

> We walked for days without meeting any people. From time to time we did meet some montagnards. We didn't speak to them because we didn't know their dialects. They only smiled at us but didn't help us with anything. We didn't consider them as either friends or enemies.[5]

North Vietnamese troops generally are told before leaving for Laos that trading with the local population there is forbidden. (One soldier said his unit had been cautioned that the enemy might bribe the local people to give poisoned food to the North Vietnamese.) However, some of the groups were not strict in enforcing this prohibition. One prisoner in South Vietnam reported that, in return for the clothes and thread which the troops in his infiltration group could offer, they received chickens, rice, green beans, vegetables, cigarettes, and flare-bomb parachutes that they used for hammocks and blankets. Another prisoner gave the following account of the trading carried on by his infiltration group:

> We had only salted meat. We continued to receive our daily ration of rice — seven hundred and fifty grams — but when cooked, its volume didn't increase enough to fill our stomachs. We ate it with a sort of soup made with seasoning powder, salted meat, water, and a plant called "rau tau bay" whenever we had time to look for it in the forest.
>
> The local inhabitants didn't give us anything, although we got some food from them by giving them our clothes in exchange. As we had only the clothes we needed, we exchanged our underclothes for food. For a pair of drawers, one got seven or eight manioc roots; for two undershirts, one got a fowl.

This same soldier reported that, although it was forbidden to trade with villagers, even some of the cadres did so. Others recalled that, when they were caught, they were subjected to criticism sessions.

Although most Vietnamese working in the Trail area or infiltrating through it have little contact with the local inhabitants, some are specifically assigned to dealing directly with the residents. For example, we interviewed a former Vietnamese supply officer (B-12) who had been responsible for purchasing livestock from local farmers and then cooking, salting, and drying these products for shipment to South Vietnam. He traded salt and clothes in return for buffalo, cows, pigs, ducks, and chickens.

In keeping with Vietnamese Communist doctrine, the military or civilian advisers in the Trail area take special pains to encourage their Lao counterparts to win over the local population through effective propaganda techniques. A notebook of a Vietnamese cadre who worked with the Lao Communists near the Lao Ngam district of southern Laos assessed the weak points of their military and propaganda operations in this area:

> The military activities at some places did not coincide with politics. They were not used for armed propaganda activities or to motivate people. Activities in the enemy-controlled areas were not undertaken. In combat, direct attack was practiced too much, while guerrilla warfare was neglected.

In some cases, especially in areas where the highland minorities live, Vietnamese cadres engage directly in propaganda addressed to the local population. The Vietnamese supply officer quoted above spent three months in propaganda and intelligence activities in the Attopeu region in southern Laos before he was assigned the supply function. The instructions he received from his Vietnamese regimental commander before his first visit to the LPLA leader in Attopeu Province reveal some of the issues that most concerned the Vietnamese:

> First, he [the Vietnamese regimental commander] told me that I should try to influence the thinking of the villagers to support us. Second, to try to stay in close contact with the villagers and with the Lao provincial authorities in order to get information about enemy activity. Third, I had to make propaganda among the villagers about enemy terrorism in the areas already bombed or about to be bombed. Fourth, I should try to watch and report the feelings of the people toward North Vietnamese personnel. Last, I should report any relations between Vietnamese personnel and the girls of the village or

any cases of North Vietnamese trying to buy or sell anything among the villagers, or stealing anything — all these things should be reported.

I did this work together with a Lao soldier because we needed a man who knew the area and operations there. It would also help the NLHS to control the population. If there were any problems with the villagers, the Lao soldier would report to the NLHS provincial authorities.

DRV Strategy and Tactics in Laos

Apart from the protection of their country's border regions against unfriendly elements (such as the forces of the anti-Communist Meo General Vang Pao), the North Vietnamese military in Laos have two principal missions: operating the Ho Chi Minh infiltration system and strengthening the position of the Lao Communists. Regarding the first, the DRV's primary interest is in a successful conclusion to the war in South Vietnam, and they judge it fundamental that they be able to move men and supplies freely from the North to the South. By its military actions in the area the North Vietnamese have made it clear to the Royal Lao Government — and the United States as well — that they will fight aggressively to protect their investment in the vital artery to South Vietnam. The government, recognizing how small would be its chances of success against such determined Vietnamese opposition (unless, of course, it were supported by outside forces), hesitates to undertake military action within the Ho Chi Minh Trail area. Baldly stated, even though the Royal Government finds any Vietnamese occupation of Lao soil repugnant, it tends in the present circumstances to look upon the Trail area as being too intimately linked to the prosecution of the war in South Vietnam to permit interference with North Vietnamese designs. Further diminishing Vientiane's inclination to confront the Vietnamese in the Lao panhandle is the fact that the area is sparsely populated by mountain tribes, to whom the Lao elite feel a less intense commitment than they do to the lowland Lao.

North Vietnam, to judge by its own statements, is understandably less worried about the FAR than it is about the possibility that American or Thai ground troops could move into southern Laos to cut off its infiltration to South Vietnam. Reflections of this anxiety are Radio Hanoi's frequent broadcasts denouncing alleged plans by the United States and Thailand to "establish bases" within southern Laos from which to attack both North and South Vietnam. After the start of construction on the "McNamara Line" between North and South Vietnam (the infiltration barrier that was begun but not completed), Hanoi intermittently accused the United States of planning to extend the barrier into Laos.

The heavy bombing of the Ho Chi Minh Trail by the US Air Force has been bitterly denounced by the North Vietnamese as a violation of the Geneva Accords of 1962. Further, they charge that the United States and Thailand have also been violating the agreements by introducing ground forces into Laos.[6] Their pronouncements on these subjects fulfill several functions. On the one hand, by focusing international attention on these issues, they hope to pressure their enemies into suspending all hostile action in Laos and, perhaps more important, to discourage future ground attacks by Americans and Thai in the Trail area. On the other hand, they appear to be signaling their enemies that they would respond to such attacks in kind. By their presence throughout Laos, NVA troops in a sense hold the Mekong Valley area of Laos hostage, for, if their enemies threaten their vital supply route, they can retaliate by attacking other areas of Laos.

Regarding the second principal mission of the North Vietnamese military in Laos — strengthening the position of the Lao Communists — we have already described the Vietnamese advisory role. In addition, the NVA has established a relatively sophisticated apparatus that serves both North Vietnamese and Lao troops and includes the necessary communications network, logistics operations, and transportation units. From a Vietnamese defector (B-21), a Black Tai who had been engaged in road repair on Route 7 in Xieng Khouang Province, we learned, for example, that the Vietnamese assign engineer units to maintaining the truck arteries to North Vietnam. This is how he described his work for one month in early 1967:

> Our function was to fill the holes in the road, and to dig drains. We all used pick and shovel. If airplanes would bomb the road, we had to fill the holes and flatten the road. We had no machines.
>
> There were no Lao — we were all Vietnamese. We were separated into squads for the work. On Route 7, Battalions 2 and 3 worked on the roads. This is Route 7, which leads to Phou Kout and on which a lot of Vietnamese troops came into Laos. I was told that we had a lot of troops in Phou Kout, so we had to work hard and pave the way for them.

The NVA commit special units to performing functions for which the Lao do not have the capability. For example, the heavy weapons and antiaircraft units are North Vietnamese.[7] As indicated earlier, the NVA have established a separate medical system to serve their own personnel and to provide assistance to the Lao troops. A Vietnamese medical technician described to us five rudimentary hospitals — three Vietnamese and two Lao — that he helped to establish in NLHS Nam Tha Province, during 1966 and 1967.

To bolster the military strength of the LPLA, North Vietnamese troops stationed in Laos coordinate their efforts with Lao units, often operating alongside them. The pattern of earlier years, when special NVA shock troops would be sent from North Vietnam to soften up RLG defense positions for later consolidation by the provincial LPLA and NVA units, has continued into the present. Against such concerted attacks, the FAR generally is a poor match for the well-trained Vietnamese. A vivid description of one Vietnamese shock-troop engagement was given us by a 19-year-old Vietnamese prisoner (B-14), who had been a member of a company of Dac Cong (commandos) when, in May 1967, his unit was assigned to what the North Vietnamese designate as "Mission C," that is, combat in Laos. The Dac Cong were elite troops who had undergone a year of intensive training in commando tactics which included work with all types of explosives. The Vietnamese informant claimed that when he graduated from his training course, his regiment was addressed by Ho Chi Minh, Vo Nguyen Giap, and Pham Van Dong, who inspired the young commandos with their great praise, telling them that the Dac Cong were the North Vietnamese answer to the American B-52s. His company was ordered to carry out an attack against an FAR post in Saravane Province early in August 1967, and succeeded in causing great destruction to the post.[8] After the attack the commandos were to withdraw, allowing Lao and Vietnamese troops to take their place. Our informant was wounded by a mortar burst during the action and lost his comrades. He dragged himself through the woods, but was discovered the next day by an FAR soldier and taken prisoner. The Royal Government confirmed the success of the Vietnamese attack described above.

The DRV uses its troops to remind RLG authorities to exercise restraint in their own military initiatives. An example of such use of military power occurred in late 1967 and early 1968, when the commander of the FAR in southern Laos was engaged in an ambitious pacification effort in the Sedone Valley. NVA troops with LPLA support attacked Lao Ngam, an important post in the area, and launched a campaign of pressure throughout the region of which the Lao Ngam assault formed a part. As a result, they wiped out much of the FAR's accomplishment in pacification.

The aim of attacks like the one on Lao Ngam is partly psychological: to demonstrate the fragility of the FAR, and to persuade the RLG to be respectful of the power of the DRV and, by extension, its Lao ally. There have been cases, however, in which NVA attacks on RLG positions in southern Laos have backfired. On March 9, 1965, for example, a North Vietnamese unit assisted by Lao elements attacked an FAR officer training school at Dong Hene in the province of Savannakhet, apparently to demoralize the FAR. This time, the FAR soldiers successfully repulsed the attackers, inflicting heavy losses on them (according to one RLG communication about the battalion-size assault, there were at least fifty enemy dead and fifty wounded) and taking nine North Vietnamese prisoners. These prisoners were then presented before the International Control Commission as proof of North Vietnamese military intervention in Laos. The ICC investigated the "Dong Hene Incident," interrogated the prisoners, and eventually transmitted a 747-page report of its investigation committee, signed by the Canadian and Indian members,[9] to the Co-chairmen of the Geneva Conference on Laos, Great Britain and the USSR.[10] Though both the DRV and the LPLA denied having been involved in the attack on Dong Hene, the overwhelming public evidence of the Vietnamese role was undoubtedly an embarrassment.[11] Moreover, this relatively rare victory by FAR troops over attacking Vietnamese was widely publicized by Vientiane, and it boosted RLG morale.

Another military effort in southern Laos that went badly for the North Vietnamese was the joint attack with LPLA units on RLG positions in Khammouane Province in November 1965. The FAR troops repulsed the attack, in the course of which they cornered a platoon of fifteen Vietnamese, including two officers, in a cave near Thakhek. The trapped men bravely fought on against a much larger FAR force for several weeks, until their food supply was exhausted and they surrendered. Testimony from these fifteen North Vietnamese soldiers captured on Lao soil was publicly presented, enabling the RLG not only to offer further evidence of the DRV's military intervention in Laos but also to feel pride in having won an engagement against the Vietnamese.[12]

The North Vietnamese role in Laos differs from region to region. The Vietnamese presence is preponderant in areas where the RLG is a serious threat to the Lao Communists, such as Xieng Khouang, or where the DRV judges its own interests to be vital, such as Khammouane Province, the northern flank of the Vietnamese strategic route complex to South Vietnam.[13] In all regions except the area of the Ho Chi Minh Trail, the North Vietnamese apparently permit NLHS officials to handle civil affairs and to deal directly with the local population, assisted, of course, by their DRV advisers.

The primary deterrent to RLG action (apart from the unfavorable geography of the country), and the guarantor of the NLHS' continuing control in its area, is the weight of North Vietnamese military strength. The NVA maintains a strategic capability that permits it to mount coordinated attacks throughout Laos. Demonstrations of that capability, though exercised with obvious restraint, were the attacks, in late 1967 and early 1968, on Nam Bac in the northern mountains, in the region of Paksane in the Center, and near Saravane in the South as well as the Plain of Jars offensives of mid-1969 and early 1970. Thus, when the RLG is tempted to move into a Communist-held area which it feels confident it could seize, it must risk either retaliation elsewhere in the country or loss of the newly gained territory a year or two later. Indeed, the war has followed a pattern that has included trade-offs, as each side has from time to time initiated a limited campaign to improve a tactical position or to gain a psychological advantage. Although the basic territorial balance between the two contending camps in Laos had changed only slightly since the days of the 1962 Geneva Conference, some important campaigns have been undertaken by both sides: these include the PL/NVA campaign of 1963–64, which deprived the Neutralists of their power position on the Plain of Jars and strengthened the Communist posture in Laos; the successful Operation Triangle by the FAR in 1964; the LPLA/NVA campaign of 1967–68, which gained the Communists territory in North and South Laos; the FAR thrust of 1969 which resulted in the reoccupation by the RLG of the Plain of Jars and, in early 1970, the ouster of the forces of General Vang Pao from the Plain by a combined North Vietnamese/Pathet Lao assault despite US air support, including the use of B-52s.

The situation in Laos is often described as a standoff, with each side holding the line while waiting for the outcome in Vietnam, which will be crucial to the future of Laos. But the apparent military balance, it is argued, should not rule out the likelihood that, if the DRV wished to increase its military effort with the aim of seizing all of Laos, the RLG could not resist for long without direct, massive outside assistance. Writing of the 1963 period, the then US Assistant Secretary of State, Roger Hilsman, stated that the "Communist North Vietnamese could easily put enough troops into Laos to take it over within two to four weeks, if they were willing to take the risk of an American intervention.[14] This assessment still appears valid today. The NVA also enjoys an advantage in its ability to shift forces in and out of Laos almost at will and to alter the military situation there at relatively low cost. This was demonstrated in early 1970 when a North Vietnamese thrust easily recaptured the Plain of Jars from the forces of General Vang Pao and pressed further toward key command posts of the non-Communist forces in northern Laos. Only massive external assistance — including ground forces — could have prevented the success of this campaign.

Even if the North Vietnamese were not inclined to overrun all the Mekong Valley, they could easily call for harassment of the urban centers[15] — Vientiane, Luang Prabang, Savannakhet, Pakse, and other towns that have so far experienced little fighting or terror — just as they have done in South Vietnam since the Tet offensive of 1968. The present military equilibrium in Laos is thus largely the product of North Vietnamese self-restraint.

If the NVA could so readily seize control of all Laos, why, we must ask, has it not done so? Leaving the discussion of the DRV's long-range aims in Laos for our final chapter, we shall merely offer here some of the reasons for the North Vietnamese self-restraint that are relevant in the present context. It must again be emphasized that the DRV's primary interests are in winning the war in the South and in defending and reconstructing the North. Any effort that would divert them from these central objectives would be considered too costly. An NVA-led attack into the Mekong Valley would create the risk of direct intervention in Laos by Thailand and the United States, Thailand being greatly troubled by the prospect of a hostile Communist enemy on its borders. In the present circumstances, the DRV's military presence in Laos actually reduces the danger of an American or Thai attempt to put in ground troops to seal off infiltration to South Vietnam, because of the threat that in the face of such an attempt the NVA would indeed overrun the rest of Laos. If the North Vietnamese were to take the initiative in widening the war in Laos, they would lose that leverage and then not only could expect to suffer greater punishment from the United States in North Vietnam but also would be inviting the direct action against their operations along the Ho Chi Minh Trail that they so intensely wish to avoid. This is certainly true since the start of negotiations between the United States and the DRV in Paris and the American decision to halt the bombing of North Vietnam. Any large-scale military action in Laos by the Vietnamese Communists might destroy the Geneva Accords. It could also provoke a US resumption of bombing in North Vietnam.

Although the 1962 Geneva Accords have been repeatedly violated, the DRV sees advantage in their being preserved. If Hanoi were to disregard the terms of the treaty *openly* by invading large areas of RLG-controlled territory, the constraints on its enemies would be lifted and the war might well be widened, forcing the DRV to spend scarce resources that it would rather commit to achieving victory in South Vietnam. Thus far, as we shall see, the North Vietnamese have zealously camouflaged their military presence in Laos, publicly maintaining that they have no troops in that country, and in every way trying to convince the rest of the world that they have respected the Geneva Accords, while the United States and its "puppets" have been violating them. An occupation of Mekong Valley Laos would cost the North Vietnamese much foreign sympathy and would counteract their attempt to create an image of themselves as the beleaguered small nation defending itself against an unjustified attack by the imperialist Americans.

On the basis of this analysis of the situation, the relative stability that has been maintained so far between government- and Communist-held territory in Laos had best be described as a political rather than a military balance.

X

The Relationship, Public and Secret

In their international propaganda, the North Vietnamese frequently plead the Lao Communists' cause, denouncing the intervention of the "American imperialists" in Laos, denigrating the government leaders in Vientiane, and insisting that "peace in Indochina is indivisible." At the same time, both the NLHS and the DRV have stated that the situation in Laos must not be made a subject of discussion in the Paris talks. Laos is a sovereign nation whose affairs can be dealt with only through negotiations between the Lao parties as is emphasized in both NLHS and DRV public statements and in the March 1970 five-point peace proposal offered by the NLHS to the Souvanna Phouma government. Obviously, to raise the issue of the future of Laos in the Paris talks would mean to touch on the North Vietnamese role in that country—something both the Lao and Vietnamese Communists are not eager to do.

At the two Geneva Conferences (1954 and 1961–62) the DRV acted as spokesman for the Lao Communists while pursuing primarily its own interests. Although since 1962 there has been less occasion for the North Vietnamese to represent their Lao allies in a diplomatic context, it is reasonable to expect that in any future negotiations on Laos they will act as the mentor of the NLHS, at least behind the scenes.

Even though DRV authorities do not publicly admit to the fact that they maintain troops in Laos, they do not deny their close spiritual alliance with the Lao Communists.

The following recent broadcast is typical of North Vietnamese propaganda statements regarding Laos:

The Vietnamese and Lao peoples have always maintained close neighborly relations, like those between lips and teeth. These are relations between kith and kin who share weal and woe and march together through life or death. The Vietnamese have always given unreserved support to the Lao people's just struggle and consider the success of the Lao people as their own.

The Lao frequently match these effusions of devotion with eloquence about their own solidarity with the Vietnamese people. A telegram from Prince Souphanouvong to President Ho Chi Minh on the occasion of Ho's seventy-seventh birthday is representative of these statements:

The Lao people who have struggled against the common enemy on the battlefield rejoice very much at the grandiose victories won by the brotherly Vietnamese people and consider these victories as their own.

So far, in struggling against the United States, the Lao people have received the sincere support and aid of the Vietnamese people and workers and the DRV government. Therefore, I take this opportunity to voice our sincere gratitude for this sincere support and aid. I hope that the friendly relations and the very close militant solidarity between the Lao and Vietnamese people will be further tightened. (Letter signed at Sam Neua, May 17, 1967.)[1]

In a speech he delivered in Sam Neua on March 19, 1968, Prince Souphanouvong publicly acknowledged the close ties between the NLHS and the North Vietnamese and the interrelationship between their two revolutionary movements:

The *victories of the Lao armed forces* and people are an *actual result of the struggle which we conduct jointly* with the brotherly Vietnamese people . . . I appeal to all our cadres, combatants, workers, and people to *strive to learn* from the lesson of sacrifices and valiant struggle provided by the Vietnamese armed forces and people . . . We consider the victories of the fraternal Vietnamese people as ours . . . We must voice and extend to them our sincere and *active support* by struggling and winning brilliant victories and by *coordinating* our struggle with theirs.[2]

The Royal Government makes intermittent efforts to document the interference of the DRV in Laos. It has submitted a number of memoranda to the International Control Commission, listing a long series of North Vietnamese violations of the Geneva Agreements of 1954 and 1962.[3] In addition, RLG spokesmen frequently make statements to the international press charging North Vietnam with intervention in Laos.[4] Both the DRV and the NLHS categorically deny these accusations, which they counter with charges of "American imperialist" military intervention in Laos and US domination of what they term the "puppet" government in Vientiane.[5]

In the pursuit of its military mission in Laos, the DRV has been masterful in camouflaging its true role. Historically, this remarkable secrecy has been part of the Vietnamese-Communist insurgent style. The Viet Minh, for example, during their struggle against the French that lasted from 1946 to 1954, received material assistance from China under strict secrecy. Although, by the end of the war, Chinese supplies had reached substantial proportions, neither the North Vietnamese nor the Chinese Communists have ever admitted that any such contribution was made.[6] This pattern of dissimulation, so effective against the French, was continued in Hanoi's subsequent campaign to seize control of South Vietnam. After the Geneva Conference of 1954, the DRV sent clandestine political agents to the South to help the insurgents' struggle against the Diem regime, and between 1959 and 1964 it infiltrated from 20,000 to 50,000 men, mostly southerners who had been regrouped in the North and were being returned to their native region.[7] Since 1964, the DRV has assigned thousands of northern troops to combat in the South. Yet, in the early part of this struggle, the North persistently denied having sent any troops to South Vietnam, and, until the widening participation of northern troops in the war in recent years, those who wished to show the true role of North Vietnamese involvement bore a difficult burden of proof.

This same pattern of secrecy has also characterized the Vietnamese Communist role in Laos. The Viet Minh cadre who in September 1945 led the group that escorted Prince Souphanouvong on his hike back to Laos to build an independence movement recalls that, when they crossed the border of Laos, the Vietnamese accompanying the Prince took off their Vietnamese insignia and "put on the three-headed elephant emblem of the Lao Liberation Army." [8] The Viet Minh's practice of changing into Lao uniforms when marching through Laos was adopted in the 1960s by soldiers from North Vietnam on their infiltration route to the South[9] and by NVA troops and advisers serving in Laos.

Because of the DRV's common frontier with Laos, the North Vietnamese can easily move their troops in and out of that country, as indeed they have done for more than fifteen years. But it is exceedingly difficult to obtain firm evidence of their troops' presence. In 1962, the DRV maintained that it had only forty troops in Laos, whom it withdrew, and though this was a patently incredible invention, the ICC had no independent means of checking this claim.[10]

A possible source might have been the testimony of NVA prisoners and defectors in Laos, had there been more of them. Indeed, to many observers the negligible number of captives suggests that the North Vietnamese were not heavily involved. The Royal Government could claim only five prisoners and one defector before the Geneva Conference of 1962, and all of these after 1959.[11] As suggested earlier, the lack of Vietnamese prisoners is more easily explained by the FAR's reluctance to engage in battle with the Vietnamese than by the absence of Vietnamese troops. As one Lao officer pointed out to us:

It was the Vietnamese who took us prisoner — we did not take them.

Even with their allies of 1960 to 1962 (the Neutralist forces of Kong Le and Souvanna Phouma) and with the Lao Communists, the North Vietnamese have been extremely secretive about their troops' disposition. In interviews with Neutralist government officials and military officers, and with Souvanna Phouma himself, we learned that access to the North Vietnamese command headquarters on the Plain of Jars had been severely restricted and that only a relatively few could gain admittance. Officers of the Neutralist army, presumably allies of the North Vietnamese as well as of the Lao Communists, reported to us that they were treated with suspicion, even hostility, when they tried to obtain some picture of the operation of their "allies." Consequently, these officers, several of whom had the rank of colonel, were remarkably uninformed about the North Vietnamese troop strength and disposition, except for the particular units with which they had had personal contact.

Yet it is not easy for DRV troops to go unnoticed in Laos. Most North Vietnamese do not speak Lao, and though they resemble the Lao racially, a close observer can distinguish Lao from Vietnamese by physiognomy and, above all, by cultural characteristics. However, as we shall show presently, the North Vietnamese take pains to camouflage their presence, and RLG intelligence is generally poor. As a result, outside observers — at least until 1962 — have tended to doubt the Lao government's reports about the North Vietnamese presence in Laos, the more so as some of its earlier claims of DRV interference had indeed been exaggerated.

Our interviews are rich in detail about the measures taken by the North Vietnamese to conceal their military presence in Laos, or at least to make it unobtrusive. Many units were required to bivouac outside populated areas, often in the jungle, so as to reduce their contact with the local population to a minimum. Vietnamese soldiers often wore uniforms resembling those of the LPLA. We had a number of statements similar to the following:

Before coming to Laos, we were issued uniforms which were made of Vietnamese material but in the style of Pathet Lao soldiers. The shirts had epaulets as the Lao uniforms have, the hats were Lao hats.[12]

Both military and civilian Vietnamese advisers took Lao names, and those who worked in a civilian capacity, even if they were military officers, wore civilian clothes similar to those of their Lao counterparts.[13]

At the time of their departure from North Vietnam, most of the enlisted men in combat or support units were not informed that they were going to Laos, and though some guessed their destination, many claimed that they had not realized it until they found themselves on Lao soil. Only a few of our informants said that they were permitted to receive mail, and a small number said that they could write home but pointed out that they were prohibited from mentioning that they were in Laos. One soldier (B-1) explained it this way:

We received explanations that we had to keep our activities in Laos secret . . . word of casualties might discourage families at home and word would get back to the troops and hurt their morale.

All Vietnamese personnel in Laos are severely cautioned against discussing Vietnamese plans, troop movements — indeed, any activities — with unauthorized persons. In short, just as in South Vietnam, the NVA's internal security in Laos, in contrast to that of its opponents, is very good.

The North Vietnamese involvement in Laos is further protected from discovery by the fact that most outside personnel is prohibited from entering the Communist-controlled zone. In the past, ICC observers occasionally gained admission to limited areas under careful scrutiny, but it has been years since the ICC was last able to go anywhere in NLHS territory, and the Commission has effectively been paralyzed. Furthermore, "unfriendly" newsmen are unwelcome in the Communist zone of Laos. Foreigners who do gain access, such as a Japanese film crew and in

1968 a French visitor, must enter from Hanoi and usually are known to be well disposed to the Communist cause. They are always carefully guarded. The few foreign residents in NLHS territory are Communists. The rare non-Communist visitor to the zone is given little opportunity to assess the extent of the Vietnamese presence in Laos, although he may occasionally and unexpectedly encounter North Vietnamese units stationed in the NLHS zone.[14] Thus, North Vietnamese measures to disguise their presence in Laos, as well as the difficulty of access and the careful screening of strangers who are permitted to enter the Communist-controlled areas, have served to make North Vietnam's activities in Laos difficult to document in their full scope.

XI

An Assessment

Though the early history of the revolutionary movement in Laos
is still incomplete, it is clear that the Vietnamese Communists
under Ho Chi Minh played the decisive role in creating that
movement and in keeping it alive in the years immediately after
the Second World War.

Between 1946 and 1949 — the formative years of the Lao Communist movement — several Lao "resistance groups" survived in
eastern Laos thanks to the leadership and aid furnished by the
Vietnamese Communists. The merger of these groups in 1950 was
effected under the guidance of the Viet Minh, and the First Lao
Resistance Congress convened on Vietnamese soil. Thereafter, the
Viet Minh invasion of Laos provided the Lao revolutionaries with
their first territorial base, in the border province of Sam Neua,
which to this day has remained the headquarters of the Lao Communists. Since then, with the advice and assistance as well as the
military might of the Vietnamese Communists, the Lao Communists have succeeded in bringing under their domination perhaps
one third of the country's population and about two thirds of its
territory.

From its inception, the Lao Communist movement was made
up of individuals closely associated with the North Vietnamese.
The two most important figures in the movement, Kaysone
Phomvihan and Nouhak Phomsavan, who lacked the attributes of
social background and status to make them part of the traditional

Lao elite, were favored in their climb to power by the Vietnamese. Prince Souphanouvong, whose aristocratic origins carried prestige in Lao society, but who apparently was not so close to or so fully trusted by Hanoi, was never more than the titular leader of the NLHS.

The political system of the Communist-controlled areas of Laos has a dual structure in which the front organization, the Neo Lao Hak Sat (NLHS) political party, is controlled by a small, semisecret Communist party, the Phak Pasason Lao (PPL) or People's Party of Laos. Vietnamese advisers are distributed throughout both organizations.

While the over-all relationship between the North Vietnamese Communists and their Lao allies is clear, the exact interaction between the two Communist organizations — the Vietnamese Workers Party (Dang Lao Dong Vietnam) and the People's Party of Laos — remains to be clarified. After the formal dissolution in 1945 of the Indochinese Communist Party (ICP), three separate Communist parties were created, at least nominally, for the three countries of Indochina. It is possible, as some observers maintain, that former Lao members of the ICP hold membership in both the Lao and the Vietnamese party and that Hanoi exercises control in Laos by this device. But, given the presence of a Vietnamese political-administrative mission (Doan 959), which guides the policy-making institutions of the Communist zone of Laos, and given the dependence of the Lao Communists on Vietnamese military and economic support, there would appear to be no compelling need for such a device; indeed, it could even have political disadvantages in ignoring certain Lao sensitivities. At any rate, we found no evidence of anyone's maintaining dual membership in the two parties (which does not, of course, rule out the possibility that such a phenomenon exists).

The external policy of the Lao Communists, not surprisingly, parallels that of the DRV. In the Sino-Soviet conflict, for example, Lao spokesmen follow the lead of Hanoi. Thus, in a broadcast of August 1968 concerning negotiations for a settlement of the Vietnam issue, Radio Pathet Lao praised the DRV decision to go to Paris, while Radio Peking was silent. Also, the Third Extraordinary Congress of the NLHS, which convened in October 1968, adopted a program that seemed to echo the earlier (1967) program of the National Liberation Front of South Vietnam (NLFSV). In internal policy, the Lao Communists have not been so orthodox; but the fact that they have not closely followed the measures of the Lao Dong Party would be attributed by a Vietnamese adviser to the more backward state of their country's economic and social development.

Our investigation shows that in virtually every important field of Lao Communist development the North Vietnamese have played a critical role. They are largely responsible for selecting the Lao Communist leadership, which has shown remarkable stability and cohesion. Like the leadership in Hanoi, these men have served together in Laos for some twenty years with dedication and self-sacrifice. The DRV also has provided facilities and guidance for the training and political indoctrination not only of the top leadership but of almost the entire cadre structure of the Lao Communists. (Only a very small group, by contrast, has received training in the Soviet Union and Communist China.) North Vietnamese advisers have helped these cadres construct an army, a bureaucracy, a Marxist-Leninist party, and political and mass organizations, all based upon the DRV model. Not surprisingly, the political system of the Communist zone of Laos is the image — if only a pale one — of that of its neighbor and mentor.

Still another important contribution of the North Vietnamese is the sense of over-all direction and cohesion they provide to the Lao Communists. Even more than on the RLG side, the population in the Communist zone of Laos is extremely diverse, divided by regional, ethnic, tribal, linguistic, and socioeconomic differences. Left to themselves, the Lao Communists might well bog down in factional disputes. The Vietnamese are sensitive to these group differences, however, and they provide the needed coordination through an effective advisory staff, which enjoys a neutral, unbiased vantage point that a Lao staff could not claim. Not only are Vietnamese advisory and control activities in Laos conducted with a view toward concealing them from outside observation, but Vietnamese policy in Laos is careful to present the picture of a partnership between equals — a difficult feat in view of the vast military, economic, and organizational superiority of one partner over the other and the impressive range of North Vietnamese assistance efforts in Laos.

It seems hardly necessary to spell out the importance to the Lao Communists of the North Vietnamese military presence in Laos. Khamtay Siphandone, the supreme commander of the Lao People's Liberation Army, sent a telegram to DRV Defense Minister Vo Nguyen Giap on January 22, 1969, in which he said:

Because of the close relations between Laos and Vietnam which have existed since ancient times, our Lao armed forces and people are always wholeheartedly supported by the fraternal Vietnamese people and armed forces.

He was more accurate in describing the present than the past. North Vietnamese military units in Laos give evidence of the same effective leadership, organization, discipline, and will to fight that they show in South Vietnam. These assets are all the more formidable in Laos, where the opposition from government forces is greatly inferior to the opposition in South Vietnam. Moreover, in its favorable location astride Laos, the DRV enjoys relative ease of supply and communication with its troops.

While it is possible that some Lao Communist leaders have grown restive about their dependence upon the North Vietnamese or that certain individuals are unhappy with their fate because of Vietnamese disfavor, one measure of their commitment to this alliance is the fact that, in the two decades since they split with the Lao Issara, there have been no defections of Lao Communist leaders to the RLG. It is true that a handful of lower-echelon cadres elected to accept integration into the Royal Government and Army in 1956, when the formal agreement — never fully implemented — was made. Since that time, the Lao Communist leadership has maintained a remarkable unity, at least outwardly.

Nevertheless, the alliance with the DRV has not been without some grave disadvantages for the Lao Communists. It has drawn them, and all of Laos, into the ugly struggle of Vietnam, first against the French and now against the South Vietnamese and the Americans. The war has brought devastation to Laos and an outpouring of more than a half-million refugees from the combat zones. Their allies cannot supply them with as abundant material resources as the Americans have lavished upon the Royal Government. Life in NLHS territory, as in North Vietnam, is austere, and its hardships contrast vividly with the relative easy life of Vientiane. In spite of sacrifices, however, we see no signs that the Communist leaders' resolve to continue their struggle has been seriously shaken.

A number of factors explain the Lao Communists' reliance upon the North Vietnamese: Their historical association has created conditions of psychological and ideological dependence on the part of the Lao and a readiness to accept Vietnamese advice. The great scarcity of human and material resources in the Communist zone has encouraged the Lao to turn for assistance to the North Vietnamese. The NLHS zone is handicapped by a small and dispersed population, a dearth of trained military and civilian personnel, and lack of organizational experience in civilian and military affairs. It has poor communications, and few production facilities that would allow the Lao Communists to maintain their political and military struggle out of indigenous resources. Since their enemy has been able to draw on the support of a rich outside power, the United States, it is not unnatural for them to look to North Vietnam for protection and a safe haven.

During the two decades that they have depended on the North Vietnamese for advice and assistance, the Lao Communists, as we have shown, found themselves sharing many of the interests of their Vietnamese allies. Both parties opposed French colonial rule, working together under the direction of Ho Chi Minh. They faced a common enemy: first France, and then the United States. They also held a similar view of the world and of the desirable solutions to its problems. In some cases, this affinity was further strengthened by Vietnamese family relations (for example, Kaysone) or marriage ties (Souphanouvong, Nouhak, and Singkapo, among others). From their own perspective, the Lao Communists have not compromised their legitimacy as a nationalist movement by their dependence on Hanoi.

The North Vietnamese, in turn, by sponsoring the Lao Communists over the past two decades have been pursuing three fundamental objectives: the protection of their borders, access to South Vietnam, and the establishment of a politically congenial regime in Laos. In its search for security, the DRV has been concerned that the areas along its borders, particularly the regions of Sam Neua and Phong Saly, not become sites for hostile activity. Hanoi has wished to prevent, for example, any attempt by the American "imperialists" and their "puppets" to mobilize ethnic minorities on both sides of the frontier in the struggle against the DRV. Access to South Vietnam through the corridor in southern Laos became especially important to the DRV in 1959, when it stepped up its delivery of supplies and personnel in support of the insurgents in the South. As the war there intensified, the North Vietnamese, not content with friendly Lao control, virtually operated as if the Ho Chi Minh Trail were in their own territory.

Hanoi's fundamental interest in Laos during the earlier, anti-French war was equally clear. The goal of the Viet Minh was the expulsion of the French from all of Indochina. Therefore, in addition to their own, important military operations in Laos, they enlisted whatever Lao support they could mobilize for this struggle.

These interests of the North Vietnamese might be defined as their minimal aspirations in Laos. An important question is whether their goals may be even more ambitious although First Secretary of the Vietnam Workers Party, Le Duan, as recently as February 1970 stressed the DRV's respect for the territorial integrity of its Indochinese neighbors.[1]

In the precolonial period, Vietnam had dominated portions of Laos and had constantly competed with other neighboring powers, particularly Thailand, for influence in the region. While the Lao may look with trepidation at the history of Vietnamese west-

ward expansion, Hanoi, by the same token, may well find it natural that it should exercise suzerainty over their divided neighbor.
Even France began by conquering Vietnam and from there expanded its colonial domination to Laos and Cambodia. Several
authors contend that the French development of Indochina was a
natural outgrowth of earlier, Vietnamese aspirations.[2]

During most of the colonial period, Laos was ruled from Vietnam, and Vietnamese were hired to serve in the more important
administrative posts not filled by the French. Two Lao provinces
were administered directly from Hanoi: Xieng Khouang until
1942, and Sam Neua still longer. Just as other newly independent
colonies have claimed all the territory relinquished by the former
colonial power — India and Indonesia, for example — some vigorous Vietnamese may feel justified in laying claim to all of Indochina. Even those Vietnamese leaders who would not press so ex-
treme a claim would not regard as sacrosanct the Lao areas on
their borders which France assigned to non-Lao tribal minorities
similar to groups in the adjacent regions of North Vietnam. These
mountain people have never shown a strong loyalty either to the
lowland Lao who rule them from the Mekong River Valley or to
Ho Chi Minh, and they might well be considered fair game for
Vietnamese rule.

North Vietnam's military record in Laos supports the argument of its expansionist designs. In 1953–54, the Viet Minh
launched a major offensive in Laos (which was to culminate in
the disaster at Dien Bien Phu) and "liberated" almost half the
country. These successful military operations would add weight to
the claim of the North Vietnamese to part of Laos. Roughly the
same area which the Viet Minh had attacked in their independence campaign, the Lao Communists and the NVA overran once
again in the offensive of 1961–62. Since then, as our study shows,
the North Vietnamese have contrived to maintain a significant
military presence in Laos.

Another argument pointing to Hanoi's ambitions in Laos is the
fact that the DRV is an outgrowth of the Indochinese Communist
Party, whose very name suggests the intention to establish a single

Communist regime, under Vietnamese control, in the former Indochinese states. The ICP was founded in Hong Kong in 1930 by Ho Chi Minh and other Vietnamese Communist leaders, many of whom are still in power in Hanoi today. At its founding, the new party was to have been called the Vietnamese Communist Party. But, according to the official DRV party history,

> Following the Communist International's instructions, the Session decided to change the Party's name to Indochinese Communist Party because the Vietnamese, Cambodian, and Laotian proletariat have politically and economically to be closely related in spite of their difference in language, customs, and race.[3]

It is true that the ICP was officially "dissolved" in 1945, but this was a tactical move designed to make more appealing to non-Communists a newly formed national united front against the French (the Viet Minh). The ICP, as Ho Chi Minh has admitted, remained underground. In 1951, a new Communist party, the Vietnamese Workers Party, was announced in Vietnam, and national Communist parties, including the People's Party of Laos and the Cambodian People's Revolutionary Party, subsequently appeared in Laos and Cambodia, no doubt a sign that the Vietnamese were aware of the neighboring states' susceptibility to nationalist appeals. However, if one puts credence in a secret directive of the Lao Dong Party dated November 1, 1951, and reportedly captured by the French Expeditionary Corps in North Vietnam during the spring of 1952, "the three revolutionary parties of Vietnam, Cambodia, and Laos" were to "be reunited to form a single party" when conditions permitted.[4] The document is said to have stated further that the Vietnamese Workers Party was still the old ICP and that it retained the right of supervision over the Cambodian and Lao parties.[5]

We have no doubt that the present leaders of the DRV would like to see Communist systems established in neighboring Laos and Cambodia, but the one-time existence of an Indochinese Communist Party is not in itself proof of their intention to bring this about by Vietnamese expansion. Communist blueprints are not always reliable guides to future behavior.

Through its relationship with the Lao Communists, the DRV has been able to play an active role in shaping developments in Laos to its own needs while maintaining the facade of noninterference. The Pathet Lao assisted the Viet Minh in the struggle against the French, if only in a minor way. The North Vietnamese energies spent in helping the Pathet Lao acquire control of the area adjacent to Vietnam have been repaid with the DRV's present security and access to South Vietnam. Moreover, apart from its pursuit of self-interest, the Vietnamese Communists, in keeping with the principles of "proletarian internationalism," would naturally be inclined to support fellow revolutionaries against the common enemy, "US imperialism," and what they consider the corrupt, feudal, Western-oriented leadership of the Royal Lao Government. The Indochinese Summit Conference of April 1970 could be interpreted in this sense.

Working intimately with the Lao Communists has also, however, posed problems for Hanoi. North Vietnamese advisers report that their counterparts are poorly organized, indolent, and lacking in ideological zeal. Frequently frustrated, many of these advisers wish for more direct intervention by their countrymen. But despite some dissatisfaction with the inadequacies of their junior partner, the leaders in Hanoi have found it desirable to continue in the advisory role.

The North Vietnamese have made a significant investment in Laos and have developed assets that keep open for them a wide range of options. How they will use these assets will be critically influenced by the course of the war in Vietnam. Though we do not intend to discuss the impact that different scenarios in the Vietnam struggle might have upon the future of Laos, we can state with considerable assurance how North Vietnam is likely to react with regard to her fundamental interests in Laos.

Whatever the outcome in Vietnam, Hanoi will continue to regard the Lao territory bordering on North Vietnam, particularly in the provinces of Phong Saly, Luang Prabang, Sam Neua, and

Xieng Khouang, as essential to its security and will strive to ensure that these areas are not controlled by hostile forces. Hanoi's interest in access to South Vietnam through Laos, on the other hand, may diminish, depending on the nature of the settlement. The DRV, having added to its stake with the Lao Communists for over two decades, cannot be expected to abandon its ally, unless the pressures to do so are great or its own interests are substantially enhanced by such a move. A Communist victory in Vietnam would appear to the Lao Communists as an immense contribution to their own cause, and the morale of the government forces would suffer correspondingly. In such circumstances, North Vietnam could expect pressure from its Lao allies for more massive assistance toward the achievement of a similar victory in Laos.

Appendixes

Appendix A

Selective List of Persons Interviewed or Consulted

A. Lao Who at One Time or Another Were with the Pathet Lao
(including Lao Loum as well as persons of Meo, Lao Theung, Black Tai, and other Tai descent)

1. Defector; b. 1944, Luang Prabang Prov; Meo
   Ed: primary, ages 9 to 10½
   Occ before joining: farmer
   PL service: 1957–Jul 1959, in PL village unit, sgt; Feb 1960–Mar 1967—Lt, asst chief QM office in KKhay
   NVN trng: mil admin course Nov 1961 for 30 mos
   Def: Mar 1967

2. Defector; b. 1940, Nong Khai, Thailand; Tai
   Ed: med trng, course at OB hosp, Vientiane; studied in Vientiane wat (about ages 15 to 19)
   Occ before joining: supply clk at OB hosp
   PL service: 1962–1966; 1962—joined Kong Le, briefly arrested by PL, given med trng & worked in villages for Kong Le Neutralists; 1963—captured by PL & Deuane Neutralists, then coolie & nurse in KKhay
   Def: Aug 1966

3. Defector; b. 1930, Sayaboury
   Ed: no formal ed
   PL service: 1954–1957, soldier; 1959—fled into jungle & stayed there as guerrilla; 1960–joined Kong Le forces; 1962–66—PL forces, 2nd Lt; 1963—asst co cmdr
   Def: Sep 1966

4. Defector; b. 1931, Khammouane Prov; Tai Dam (moved with family to SVN in 1937)
   Ed: ages 6 to 18, in SVN
   Occ before joining: 1949–1953—served in French Army until captured by VM; 1955–1957—prisoner in NVN; 1957–1962—released and served in NVA (squad ldr, taught mil subjects to Lao, interpreter at Son Tay)
   PL service: 1962–1966, cmdr of Lao 2nd Co under NVA 36th Bn; later, asst co cmdr in PL bn in Saravane
   Def: Jun 1966

5. Defector; b. Jun 1937, Xieng Khouang Prov
   Ed: learned to read & write Lao at local temple
   Occ before joining: farmer
   PL service: 1953–57, sgt & chief cook in PL bn; 1961–63—mil pol with Kong Le faction until captured by PL; 1963–67—S/Lt & propagandist
   Def: Feb 6, 1967

6. Prisoner; b. 1946, Sedone Prov
   Ed: 2 yrs (1957–59)
   Occ before joining: student
   PL service: 1959–1966 or 1967; 1966—chief of QM with regional hq at Lao Ngam
   Cap: 1966 or 1967

7. Defector; b. about 1948, Luang Prabang Prov
   Ed: 3 mos primary sch; can read & write; med trng for 7 mos under PL
   PL service: 1961–1967; in dance show for propag purposes; 1964—Nam Tha hosp where she met Ngo Van Dam (see Appendix A, B–10) in late 1966
   Def: May 1967

8. Defector; b. 1938, Luang Prabang Prov
   Ed: can read & write
   Occ before joining: farmer
   PL service: 1960–1966, soldier & propagandist
   Def: Sep 1966

9. At present high police official, Pakse; b. 1930, Sedone Prov
   Occ before joining: schoolteacher
   PL service: 1950–1955, cadet sch; Co Cmdr; 1953—to VN; 1954—C/S of southern Laos, representative of Lao Issara in Central Commission & member of Mixed Sub-Commission in Paksong; member of PPL
   Def: Oct 1955

10. Defector; b. 1938, Attopeu Prov
    Ed: 3 yrs as novice monk until age 21
    Occ before joining: student
    PL service and NVN trng: 1959–1966; 1959–1964—med student
    in Ha Dong; chief of med unit in Attopeu after 1964 grad; capt.
    Def: Sep 1966

11. Prisoner; b. 1930, Khammouane Prov
    Ed: 2 yrs formal, 3 mos French Army trng (1944)
    Occ before joining: farmer, then volunt'd for French Army (1951–
    53)
    PL service: 1953—fled to VN, worked as cook to wealthy Lao, then
    sent to Savannakhet Prov as warehouse keeper for PL; 1956—
    PL driver; 1958—demob'd; 1960–1966—Kong Le driver & laborer
    in tool shop for PL
    NVN trng: 1955—mechanic
    Cap: May 1967

12. Defector; b. Attopeu Prov
    Ed: learned to read & write in war
    PL service: 1954–1957, soldier in inf unit; 1957–1959—sent home,
    farmer; 1959–1967—M/Sgt, asst cmdr, 1st Lt of Ind Co; 1966—
    assigned to regional hq in Savannakhet Prov
    NVN trng: 1954—post-Geneva; 1955—6 mos at Muong Vinh
    Def: Spring 1967

13. Defector; b. 1937, Khammouane Prov
    Ed: taught self to read & write; 1955–1958—novice monk (2½
    yrs)
    Occ before joining: farmer
    PL service: 1959–1967—propagandist, Lt
    Def: Apr 1967

14. At present in Min of Info, RLG; b. Dec 1931, near Tchepone
    Ed: sch in Savannakhet, Pakse, & Vientiane
    Occ before joining: student
    PL service: 1945–1957, Issara guard under Thao O; 1946—moved
    with unit to VN; next few years, into Laos for propag work;
    1948—head of polit section in Exec Cmte for Nat'l Liberation
    organized in VN
    NVN trng: 1954–1957; 1952—propag chief of subdiv in Mahaxay;
    on ed staff of *Neo Lao Hak Sat* newspaper

15. Defector; b. 1941, Savannakhet Prov; Lao Theung
    PL service: 1957–Jan 1967; 1958—propagandist; asst plat ldr,
    2nd Lt

NVN trng: 1958 (3 mos); 1959 (5 mos)
Def: Jan 1967

16. Defector; b. 1927, Luang Prabang Prov
Ed: literate
PL service: 1953–1964; 1953—appt'd canton chief by VM; 1957—
worked in devl section of LPrabang Prov cmte; 1963—named
dist chief of Pakseng until 1964, when asked to resign; then a
farmer
Def: Feb 1967

17. Defector; b. 1939, Luang Prabang Prov
Ed: to elem grade 4
Occ before joining: student
PL service: 1959–1966; 1965—chief of QM unit, LPrabang region
NVN trng: 1959 (3 mos); 1963—cadet sch near Hanoi; 1 ½ yrs
polit, mil, and QM courses
Def: Aug 1966

18. At present RLG Lt Col; b. about 1925, Savannakhet Prov
Occ before joining: in father's opium business
PL service: 1946–1957
NVN trng: 1946–48; 1951—member of mil cmte for Sam Neua
Prov; 1955—Director of Khommadam Sch for off trng; then
directed guerrilla troops in SNeua & PSaly; rank of major when
he rallied to RLG in 1957

19. Defector
PL service: 1945–49 & 1952–56; dir of off sch, med sch, & QM of
Xieng Khouang area
Def: 1956

20. Defector; b. 1942, Luang Prabang Prov
Ed: elem until age 12
Occ before joining: student
PL service: Oct 1954–Jan 1967; 1962—capt & co cmdr; 1964—
cmdr of protection co with Souk Vongsak in Vientiane
NVN trng: 1955—DBPhu (6 mos); 1957—adv trng (18 mos);
1961—Son Tay, adv trng (10 mos)
Def: Jan 1967

21. Defector
Ed: grade 2 (French system)
Occ before joining: student
PL service: 1952–Sep 1965, bodyguard, medic; 1960—co cmdr;
1962—mil staff member, Attopeu Region; Lt cmdr, Sithandone;
Dec 1964—chief of combat section under Gen Phomma

NVN trng: 1953–55; 1958–59 (1 yr 2 mos) medical course; 1960–61—Dong Hoi (8 mos adv trng)
Def: Sep 1965

22. Defector; b. 1936 or 1937, Sedone Prov
Ed: 1 yr in monk's sch for elem ed; 4 yrs monk trng in 'Thailand (1947–51)
Occ before joining: student monk
PL service: 1954–67, C/S 2nd PL prov bn
NVN trng: 1954–57, automechanics at Bac Yang (3 yrs); about 1959—at Son Tay for off trng, graduated as capt & co cmdr
Def: Feb 1967

23. Defector; b. 1940, Sam Neua Prov
Ed: 6 yrs from ages 12 to 18; also teacher trng course in Sam Neua
Occ before joining: trader in clothes and opium (3 yrs)
PL service: Nov 1960 to 1966—PL teacher, with ed dept in Sam Neua, sch director in Sam Neua
Def: 1966

24. At present official in RLG judiciary, Savannakhet; b. 1919, Tchepone
Ed: Savannakhet (1928–31); Hanoi (l'Ecole des Frères and Institut Gia Long, 1931–37)
Occ before joining: commerce; with French company operating a lead mine near Tchepone as liaison agent
PL service: 1945–57; 1945—chosen cmdr of Issara forces of Tchepone; 1946–49—to VN to organize forces and direct guerrilla and propag forces in Laos; formed Cmte for Nat'l Liberation with Nouhak as chief, while maintaining liaison with Issara govt in Thailand; 1949–57—returned to Laos to command local troops in Tchepone; from there to NVN, where interned with family (about 3 yrs); then served in minor functions, including liaison to ICC, until his integration into RLG in 1957

25. Defector; b. 1935, Vientiane Prov
Ed: elem
Occ before joining: 1960–63, in Kong Le's Neutralist police until taken prisoner by PL
PL service: 1963–65, warrant officer; 1964—policeman in KKhay; Apr 1965—polit instructor to ex-RLG personnel in Deuane forces
Def: Dec 1965

26. Defector; b. probably late 1940s, Sam Neua Prov
Ed: can read & write
Occ before joining: farmer

PL service: 1960–66, soldier & propagandist
Def: Sep 1966

27. Defector; middle-aged; b. near Muong Hong, NE Laos; Meo
Ed: cannot read or write
Occ before joining: farmer, asst village chief (1954–58), Xieng
Ngeun
PL service: 1958–66, propag agent near native village
NVN trng: 1961–62, Hanoi & Haiphong
Def: Oct 1966

28. Defector; b. 1940, Xieng Khouang Prov
Ed: grade 6, elem
Occ before joining: teacher
PL service: 1962–66; 1962—village captured by PL, served as PL
instructor
Def: Sep 1966

29. Defector; b. 1929, Saravane Prov; Lao Theung
Ed: learned to read & write in wat; novice monk (3 yrs)
Occ before joining: farmer
PL service: 1950–54, propagandist; 1960–66—soldier
Def. 1966

30. Defector; b. 1921, Khammouane Prov
Ed: self-educated, reads & writes Lao
Occ before joining: farmer, after being RLG asst platoon ldr of
home guards
PL service: 1962–66, PL canton chief
Def: Nov. 1966

31. Defector; b. Sep 1942, Sedone Prov
Ed: 1948–61; attended Collège of Pakse and spent 4 mos at wat as
novice monk
Occ before joining: student
PL service: 1961–66, mechanic & asst platoon ldr; 1963—S/Lt
NVN trng: 1961–63, Dong Hoi and Thai Nguyen Tech Sch, auto-
mechanics
Def: Dec 1966

B. Members of North Vietnamese Army (NVA) in Laos

1. Defector; b. 1946, Thanh Hoa, NVN; Tai Dam
Ed: 6 yrs village sch
Occ before joining: farmer
NVA service: Apr 1963–Mar 1967; 1964—to Laos as soldier; 1965—

made cpl & stationed at Muong Sa, Laos; 1966—2nd Lt, asst co cmdr, Bn 923, Laos; 1967—in Houei Tom attack when defected
Def: Mar 1967

2. Prisoner; b. 1943, NW NVN; Chinese-Tai Dam
Ed: 5th class, DRV
Occ before joining: oxcart driver in cooperative
NVA service: Jul 1966–Jan 1967, private; Jan 1967—to Laos, taken while attacking FAR post
Cap: Jan 1967

3. Prisoner; b. 1947, Yen Bai, NVN; Vietnamese
Ed: about 3 yrs
Occ before joining: farmer
NVA service: 1966–Jan 1967, soldier; Oct 1966—to Laos; Jan 1967—wounded and taken in attack by FAR
Cap: Jan 1967

4. Defector; b. 1943, Xieng Khouang Prov, Laos; Tai Deng (Red Tai); moved with family to VN in 1951 (move forced by VN troops)
NVA service: 1959–66; orderly to VN adviser in Xieng Khouang Prov, Laos, & also with VN adviser to 17th PL Bn, Khammouane Prov; propagandist & soldier in Thakhek area until defection
Def: Jul 1966

5. Prisoner; b. 1946, NVN; Vietnamese
NVA service: 1965–Feb 1966, soldier; Jan 1966—to Laos, wounded and taken prisoner
Cap: Feb 1966

6. Defector; b. 1945, Vientiane Prov; Vietnamese
Ed: speaks, reads, writes Thai & Vietnamese (moved with family to Thailand 1945–62); also 10 mos mech trng Phu Tho, NVN
Occ before joining: mechanics student
NVA service: 1962—recruited by VN agents in Thailand & sent to NVN; 1965—recruited into NVA; 1965—assigned to SVN; defected while going through Laos
Def: Apr 1966

7. Prisoner; b. 1930, Nghe An, NVN; Vietnamese
NVA service: capt; 1965—arr in Laos, fought in Thakhek battle
Cap: Nov 1965

8. Defector; b. 1942, Muong Lan, NVN; Vietnamese-Tai Dam
NVA service: 1962–66; 1965—squad ldr & jr off after grad from cadet sch, Thanh Hoa; Sep 1965—to Laos
Def: Dec 1966

9. Defector; b. Dec 1930, Thanh Hoa, NVN; Vietnamese
   NVA service: Jan 1950–Dec 1966; 1958–60—off sch at Son Tay &
   promoted to 1st Lt; 1963—acted as C/S to Bn 1; Feb 1964—to
   Laos as adviser to PL Bn 408; Oct 1966—Sr Capt
   Def: Dec 1966

10. Defector
    Occ before joining: med student finishing 1st yr of 5 yr course at
    Ha Dong
    NVA service: Oct 1966–May 1967; Oct 1966—to Laos to head
    Nam Tha Prov med services for VNese and to advise PL
    Def: May 1967

11. Prisoner; b. 1942, Vinh Phuc Prov, NVN; Vietnamese
    Ed: completed 5th grade
    Occ before joining: farmer (1960–64)
    NVA service: 1964–Jul 1966, soldier; May 1966—to Laos
    Cap: Jul 1966

12. Defector; b. 1937, Thanh Hoa, NVN
    Ed: 3 yrs (1952–55)
    NVA service: 1959–67, S/Lt, subaltern in QM service; May 1964—
    to Laos, Attopeu Prov; Feb 1965—polit agt for VNese with PL
    Married: Mar 1966
    Def: Apr 1967

13. Prisoner; b. 1949, NW NVN; Vietnamese
    Ed: 5 yrs (1960–65)
    NVA service: Jan 1966–Mar 1967, private; Jul 1966—to Laos, in
    combat about 5 days after trng about 6 mos
    Cap: Mar 1967

14. Prisoner; b. 1948; Vietnamese
    NVA service: 1966–Aug 1967; May 1967—intel recce mission to
    Laos in commando co when taken following NVA attack in
    Saravane on FAR post
    Cap: Aug 1967

15. Prisoner; Vietnamese
    NVA service: Aug–Sep 1966, soldier; Aug 1966—to Laos when
    wounded and taken prisoner
    Cap: Sep 1966

16. Prisoner; b. 1940; Vietnamese
    Ed: 3rd grade
    NVA service: 1963–65; assigned to 1st Ind Bn & then to Laos, cpl;
    in Thakhek battle
    Cap: Nov 1965

17. Prisoner; b. 1946, NVN; Vietnamese
    Ed: 4 yrs
    NVA service: 1964–65; 1965—sent to Laos, wounded and taken
      at Dong Hene
    Cap: Mar 1965

18. Prisoner; Vietnamese
    NVA service: 1958–65, low-level comm off; 1965—arr Laos, in
      Thakhek attack
    Cap: Nov 1965

19. Defector; b. NVN; Meo
    Ed: no formal ed
    NVA service: 1962–67, sgt; propagandist amg Meo in Laos
    Def: after Tet 1967

20. Prisoner; b. 1947 (approx); Vietnamese
    NVA service: 1964–65, soldier; Oct 1965—entered Laos and taken
      prisoner after wounded
    Cap: Dec 1965

21. Defector; b. 1945, Nghe An Prov, NVN; Tai Dam
    Ed: primary (1959–66)
    NVA service: Jan–Feb 1967, private; assigned to road repair unit
      near Ban Ban, XKhouang, Laos
    Def: Feb 1967

22. Defector; b. 1947, Xieng Khouang Prov; Lao Loum
    Ed: 1953–63, in Hanoi, thru 8th grade under govt sponsorship,
      grew up in orphanages
    NVA service: 1964–67; Spring 1964—to Laos, aspirant, platoon ldr
    Def: Jun 1967

Appendix B

The Lao Communist Movement—
A Basic Chronology

I	II
Important Events in the Evolution of the Movement	**Important Events Outside the Movement**

<table>
<tr><td></td><td>

March 1945

Japanese defeat of French in Indochina

April 8, 1945

King Sisavang Vong proclaims the independence of Laos

Summer 1945

Japanese surrender

September 1945

Ho Chi Minh proclaims Democratic Republic of Vietnam in Hanoi

</td></tr>
<tr><td>

October 12, 1945

Lao Issara Provisional Constitution adopted and government formed; Phaya Khammao, Premier

Date is celebrated in NLHS-controlled zone as National Day

</td><td></td></tr>
<tr><td></td><td>

November 11, 1945

Ho Chi Minh formally dissolves Indochinese Communist Party

</td></tr>
</table>

March 21, 1946
Prince Souphanouvong wounded in Lao partisan attack against French in Thakhek

April 23, 1946
Constitutional monarchy proclaimed in Luang Prabang

April 24, 1946
Issara government flees to Thailand after French enter Vientiane

April 24, 1946
French troops enter Vientiane

May 13, 1946
French troops enter Luang Prabang

July 1946
Souphanouvong goes to Hanoi where he is in touch with Viet Minh; is also in contact with Viet Minh representative in Bangkok, Nguyen Duc Quy

August 1946
Laos becomes member of Indochinese Federation

September 23, 1946
With the occupation of Houei Sai (in northwest Laos), the French regain control over all of Laos

October 1946
People's Committee of East Laos, headed by Thao O, starts military activities on Route 7

December 1, 1946
Direction of the Lao Issara exile government, while continuing to be officially headed by Phaya Khammao, is assumed by Prince Phetsarath, elder brother of Prince Souvanna Phouma and half-brother of Prince Souphanouvong

December 1946
Outbreak of Indochina War

end 1946
Souphanouvong, with Viet Minh advisers, heads guerrilla raids in Laos against French

May 11, 1947
Constitution is promulgated by King in Laos

late 1947
Revolutionary forces in western Laos, because of unfavorable political situation in Thailand, shift to eastern Laos to create resistance bases

End 1948–beginning 1949
Lao Communist forces create military zones of Southeast and Northeast (Sam Neua) Laos and step up armed propaganda activities

January 20, 1949
Armed forces now entitled Lao Issara Armed Forces

February 1949
Souphanouvong establishes separate political front for Issara guerrilla army he commands, calling this the Progressive People's Organization

May 1949
Souphanouvong splits with Lao Issara and is removed (or resigns) from posts

July 19, 1949
In Paris King Sisavang Vong and French President Vincent Auriol sign the General Franco-Laotian Convention, which recognizes the independence of Laos within the French Union

October 24, 1949

Phaya Khammao, Prime Minister of the Lao Issara provisional government, signs a decree in Bangkok announcing the dissolution of the Issara government. Subsequently Souvanna Phouma and other Issara moderates return to Vientiane

November 1949

Souphanouvong meets Ho Chi Minh at Tuyen Quang, North Vietnam, and receives promise of support

January 14, 1950

Ho Chi Minh appeals to all foreign powers to recognize DRV

February 1950

US recognizes French-sponsored governments in Phnom Penh, Vientiane and Saigon

March 1950

US mission to Saigon to explore granting economic aid to Phnom Penh, Vientiane, and Saigon governments

August 13, 1950

Laos National Assembly of over 100 representatives convenes and forms a Resistance Coalition Government, headed by Souphanouvong and the Free Laos Front (Neo Lao Issara), issuing a manifesto and adopting a national flag and hymn

November 19, 1950

National Peace Congress in North Vietnam is attended by delegates from Cambodia and Laos. On November 20–22 there reportedly follows a three-day conference of representatives of national fronts of the three Indochinese countries who decide to set up a united front; meeting is attended by Prince Souphanouvong for Laos, Sieu Heng, head of the Cambodian Liberation Committee, and Ton Duc Thǎng (in 1969, President of the DRV), representing the Viet Minh

December 1950

The US signs a Mutual Defense Assistance Agreement with France, Vietnam, Cambodia, and Laos for indirect American military aid to the three Southeast Asian countries

1951

Four DRV battalions are stationed in Laos but, until early 1953, avoid contact while concentrating on training Pathet Lao

February 1951

Indochinese Communist Party reconstituted as Dang Lao Dong Viet Nam (Vietnamese Workers' Party); Souphanouvong attends meeting as do other Lao and Cambodian observers

March 1, 1951

Representatives of national united fronts of Vietnam, Cambodia and Laos meet and establish an alliance

November 1951

Souvanna Phouma, as Prime Minister, succeeds Phoui Sananikone government

October 1952
Lao delegation appears at Peace Conference of Asian and Pacific Area; Laos question is discussed and resolution adopted demanding foreign troop withdrawal

Winter 1952–1953
Viet Minh turn to Laos with guerrilla infiltration and obtain allegiance of small group of Lao agents

March–April 1953
Viet Minh forces invade Laos; Sam Neua falls into Viet Minh hands; Souphanouvong establishes his seat of government there

April 13, 1953
French abandon Sam Neua

April 30, 1953
Luang Prabang falls

May 1953
Viet Minh advance through northeastern, central, and southern Laos

October 1953
French are compelled to protect Laos from invasion under mutual defense treaty. Treaty with France affirms Laos' full independence in French Union

end 1953
Viet Minh occupy Thakhek, then disperse into southern Laos hills after French reinforcements arrive

March–May 1954
Battle of Dien Bien Phu

July 1954
Geneva Conference; certain areas of Phong Saly and Sam Neua provinces assigned to Pathet Lao for regroupment

July 21, 1954
Geneva Agreements accepted by most major powers

August 1954
Joint Armistice Committee provided by Geneva Accords appoints joint commissions in central and lower Laos to supervise troop movements

September 1954
SEATO Treaty (includes protocol extending protection to the three Indochinese countries)

November 19, 1954
French Union and Viet Minh troops complete withdrawal, and Pathet Lao units regroup in Phong Saly and Sam Neua

November 1954
Katay Sasorith becomes Prime Minister when Souvanna Phouma resigns

1955
(Neo) *Lao Hak Sat* newspaper founded

March 22, 1955
Formation of *Phak Pasason Lao* (People's Party of Laos)

April 13, 1955
RLG White Paper published, a memorandum to ICC about North Vietnamese interference

April 18–24, 1955
Bandung Conference; Chou En-lai at Bandung proclaims that China does not desire to interfere in Laos affairs

April 23, 1955
Prime Minister Katay Sasorith and DRV Foreign Minister Pham Van Dong reach agreement that the political settlement in Laos is an internal affair

October 1955
Meeting of Katay Sasorith and Souphanouvong in Rangoon

December 25, 1955
Katay Sasorith organizes election; Pathet Lao do not participate

January 6, 1956
National congress of the Neo Lao Issara, held in Sam Neua, changes name to Neo Lao Hak Sat (Lao Patriotic Front) and elects a 47-man Central Committee headed by Souphanouvong and Deputy Kaysone; congress adopts "10 practical policies"

March 1956
Souvanna Phouma becomes Prime Minister

July 1956
Santiphab Party established, headed by Quinim Pholsena; party works closely with NLHS

August 1956
New round of negotiations and signature of final agreement to integrate Pathet Lao into RLG

August 25, 1956
Premiers Chou En-lai and Souvanna Phouma sign joint statement stressing "traditional friendly ties" between Laos and China

August 29, 1956
Souvanna Phouma signs joint statement with Pham Van Dong in Hanoi

December 24, 1956
Agreement between RLG and Pathet Lao barring discrimination and reprisals against the Pathet Lao

November 12, 1957

Agreement reached between Souvanna Phouma and Souphanouvong to form coalition government with participation of Pathet Lao fighting units; NLHS is to be recognized as a legal political party, Phong Saly and Sam Neua to be handed over to RLG, and 1500 Pathet Lao forces to be integrated; elections set for May 1958 to add 21 members to 38-man National Assembly

November 18, 1957

Investiture of coalition cabinet; Souphanouvong formally returns the provinces of Sam Neua and Phong Saly to the authority of the King

February 18, 1958

In ceremony in Plain of Jars, 1501 Pathet Lao soldiers are formally (though not in actual fact) integrated into RLG army

May 1958

NLHS wins 9 seats and affiliated Santiphab Party 4 seats of total of 21 seats in national (supplementary) elections

1958

Committee for Defense of the National Interests (CDNI) is set up with Phoumi Nosavan as its head

July 19, 1958

ICC for Laos is adjourned over the objection of its Polish member

July 23, 1958
Souvanna Phouma as Prime Minister acts as caretaker until August 18 when Phoui Sananikone is appointed Prime Minister

1959
NLHS states that in 1959 US revived war in Laos

1959
Regroupees from North Vietnam infiltrate through Ho Chi Minh trail in increasing numbers to South Vietnam

February 1959
Sananikone government denounces Geneva Agreements

May 11, 1959
RLG orders two battalions of former Pathet Lao fighting units to surrender their arms within 24 hours; Pathet Lao Second Battalion escapes to North Vietnam

May 13, 1959
Souphanouvong is put under house arrest by RLG authorities

May 18, 1959
The Ministry of Foreign Affairs of the Chinese People's Republic issues stern warning to RLG that its "persecution of Pathet Lao amounts to the open launching of civil war"

May 25, 1959
Chinese Foreign Minister Chen Yi, in a letter to the Co-chairmen of the Geneva Conference, protests RLG armed attack on Pathet Lao units and house arrest of NLHS Party leaders

May 28–31, 1959

Major offensive unleashed against RLG, carried out primarily by North Vietnamese units against RLG frontier posts

July 29, 1959

Souphanouvong and other NLHS leaders imprisoned following emergency measures by RLG

August 8, 1959

Part of Pathet Lao first battalion escapes into jungles

July 1959

RLG protests to United Nations about North Vietnamese invasion

Autumn 1959

UN investigating team sent to northeast Laos

October 1959

Laos establishes diplomatic relations with the USSR

October 14, 1959

Prince Phetsarath dies

October 29, 1959

King Sisavang dies

December 1959

Phoumi Nosavan takes over control of the government

April 24, 1960

Elections in Laos; Pathet Lao representatives eliminated from National Assembly

May 22, 1960

Souphanouvong and other NLHS leaders escape with guards from prison in Vientiane

August 9, 1960

Kong Le coup

August 31, 1960

Souvanna Phouma gets vote of confidence from National Assembly and takes oath of office on September 2

September–October 1960
Thai economic blockade of Laos

October 12, 1960
Negotiations between RLG and NLHS in Vientiane

October 1960
Soviet Union appoints first Ambassador to Laos

October 27, 1960
Soviet airlift from Hanoi to Kong Le forces begins

October 1960
US suspends military aid to Laos

November 1960
Committee for Peace, Neutrality, Concord, National Union established under joint Presidency of Souvanna Phouma and Souphanouvong; made up of NLHS and Santiphab Party

November 11, 1960
Boun Oum's Revolutionary Committee seizes control of Luang Prabang

November 18, 1960
Souvanna Phouma meets Souphanouvong at the latter's headquarters in Sam Neua, agreeing to a Government of National Union including the NLHS

December 1960
Boun Oum and Phoumi Nosavan forces retake Vientiane; Souvanna Phouma and Kong Le flee

January/February 1961
Soviet airlifts to Pathet Lao

Spring 1961
Communist seizure of Tchepone and Muong Phine; North Vietnamese and Pathet Lao push RLG forces back to Hien Heup from north of Vang Vieng on Route 13; right wing almost completely defeated, losing effective administrative control of nearly all upland Laos

April 2, 1961
Foreign Minister Chen Yi, in Djakarta, states that "China will not remain idle" if SEATO takes part in Laos civil war

April 1961
Souvanna Phouma and Chou En-lai agree to establish diplomatic relations and exchange cultural and economic missions

April 24, 1961
US and USSR agree on cease-fire in Laos

May 1, 1961
Cease-fire negotiated between warring factions

May 7, 1961
ICC returns to Laos

May 1961
Geneva Conference on Laos opens

May 26, 1961
Founding of Laotian Neutrality Party

June 22, 1961
Zurich Agreement to form tripartite government

June 1961
President Kennedy and Chairman Khrushchev meet in Vienna and issue joint statement reaffirming support for a neutral and independent Laos

October 1961
Meeting at Hien Heup and Ban Namone and agreement to establish coalition government

October 1961
China and Laos agree to establish consulates-general at Phong Saly in Laos and at Kunming in Yunnan, China

November 1961
Chinese appoint an economic and cultural mission to Laos headed by Ho Wei and Liu Ch'un, who are received in Xieng Khouang by Souvanna Phouma and Souphanouvong

December 1961
First Vietnamese prisoner captured by RLG

December 1961
Geneva Conference drafts Declaration of Neutrality of Laos

January 1962
Prince Souphanouvong visits Moscow

May 1962
Nam Tha seized by Communist forces

Spring 1962
President Kennedy sends some 5,000 troops to northeast Thailand in response to Nam Tha attack by Communists; these forces are withdrawn after July

June 2–3, 1962
Khrushchev receives Kong Le and General Singkapo Chounramany

June 12–24, 1962
Plain of Jars agreement; coalition government formed including NLHS, with Souvanna Phouma as Premier and Souphanouvong and Phoumi Nosavan as Vice Premiers

July 1962
Pathet Lao army now has almost 20,000 soldiers armed with Soviet weapons; Pathet Lao ministers control Economic Planning, Information, Transport, and Public Works in coalition government

July 9, 1962
RLG signs Declaration of Neutrality

July 23, 1962
Geneva Agreements signed, including Declaration of Neutrality of Laos

August 1, 1962
Lao Women's Federation founded in Khang Khay with Phayboun (Madame Quinim) Pholsena as chairman of its 10-member Central Committee

September–October 1962
Prince Souphanouvong in Moscow, received by Khrushchev on October 14

September 1962
Taiwan regime severs diplomatic relations with Laos, and Communist China announces ex-

change of diplomatic missions between China and Laos

October 8, 1962
Lao National Assembly meets and agrees to grant Souvanna Phouma full powers for one year

November 27, 1962
Joint agreement between NLHS and RLG to set up tripartite police and armed forces in Vientiane

late November–early December 1962
Phoumi Nosavan visits Moscow, is received by Khrushchev, and concludes an economic agreement

February 11–18, 1963
King Savang, Premier Souvanna Phouma, and Phoumi Vongvichit visit the USSR, are received by Khrushchev and Brezhnev

February 12, 1963
Kong Le's Chief of Staff, Colonel Ketsana Vongsouvan, is killed on Plain of Jars, provoking breach between Kong Le and Pathet Lao

February–March 1963
Kong Le makes trip to Hanoi, Peking, Moscow

March 31, 1963
Fighting breaks out between Deuanist and Kong Le Neutralists on Plain of Jars

April 1, 1963
Assassination of Quinim Pholsena

April 1963
Souphanouvong and Phoumi Vongvichit leave Vientiane government for Khang Khay, claiming security inadequate in Vientiane

April 20, 1963

Kong Le loses Xieng Khouang airfield to Deuanist-Pathet Lao forces, beginning gradual elimination of Kong Le forces from Plain of Jars; North Vietnamese also engage in attack on Kong Le

May 1963

Chinese complete strategic road from Yunnan to Lao provincial capital of Phong Saly

May 3, 1963

An ICC helicopter is destroyed; each side blames the other and talks finally break down; Pathet Lao demand establishment of tripartite Vientiane police force and claim that National Assembly formed on basis of 1960 elections is illegal

Summer 1963

Small-scale clashes continue on Plain of Jars and elsewhere in Laos

August 1963

Souvanna Phouma at UN calls for end of foreign interference

October 30–November 3, 1963

Souvanna Phouma visits Moscow and is received by Khrushchev

April 10, 1964

Second National Congress of NLHS, held in Sam Neua, elects a Central Committee of 63 members; 10-point program adopted

April 1964

Souvanna Phouma makes goodwill visit to Peking

April 17, 1964

Tripartite talks on demilitarization and neutralization of Luang Prabang

April 19, 1964
Kouprasith-Sananikone coup, destroying thereby, in the view of the Pathet Lao, the Zurich and Plain of Jars Agreements

May 17, 1964
Pathet Lao claim that since this date, US has openly used air force to bomb liberated areas

May 24, 1964
Inauguration Congress of Lao Youth Federation in Khang Khay

May 25, 1964
Souvanna Phouma asks USSR for additional military aid

May 31, 1964
ICC, French and Indian ambassadors visit Khang Khay to meet with Souphanouvong

June 4, 1964
Six-nation talks in Vientiane to discuss pre-conditions for international conference on Laos

June 11, 1964
T-28s bomb Khang Khay, hitting Chinese Mission, killing one Chinese, and wounding five others

June 1964
Souvanna Phouma calls for urgent Zurich conference on Laos

June 16, 1964
Representatives of Geneva Conference Co-Chairmen and ICC visit Khang Khay

August 22, 1964
Souphanouvong and Phoumi Vongvichit confer with Chen Yi in Peking

August 1964
Gulf of Tonkin crisis

August 25, 1964
Patriotic Neutralist forces hold first congress in Khang Khay

September 21, 1964

Formal talks of the three Lao factions begin in Paris (Souvanna Phouma; Souphanouvong, Phoumi Vongvichit, Khampheuan Tounalom; Boun Oum na Champassak, Ngon Sananikone). Subsequently Souphanouvong visits Moscow

October 1964

Upon his return from Paris meeting where they failed to reach agreement, Souphanouvong attends 15th anniversary of Chinese People's Republic in Peking. At October 16 press conference, Souphanouvong terms the Vientiane government formed after the 1964 coup "illegal," urges the reconvening of the Geneva Conference on Laos, and denies that Vietnamese forces are on NLHS territory. Subsequently Souphanouvong visits Moscow

December 8, 1964

Phoumi Nosavan reads RLG *White Paper* on DRV interference in Laos before 19th session of UN General Assembly

December 1964

Hanoi radio reports establishment of Thai independence movement, aimed at driving US out and overthrowing Thai administration

1965

Pathet Lao control large areas of Laos; at least 11 Pathet Lao province administrations (out of 16 total Lao provinces)

January 1965
White Paper published by NLHS

February 3, 1965
Phoumi-Siho coup attempt

late February–early March 1965
Delegation of Patriotic Neutralist Party and Party of Peace and Neutrality attend Indochinese People's Conference in Phnom Penh; chief NLHS delegate, Secretary-General Phoumi Vongvichit

March 1965
Souvanna asks ICC to inspect Vietnamese prisoners

April 17, 1965
Souphanouvong heads NLHS delegation at 10th anniversary of Bandung Conference at Djakarta

June 1, 1965
Thai Patriotic Worker's Federation created

July 23, 1965
First NLHS Congress on Education opens in Sam Neua

October 1, 1965
Name of "Pathet Lao Fighting Units" changed to "Lao People's Liberation Army" and decision made to publish a People's Liberation Army newspaper

October 1965
Talks among representatives of three parties resumed in Vientiane

October 13, 1965
National Political (consultative) Joint Conference of Patriotic Neutralists and NLHS held in Sam Neua; "four points and five principles" issued as part of program

November 1965
Proclamation of state of emergency by Vientiane authorities in Khammouane and Savannakhet provinces

November 25, 1965
Geneva Conference Co-Chairmen propose that ICC continue for another year in Laos if no objection from signatories (Souphanouvong protests January 1966)

December 28, 1965
Khang Khay journalists' school opens

January 6, 1966
NLHS convention marking Front's 10th anniversary; adopts ten-point program which is a restatement of the 1964 Second Congress program

January 13–15, 1966
Afro-Asian and Latin American Solidarity Conference in Havana with Pathet Lao delegation led by Phoumi Vongvichit

February 1966
Chinese Yunnan Art Troupe visits Xieng Khouang

February–March 1966
Air attacks damage Chinese Consulate-General of Phong Saly and Economic and Cultural Mission at Khang Khay

March 21, 1966
NLHS Youth Association holds first youth congress in Xieng Khouang

April 22, 1966
NLHS Cultural Congress; NLHS Cultural Association formed

May 1966
King Savang and Premier Souvanna Phouma visit Soviet Union at the invitation of President Podgorny

June 2, 1966
RLG General Thao Ma rebels and seizes Savannakhet airport

June 17, 1966
Ex-General Siho gives himself up to government authorities

July–August 1966
RLG retakes Nam Bac region (north of Luang Prabang) which Pathet Lao had controlled for several years

August 29, 1966
NLHS Central Committee declares June ICC report "completely illegal"

September 4, 1966
Siho killed during alleged escape from RLG prison

October 1966
NLHS delegation to Cuba; Lao Day of Independence adopted by Havana Conference

November 17, 1966
Souphanouvong broadcasts telegram rejecting general election call

November 21–27, 1966
Representatives of NLHS and Neutralist Forces hold second joint political conference

November 1966–February 1967
Chinese Yunnan Art Troupe tours NLHS areas

December 15–21, 1966
NLHS Central Committee conference in Sam Neua Province; Souphanouvong reports on military, political, and economic situation in liberated areas

December 16, 1966
Souphanouvong invites ICC chiefs to visit him in Khang Khay

December 19, 1966
DRV chargé in Vientiane denies that there are any North Vietnamese prisoners in Laos, in answer to RLG claim

January 1967
Sisana Sisane and Sithon Khommadam visit Peking, meeting with Foreign Minister Chen Yi

January 1967
National elections in RLG territory, boycotted by NLHS

May 6, 1967
In an interview broadcast by Radio Prague Souphanouvong makes first public statement expressing allegiance to Marxism and Communism

July 1967
Souphanouvong sends message to Havana Conference of Latin American Solidarity Committee

July 29, 1967
Supreme Commander of LPLA, Khamtay Siphandone, sends telegram to Lin Piao on 40th anniversary of Chinese People's Liberation Army

September 1967
Moscow stage artists tour NLHS zone and are received by Souphanouvong

January 6, 1968
NLHS Central Committee, on 12th anniversary of the founding of the NLHS, establishes Pathet Lao News Agency (*Khaosan Pathet Lao*) under Central Committee member Sisana Sisane

January 13, 1968
Pathet Lao take back Nam Bac region they had lost in 1966; RLG suffers substantial losses

Dry season (ending about June) 1968
Communist forces in Laos mount strong attacks against RLG

Summer 1968
NLHS indicates that settlement of Laos issue must take into account "the realities of the current situation"

Rainy season (ending about October) 1968
RLG unable to take back positions lost to enemy during dry season

September 5–26, 1968
NLHS delegation under Sithon Khommadam visits North Korea to participate in the 20th anniversary celebrations of the DPRK and is received by Kim Il-Song

September 7–13, 1968
Third National Political Joint Conference of NLHS and Patriotic Neutralists

September 13, 1968
Souphanouvong sends letter to King of Laos

1968
RLG issues *White Paper* on violations of Geneva Accords by the DRV

March 31, 1968
President Johnson announces partial bombing halt of North Vietnam

October 25–November 1, 1968
Third Extraordinary NLHS Congress is held in Sam Neua and adopts 12-point political program; Souphanouvong delivers political report on the situation in Laos

October 31, 1968
President Johnson announces cessation of bombing of North Vietnam

January 14, 1969
Communists blow up RLG ammunition depot outside Vientiane

January–February 1969
Tiao Souk Vongsak, leading delegation of Lao Afro-Asian Solidarity Committee, visits USSR

February 1969
Victor Minin, Soviet Ambassador to Laos, accompanied by Soviet military attaché, visits Hanoi and Pathet Lao-controlled zone

March 1–2, 1969
Meo anti-Communist guerrilla base of Na Khang in Sam Neua Province falls to Communists

April 1969
RLG forces evacuate town of Thateng, north of Bolovens Plateau, as a result of Communist effort (started in late 1967) to isolate the Bolovens

early April 1969
National Political Conference of Patriotic Neutralist Forces held in Xieng Khouang Province

late April 1969
RLG forces take Xieng Khouang town but evacuate it a month later

May 1969
US jets blast Communist-held town of Xieng Khouang on Plain of Jars

May 19–26, 1969
Soviet Afro-Asian Solidarity Committee delegation visits NLHS zone

May 1969
Le Van Hien, DRV Ambassador to Laos, long absent from his post, returns briefly and is received by Souvanna Phouma on May 14 (Le Van Hien's previous visit was July 26–September 3, 1968)

May 15, 1969
Souvanna Phouma gives banquet for Peter Kapitsa, Chief, Southeast Asia Division of the Foreign Ministry of the USSR, who visits Laos and nearby countries

June 11–24, 1969
A 15-member Soviet artist ensemble tours the Sam Neua area at invitation of the NLHS

June 27, 1969
Communist forces take Muong Soui, the last RLG Neutralist-held stronghold on the Plain of Jars

July 8, 1969
NLHS Central Committee issues memorandum stating position on Tripartite Government in Laos

July 21, 1969
Under the presidency of Souphanouvong and with the attendance of Sithon Khommadam,

Phoumi Vongvichit, Khamsouk Keola and other NLHS and Patriotic Neutralist dignitaries, mass meeting is held in Sam Neua commemorating the 15th anniversary of the 1954 Geneva Agreements and inaugurating the "Month of the Lao People's Solidarity with the Vietnamese People"

late July 1969
Souphanouvong receives the editor of the Austrian newspaper *Volksstimme*, Otto Janecek, in Sam Neua

August 1969
Communist forces capture Xieng Dat (20 km south of Muong Soui) from the RLG Neutralists

August 15–23, 1969
A NLHS delegation, headed by Tiao Souk Vongsak, visits North Korea at the invitation of DPRK

September 5, 1969
A solemn mourning ceremony for Ho Chi Minh is held in Sam Neua by the NLHS; speeches made by Phoumi Vongvichit, Souphanouvong, and Kaysone

September 7, 1969
Souphanouvong heads NLHS delegation to Hanoi for Ho Chi Minh's funeral; accompanied by Sithon Khommadam, Faydang, Phoumi Vongvichit and other members of the NLHS Central Committee, Souphanouvong meets with Nguyen Huu Tho, President of NLFS,

September 1969
Ho Chi Minh dies

and Pham Van Dong, Premier of the DRV; he also confers with Soviet Premier Kosygin, Chinese Vice Premier Li Hsien-nien and Prince Sihanouk of Cambodia

September 8, 1969

RLG forces capture Muong Phine (east of Savannakhet and close to Ho Chi Minh Trail), a Pathet Lao headquarters for past 7 years; RLG forces also move against Tchepone base

September 1969

New York Times reports large-scale US-backed RLG operations under way to recapture important areas from the Pathet Lao; RLG forces take Plain of Jars, including Khang Khay, Xieng Khouang Ville, Ban Ban, and Phongsavan as well as Communist strongholds in southeast Laos

October 2, 1969

NLHS spokesman reiterates that Vientiane administration of Souvanna Phouma is not legitimate government of Laos and has no right to act as such at the UN or elsewhere. Radio Pathet Lao declares that Souvanna Phouma has no right to dismiss the Patriotic Neutralist ministers and deputy ministers from their posts in the national coalition government since they became the "actual representatives" of the Neutralists when Souvanna Phouma's neutralist status came to an end with the April 1964 coup

October–November 3, 1969
NLHS delegation headed by Tiao Souk Vongsak and deputy leader Nhia Vu visit China.

October 11–22, 1969
Soviet Communist Youth League delegation visits Sam Neua

November 3, 1969
Soviet Foreign Minister Gromyko expresses concern about the situation in Laos

December 15, 1969
US Senate votes 73–17 that none of the funds of the Defense Department's appropriation bill "shall be used to finance the introduction of American ground combat troops into Laos or Thailand"

end January 1970
CPSU Sec. B. N. Ponomarev receives delegates to Third Conference of Asian and African People's Solidarity including representative(s?) of NLHS. Souk Vongsak makes a speech of greetings on January 27

February 1970
Pathet Lao/North Vietnamese forces recapture the Plain of Jars, which they had lost to the RLG in September 1969

February 24, 1970
Pathet Lao/North Vietnamese forces recapture the important town and airport of Muong Soui, 15 miles west of the Plain of Jars

early February 1970
Souvanna Phouma calls for neutralization of Plain of Jars; appeal directed to Hanoi

February 28, 1970

Souvanna Phouma sends letters to Britain and the USSR officially requesting Geneva-style consultations on the situation in Laos

March 6, 1970

NLHS makes public a 5-point peace proposal (described by Hanoi as "very logical and reasonable" and "fully consonant with the interests of peace and security in Indochina and SEA" subsequently also supported in similar terms by the USSR)

March 6, 1970

President Nixon releases a lengthy statement regarding the US involvement in Laos, indicating that US air operations over Laos have resulted in the loss of about 400 aircraft and 400 airmen; also reveals that he had written to Prime Minister Harold Wilson and Premier Kosygin to enlist the Geneva Conference cochairmen's efforts to end fighting in Laos

March 8, 1970

Souphanouvong invites Souvanna Phouma to exchange views on peaceful settlement and Souvanna accepts (first message from Souphanouvong to Souvanna Phouma since February 1969)

March 9, 1970

The US Government states it will henceforth announce American casualties and aircraft losses in Laos (previously combined with losses in Vietnam)

March 11, 1970

Sot Phetrasy, NLHS representative in Vientiane, announces that proposed all-Lao political conference can take place only after complete cessation of US bombing in Laos

March 11, 1970

Senator J. W. Fulbright introduces a resolution expressing "sense of the Senate" that the President cannot commit US armed forces in combat in or over Laos without Senate affirmative action

March 15, 1970

Moscow Radio announces that Premier Kosygin has sent a message to President Nixon (in reply to the latter's letter of March 6) rejecting Geneva-type consultations on Laos and calling for a halt to US bombing in Laos

mid-March 1970

Pathet Lao/North Vietnamese forces resume their drive in northern Laos and approach the important US-supported supply base of the Meo guerrilla forces, Sam Thong (southwest of the Plain of Jars), and the nearby headquarters of General Vang Pao at Long Chien

March 18, 1970

Prince Sihanouk is ousted as Chief of State by Premier (Lt. General) Lon Nol, an anti-Communist who in the 1950's had fought against the Viet Minh. From Peking, Sihanouk calls for a national liberation struggle to unseat the Lon Nol government

March 22, 1970

The Pathet Lao courier Col. Pradith Tiengtham hands Souvanna Phouma a letter from Souphanouvong repeating the 5-point peace formula of the Pathet Lao announced earlier that month.

The Pathet Lao conditions are subsequently rejected by Souvanna Phouma

March 23, 1970

President Nixon sends another letter to Premier Kosygin urging international consultation to solve the conflict in Laos

The Soviet response is negative

April 20, 1970

A sanitized text of the hearings of the Symington Senate Subcommittee held in the fall of 1969 is released clarifying the US role in Laos

April 22, 1970
Nouhak, representing the NLHS, makes a speech at the Lenin celebrations in the Kremlin

April 23, 1970
North Vietnam's Party Chief First Secretary Le Duan in a speech at the Lenin anniversary in Moscow calls for closer cooperation of Vietnam, Cambodia, and Laos in the struggle against the US

April 24–25, 1970
An "Indochinese Summit Conference" is held somewhere in the vicinity of the tri-border area of Vietnam, Laos, and China (probably in Chinese territory); it is attended by Prince Sihanouk, Prince Souphanouvong, and Nguyen Huu Tho (Chairman of the Presidium of the Central Committee of the South Vietnamese National Liberation Front) representing the three Indochinese "liberation movements," as well as by a North Vietnamese delegation headed by Premier Pham Van Dong, and, at the final session, also by Chinese Premier Chou En-lai. A joint declaration is issued calling for intensified joint struggle against the US A Chinese government declaration subsequently pledges support for this struggle

April 29, 1970
The provincial capital of Attopeu, near the Cambodian border, is taken over by Pathet Lao/North Vietnamese forces

April 29, 1970
The US government confirms that the US is providing "advisers, tactical air, air coordinators, medical evacuation and some

logistics assistance" to large-scale South Vietnamese sweeps across the Cambodian border aimed at North Vietnamese sanctuaries

The following day, President Nixon announces that US combat forces are entering the Cambodian border areas

May 18, 1970

Secretary of Defense Melvin Laird says that US and South Vietnamese forces had in the past made incursions into Laos, but that there are no Americans engaged in ground combat in Laos now. US forays into Laos are confined to "hot pursuit," "protective reaction," and rescue missions

Appendix C

Partial List of Participants in the First Resistance Congress of Laos (August 13, 1950)

The following listing, furnished by a former Pathet Lao official who attended the meeting, includes more than a third of those who were present and indicates the provinces they represented. The starred names are those of persons who are now prominent in the Lao Communist movement. The spelling provided by the informant has been corrected to conform to the authors' system of transcription. (Further research is required to establish in all cases beyond doubt the identity of the individuals listed and the correct rendering of their names.)

Attopeu Province

(1) Phoun Sipaseuth*
(2) Khamtay Siphandone*
(3) Boun
(4) Suan
(5) Chareun

Khammouane and Savannakhet Provinces

(1) Nouhak Phomsavan*
(2) Khamfeuane Tounalom*
(3) Som Phommachan
(4) Toulan
(5) Singkapo Chounramany Sikhot*
(6) Sot Phetrasy*

(7) Sisana Sisane*
(8) Ounheuane Phomsavan
(9) Nouankham Anourak
(10) Maha Phamone
(11) Nakhonkham Bouphanouvong
(12) Apheui*
(13) Boun Nhong Vorasane

Vientiane and Houei Sai Provinces

(1) Prince Souk Vongsak*
(2) Phoumi Vongvichit*
(3) Inta
(4) Mun
(5) Saly
(6) Outtama*
(7) Sithong
(8) Thongchanh

Sam Neua Province

(1) Kaysone*
(2) Ma
(3) Sawath
(4) Nang Khamla
(5) Phya Thomsombat
(6) Chanthavong
(7) Maisouk*

Xieng Khouang Province

(1) Faydang*
(2) Thit Khamphong
(3) Nhia Vu*
(4) Lo Fung*
(5) Ba Tou

Appendix D

North Vietnamese Prisoners
and Defectors in Laos Prior
to the 1962 Geneva Conference

1. Nguyen Van Nham. 2d Lt., 335th Division. Captured at Ban Van Vieng, 70 km. north of Vientiane, by BV 53 about January 31, 1961. Sent to Hanoi at the end of 1962, after the formation of the Government of National Union.

2. Dinh Van Quang (also known as Manh Ha). 2nd-class soldier, 1st Bn., 316 Brigade, of NVA. A radio operator captured at Ban Na Pa by an FAR unit in December 1961. Sent to Hanoi in 1962.

3. Ne Tong. An ethnic Jaray from Darlac Province in South Vietnam who had been regrouped to the North with Viet Minh troops in 1954. Served in Laos with the 120th Independent Regiment. Captured by the 10th Infantry Bn., of the FAR, at Nong Het on Route 7.

4. Tran The Trung. Served with 927th Bn., 359th Regiment, a frontier defense unit. Captured by an FAR unit at Ban La The, in Laos, near the Mu Gia Pass leading to North Vietnam. Liberated from prison by Kong Le forces in 1960, and thereafter worked in Vientiane as a barber. After the coup by Phoumi Nosavan in December 1960, arrested once again and kept in prison until 1962. Chose to go to Saigon in 1962.

5. Vi Van Lang. A Red Tai, Sgt., serving with the 925th Bn., 359th Independent Regiment (a frontier defense unit). Captured at the battle of Ban Pha Tang in late April. Sent to Hanoi in 1962.

6. Linh (family name unknown). Intelligence agent of the 4th R.M. of NVA. Defected to RLG near Thakhek, in Khammouane Province in 1961 or 1962. Chose to go to Saigon after the Geneva Conference.

Notes

Selected Bibliography

Index

Notes

Chapter 2

1. The spelling "Tai" is used throughout this study to designate a distinct ethnic group of populations to whom belong among others the lowland Lao as well as the inhabitants of Thailand, the Thai.

2. For an excellent discussion of the ethnic situation in Laos see Frank M. LeBar, Gerald C. Hickey, and John K. Musgrave, *Ethnic Groups of Mainland Southeast Asia* (New Haven, Conn., 1964) and the relevant portions in Peter Kunstadter (ed.), *Southeast Asian Tribes, Minorities and Nations* (Princeton, N. J., 1966).

Chapter 3

1. The King of Luang Prabang was allowed to rule the northern part of the country under French supervision. The central and southern provinces of Laos were placed under the direct jurisdiction of a French administrator, who in turn was responsible to the French Governor General in Hanoi.

2. From an original French manuscript, handwritten and unpublished. (This and subsequent translations from the French are by the authors.)

3. See Hugh Toye, *Laos — Buffer State or Battleground* (London and New York, 1968), p. 45.

4. Information based on personal interview with the former leader of this group, Tham Sayasithsena (now Colonel Tham), who was later to become Deputy Minister of Defense in the Lao Issara (Free Laos) government.

5. E. Pietrantoni, "La population du Laos en 1943 dans son milieu géographique," *Bulletin de la société des études Indochinoises,* XXXII, iii (1957), as quoted by Toye, *Laos,* p. 45.

The six chief towns of Laos — Vientiane, Luang Prabang, Thakhek, Savannakhet, Pakse, and Xieng Khouang — had in 1943 a total population of 51,150, of whom 30,300 were Vietnamese.

6. Quoted from documents in the collection of the late Nhouy Abhay.

7. To this day, the Lao revolutionaries celebrate October 12 as national independence day.

8. In Vientiane there were three principal factions: the Committee of the People, headed by Phagna Khammao Vilay (Xiengmao), a former high government official under the French and a political moderate; the Committee of Laos for the Lao, in which a young military man by the name of Sing (now ex-Major General Sing Rattanasamay) played the leading role; and the Committee for a Free Laos, headed by a young man, Tham Sayasithsena (now Colonel Tham). It was this latter group which in the late 1940s gave the name Lao Issara (Free Laos) to the entire Lao independence movement.

9. Kaysone, whose Vietnamese father lives in Savannakhet on the Mekong, attended the Faculty of Medicine in Hanoi in the early 1940s. He reportedly was active in the radical student movement associated with the Indochinese Communist Party and later joined that party. During this period, he is said to have known Vo Nguyen Giap.

Nouhak, a Lao whose trucking business involved frequent dealings with Vietnam, is said to have become a member of the Vietnamese (Communist) Lao Dong Party in 1946, when he became an arms supplier for the Viet Minh.

10. Bounkhong was the "King of the Front" (Vangna), a hereditary position of a collateral branch of the royal house. Through his father, Souphanouvong could trace his origin to a King of Laos who had ruled in the late eighteenth century.

11. The term "Mom" designates the commoner wife of a prince.

12. It is said that Souphanouvong's mother was not taken into the Viceroy's household. At any rate, his father, Bounkhong, apparently paid little attention to him and even was rumored not to be his real father. Phetsarath, Souphanouvong's much older brother, in many ways acted as a father to him. Nevertheless, the youth reportedly suffered discrimination because of his origins, and his financial and social standing consequently was not as substantial as that of his older brothers.

13. An event of his schooldays in Hanoi reportedly had a marked influence on the young Lao, as it involved his rejection by a French métisse who apparently, despite her own mixed blood, felt superior to the "indigène."

14. This information is challenged by a Vietnamese source who states that the Prince attended a private engineering college of lesser renown in Paris. Even this informant, however, confirms that Souphanouvong obtained his French engineering license.

15. The Communist writer Wilfred G. Burchett, who frequently interviewed Souphanouvong in later years, reports that the Prince worked on

the docks during his holidays to defray the cost of his studies. See, for example, Burchett's account in *Schatten über dem Dschungel* [Shadows Over the Jungle] (Berlin, 1963), p. 212. Arthur J. Dommen, in *Conflict in Laos* (New York, 1964; rev. ed. in preparation) supports this story.

16. Wilfred G. Burchett, *The Furtive War: The United States in Vietnam and Laos* (New York, 1963), p. 177. Arthur Dommen also contends that the Prince was active in the French anti-Fascist popular-front movement and that it was in France that he "made his first acquaintance with Communists." (*Conflict in Laos*, p. 21.) A Lao government official who associated with Souphanouvong in Vietnam shortly after his return from France reported that the Prince was then a reader of the French Communist newspaper *l'Humanité*.

17. In this connection it is interesting to note that the Prince in one of his letters proudly refers to his having attended an international Buddhist congress in France in 1937.

18. A US military officer who knew the Prince well during his days of exile in Bangkok in the late 1940s, and again in the period of the coalition government of the late 1950s, confirms this assessment.

19. A Vietnamese informant who in his youth resided near the village of Au-Hien (about ten miles northwest of Thanh Hoa) remembers the Prince as having been the head of the irrigation service at this small post.

20. A document in Vientiane, purporting to reproduce autobiographical comments written by the Prince in 1943, has him describing his state of mind after his return to Indochina as "bitterness, revolt, discouragement."

21. Letters in the possession of the Nhouy Abhay family in Vientiane.

22. There exists, for example, an interesting exchange of letters between the conservative politician Katay Don Sasorith — himself half Vietnamese — and the Prince, in which the former makes critical remarks about this marriage and Souphanouvong defends himself against the accusation of being unduly under the influence of the Vietnamese. As for Le Thi Ky-Nam, the daughter of a hotel owner from Central Vietnam, she gave her husband at least nine children. An official document attesting to the Prince's clean criminal record, issued in Vientiane on December 5, 1957 (in connection with his candidacy in national elections), shows him as having nine children as of that date. Apparently another child was born thereafter.

23. An American who had occasion to observe the couple in 1946 in Bangkok gained the impression that the Prince was at that time actually somewhat in awe of his wife's dominant personality.

24. From a speech reported in *Lao Presse*, November 3, 1967.

25. In the possession of the Nhouy Abhay family.

26. Burchett, in his *Schatten über dem Dschungel*, suggests this when he states that the Prince was deeply impressed with the miserable condition

232 NOTES TO PAGES 32–39

232 | NOTES TO PAGES 32-39

of the Vietnamese workers he encountered in his travels during the war years.

27. Souphanouvong's wife was acquainted with Le Van Hien, an associate of Ho Chi Minh and at present the North Vietnamese Ambassador to Laos.

28. Souphanouvong flew from Vinh to Hanoi to meet Ho Chi Minh on an airplane provided by General Philip E. Gallagher, chief of a small American military observer team in Vietnam. (See Dommen, *Conflict in Laos*, p. 23.)

29. Nhouy Abhay, for example, one of the Lao who knew him well during this period, has said that "under the influence of his wife, he spoke only of total independence [from France] and of resisting to the death — veritable Viet Minh commands — forgetting that Laos is not Vietnam."

30. One might wonder why the Prince never sought United States aid since the Office of Strategic Services (OSS) had shown an interest in the Southeast Asian nationalist groups during the war. Actually, from 1946 to as late as 1949, Souphanouvong did make approaches to American authorities in Bangkok to obtain support. His requests were refused, even though the Prince impressed his American contacts, military officers in Thailand, as a genuine Lao nationalist with outstanding qualifications for leadership. However, US policy at the time was reluctant to interfere with French colonial policies.

31. One of our sources, who was in Hanoi at the time, indicated that on at least one occasion Souphanouvong received from the Viet Minh a sum of between 500,000 and 1 million piastres.

32. For a discussion of guerrilla activity in Laos during this period from a French point of view, see Michel Caply, *Guérilla au Laos* [Guerrilla in Laos] (Paris, 1966).

33. See the official Communist publication *Su That* [Truth], No. 154 (n.d.). [Viet-Nam Central Information Service. *Cambodia and Laos Fight Hand in Hand with Viet-Nam for Freedom* (N.p., 1951), p. 18.]

34. Although these claims may sound exaggerated, our interviews dealing with the early period of partisan activity in the Laos-Vietnam border region suggest that there was some substance to them.

35. This day is celebrated in Lao Communist territory as the anniversary of the founding of what was to become the Lao People's Liberation Army (LPLA).

36. The document, written in French, and in the possession of the family of Nhouy Abhay, is numbered No. 3235/KT, confidential. It bears the letterhead "Kingdom of Laos — Provisional Government of the Free and Independent Government of Laos — Ministry of Foreign Affairs" (Souphanouvong was Minister of Foreign Affairs as well as Minister of

Defense), and is addressed to Prince Phetsarath, "Chef Effectif du Gouvernement."

37. The letters exchanged between Souphanouvong and the Lao Issara government in Bangkok indicate that this particular instance of insubordination on the part of the Prince increased in early 1949 the mutual bitterness that had been building up over time between Souphanouvong and the other members of the Lao Issara government. This impression is confirmed by the testimony of eyewitnesses.

38. Today both these men are top military figures in the LPLA. Sithon, less influential, is the son of a famous anti-French rebel tribal leader of Lao Theung origin, who was very powerful in an area contiguous to Vietnam. Khamtay, an ethnic Lao, is Commander-in-Chief of the LPLA forces and wields political influence. He is one of the leading members of an important clan of Sithandone Province.

39. It should be noted, however, that, in the eyes of former members of the Lao Issara government, they had by that time already effectively severed their relations with the fractious Prince because of a long series of insubordinations on his part.

40. Unnumbered letter marked "confidential" and signed by Katay Sasorith, a member of the Lao Issara cabinet (later to become Prime Minister of Laos), on May 12, 1949; Souphanouvong's reply (letter No. 3280 of May 13, 1949), bearing his seal and signature; and another letter by Katay, dated May 16, 1949. Both men apparently were then residing in Bangkok.

41. From a speech delivered by Prime Minister Souvanna Phouma at Canberra, Australia, on November 2, 1967, as carried in the official *Lao Presse* of November 3, 1967.

Chapter 4

1. For example, RLG Minister of Finance Sisouk na Champassak has written: "But strangest of all was a patriotism so suspicious of even a provisional collaboration with France (whose authority in Laos, especially of late years, had been diminishing), but able to accommodate itself so easily to a powerful ally like the Viet Minh, which made no secret of its plans for the entire peninsula (including Laos)." (*Storm over Laos* [New York, 1961], p. 24.)

2. George K. Tanham, *Communist Revolutionary Warfare: The Vietminh in Indochina* (New York, 1961), pp. 68–69.

3. For a partial list of participants see Appendix C.

4. See, for example, the official Communist account of these events in *20 Years of Lao People's Revolutionary Struggle* (Neo Lao Haksat Publications,

1966). Our interviews and evidence from other, non-Communist sources confirm this information.

5. According to a participant at the meeting, the Central Committee included (1) Souphanouvong, President, (2) Phoumi Vongvichit, Vice President, (3) Nouhak Phomsavan, (4) Prince Souk Vongsak, (5) Kaysone, (6) Sithon, (7) Faydang, (8) Khamtay Siphandone, (9) Phoun Sipaseûth, (10) Mun, (11) (Phra Maha) Kham, (12) Ma, (13) (May) Souk. There were probably other members whose names we do not know.

6. See *Cambodia and Laos Fight Hand in Hand with Vietnam for Freedom* (Vietnam Central Information Service, 1951), a pamphlet issued by the insurgents, which lists no place of origin.

7. *Internal Policy:* 1. Widen the circle of unity throughout the country to include those of all races and religions, of both sexes and all ages, to defeat the French imperialists and their puppet government, and to make the country independent, free and strong. 2. Open the opportunity for people of all tribal groups to the right of liberty and democracy for all. 3. Eliminate illiteracy, which makes men deaf and blind. 4. Develop handicrafts and commerce. 5. Sweep out the backward French colonial rule. 6. Get rid of gambling and drunkenness. 7. Develop guerrilla forces into regional forces, and further develop these into a national army.

Foreign Policy: 1. Develop unity and cooperation with countries fighting for their independence. Help, for example, the resistance struggle of the Vietnamese and Cambodian peoples on the basis of equality, each side sharing benefits. 2. Demand independence from the French and insist that the French nullify the agreement of the French Union. 3. Establish good relations with all countries of the world on the basis of mutual respect for sovereignty.

This version of the policy statement was furnished by the aforementioned participant, A-14. A similar summary of the same policy declaration can be found in *A Chronicle of Principal Events Relating to the Indochinese Question, 1940–1954* (Peking, World Culture Publishing House, 1954), p. 35.

8. Bernard B. Fall (ed.), *Ho Chi Minh on Revolution* (New York, 1967), p. 214.

9. Vietnam Central Information Service, *Manifesto and Platforms of the Vietnam Lao Dong Party* (no place of publication given), April 1952.

10. Wilfred G. Burchett, *Mekong Upstream: A Visit to Laos and Cambodia* (Berlin, 1959), p. 239.

11. The vital role of the Vietnamese in the military struggle in Laos during the years preceding the Geneva Conference of 1954 is also acknowledged by Soviet writers on the subject. V. V. Pavlovskii, for example, in his *Laos v bor'be za svobodu* speaks of the united front of the revolutionary movements of the three Indochinese countries as having been created in 1951 and of the fact that Vietnamese "volunteers" came to the

aid of their Lao and Cambodian allies: "the struggle of the peoples of Vietnam, Cambodia and Laos emerged into a single powerful current" (p. 35). The same author also speaks of the joint attacks in Sam Neua and Phong Saly provinces by Pathet Lao and Vietnamese volunteers in the spring of 1953 (p. 36). See also *Sovremennyi Laos* (pp. 87 ff.) on this subject.

12. Dinh's activity in that respect is confirmed by the accounts of other informants.

13. We are much indebted to Anita L. Nutt for suggestions she contributed to our discussion of the Geneva Conference.

14. See Dommen, *Conflict in Laos,* p. 52.

15. See the *US Verbatim Minutes of the Geneva Conference,* Second Plenary Session, Indochina Phase, of May 10, 1954, p. 61. See also Jean Lacouture and Philippe Devillers, *La fin d'une guerre* [The End of a War] (Paris, 1960), p. 140.

16. *US Verbatim Minutes,* First Plenary Session of May 8, 1954, p. 16.

17. Royaume du Laos, *Memorandum, adressé le 13 avril 1955 à la Commission Internationale de Surveillance et de Contrôle au Laos* [Royal Lao Government, Memorandum of April 13, 1955, to the ICC in Laos, Vientiane] (May 1955), p. 55.

18. *US Verbatim Minutes,* First Session, p. 35.

19. *Ibid.,* Second Session, pp. 80–81.

Chapter 5

1. For Ho Chi Minh's evaluation of the postrevolutionary years, 1954 to 1960, see Part IV, "Reconstruction and Errors (1954–60)," in Fall, *Ho Chi Minh on Revolution,* pp. 281–341. See also Hoang Van Chi, *From Colonialism to Communism* (New York, 1964).

2. Also written Neo Lao Hak Xat, or Neo Lao Hakxat, and abbreviated NLHX. Neo Lao Haksat represents the official Communist version. In this report we have adopted this spelling, although, in line with our principle of separating words that have distinct meaning, we are writing the term in four words rather than three.

3. See the section "Communist Instruments of Policy Control in Laos," Chapter 6, below.

4. According to Dommen (*Conflict in Laos,* p. 82), by mid-1956 more than 3,000 partisans had been recruited from the populations of Sam Neua and Phong Saly, neither of which totaled more than 100,000.

5. Named after the famous tribal leader Khommadam.

6. Among those elected were: (1) Souphanouvong, (2) Phoumi Vongvichit, (3) Nouhak Phomsavan, (4) Sithon Khommadam, (5) Phoun Sipaseuth, (6) Khamphai Boupha, and (7) Sisana Sisane. All are important figures to this day.

7. The group also included Singkapo Chounramany.

8. A widely quoted story holds that Souphanouvong and his coprisoners carried off a dramatic escape during a violent tropical storm, after the Prince had persuaded some prison guards to join the fugitives. A less romantic account suggests that a substantial number of kip changed hands before the prison gates opened.

9. For a description of this military campaign, see A. M. Halpern and H. D. Fredman, *Communist Strategy in Laos,* The RAND Corporation, RM-2561, June 14, 1960, Chapter 5.

10. *Report of the United Nations Security Council Subcommittee on Laos,* November 3, 1959, UN Document S/4236, dated November 5, 1959, pp. 30–32.

11. For example, Roger Smith, after discussing this UN report, writes the following regarding Viet Minh involvement in Laos: "Most observers now agree that nothing more than a reactivation of PL activity had taken place and that North Vietnam was providing aid that it had in the past." He cites E. H. S. Simmonds, "A Cycle of Political Events in Laos," *World Today,* vol. 17, no. 2, February 1961, pp. 63–64. (Roger M. Smith, "Laos," in George McT. Kahin [ed.], *Government and Politics of Southeast Asia,* [2nd ed.; Ithaca, N.Y., 1964], p. 550.) See also Dommen, *Conflict in Laos,* pp. 123–124, and Bernard B. Fall, "The Pathet Lao," in Robert A. Scalapino (ed.), *The Communist Revolution in Asia,* (Englewood Cliffs, N.J., 1965), pp. 187–188.

The German writer Eckhard Budewig, who had occasion to talk to Prince Souphanouvong, reported in his book *Wird Asian Rot?* [Is Asia Going Red?] (Stuttgart, 1961), that the Pathet Lao did not admit having received support by Viet Minh units in their combat operations, but that they conceded that weapons, ammunitions, and supplies reached them from across the Vietnamese borders.

12. This key staff member was a captain, who was then and is still an officer in the G-2 section of the FAR. The captain, a Black Tai, born in North Vietnam near Laos, had served in the intelligence branch of the French army in Vietnam from 1949 to 1954. From July 1954 to March 1955, he was a staff member on the French-Lao side of the Mixed Armistice Commission while still a member of the French army, acting as interpreter in Lao, Vietnamese, and French. He was integrated into the FAR in June 1955 and continued to serve in intelligence posts, keeping close track of North Vietnamese involvement in Laos. The captain is a respected and competent intelligence officer, whose information has generally proved reliable. We had frequent conversations with him over an eight-month period. He is a principal source of our information concerning the North Vietnamese role during this period.

13. The first Vietnamese prisoner was not taken in Laos by the Royal Army until December 1961. This fact is sometimes cited to add weight to the claim that no North Vietnamese were fighting in Laos during this period. However, the absence of Vietnamese military prisoners in Royal Army prisons was attributable to the Royal Army's reluctance to accept battle with the Vietnamese and its failure to fight with great conviction whenever battle was thrust upon them, rather than to the absence of North Vietnamese troops in Laos.

14. For a brief discussion of the US role in Laos in the 1950s, see Roger M. Smith's discussion in *Governments and Politics of Southeast Asia*, pp. 546–551. See also Arthur M. Schlesinger, Jr., *A Thousand Days* (New York, 1965), pp. 323–334.

15. According to Schlesinger (*A Thousand Days*, p. 331), G. M. Pushkin, the Soviet Deputy Foreign Minister, told Averell Harriman later that "apart from the Second World War, this was the highest priority Soviet supply operation since the Revolution." Dommen (*Conflict in Laos*, p. 178) reports that during the period from December 1960 through January 1961, Soviet aircraft flew 184 supply missions into Laos from logistic bases in North Vietnam. For President Eisenhower's account of US policy at this time, see Dwight D. Eisenhower, *White House Years*, Vol. 1: *Waging Peace, 1956–61* (Garden City, N.Y., 1965), pp. 609 ff.

16. For a discussion of the relative secrecy of these three headquarters at Khang Khay see Chapter 10, below.

17. Details about the North Vietnamese units participating in these attacks was provided by the previously mentioned captain (see note 12 above), who pieced this information together from LPLA prisoners and defectors and four Vietnamese prisoners captured during this period, as well as from interviews with some of the 180 RLG prisoners who were taken by the North Vietnamese in the Pha Tang engagement described above. These POWs reported that they had been taken prisoner by the North Vietnamese and led through the Plain of Jars by the North Vietnamese, who turned them over to the Kong Le Neutralists and to the Pathet Lao.

18. As early as September 1960, Prince Sihanouk of Cambodia, concerned about the effect on his country of the continuing turbulence in neighboring Laos, had proposed at the United Nations that an international agreement remove Laos and Cambodia from the international power struggle by neutralizing these two countries. On January 1, 1961, he had followed up with a concrete proposal for an enlarged conference at Geneva — patterned after that of 1954 — to take up the Laos question. A week earlier, the USSR and North Vietnam had made similar proposals.

19. The Western powers agreed to set a date for the conference, while the Communists agreed that a cease-fire would be put into effect between the time of the announcement of the conference and its actual opening. This solution was promptly accepted by the Royal Lao Government, but the Pathet Lao and their Neutralist allies insisted that negotiations on political and military issues must precede any agreement to end hostilities. Finally, probably as a result of combined Soviet and Vietnamese pressure, the three factions agreed to instruct their respective forces to cease fire. This was done on May 3, 1961. Five days later, the International Control Commission resumed its activity in Laos. (The complex maneuvering involved in these arrangements and subsequent negotiations in Laos and at Geneva are discussed in considerable detail in Anita Lauve Nutt, *Troika on Trial — Control or Compromise?* a study of the ICC prepared for the Office of International Security Affairs, Department of Defense, September 1967. Our account has greatly benefited from this valuable study.)

20. Conference participants, apart from Laos, were the following: four Communist powers (the Soviet Union [Co-chairman of the Geneva Conference], Communist China, the DRV, and Poland [the Communist member of the ICC]); four Western powers (the United Kingdom [the other Co-chairman of the Geneva Conference], the United States, France, and Canada in its capacity of ICC member); two Asian allies of the United States and neighbors of Laos (South Vietnam and Thailand); and three neutralist nations with interests in the area (Burma, Cambodia, and India [the ICC Chairman]). Arthur Lall, who served as Chairman of the Indian delegation, recently revealed that, in an effort to speed up agreement, the "inner six," i.e., the chiefs of the delegations of the United Kingdom, Soviet Union, United States, Communist China, France, and India, met in off-the-record sessions and in strictest secrecy to hammer out the Conference declaration on the Laos question; "though some twenty meetings were held, their existence did not become known to any delegation that might have taken exception to them." (Arthur Lall, *How Communist China Negotiates* [New York, 1968], p. 131.)

21. The Geneva delegation of the NLHS was headed by Phoumi Vongvichit. Meanwhile, Nouhak was representing the Communists in the more important and intricate negotiations with the Neutralist and Rightist factions.

22. *A Thousand Days,* p. 516.

23. The agreement specified that, of the 19 cabinet posts (including those of the Prime Minister and his two deputies), 4 should go to the Rightists, 4 to the NLHS, and the remaining 11 to the Neutralists. (The last were in turn split into two factions, of which the Souvanna Phouma

faction was allocated 7 seats and the so-called Vientiane faction received 4.) The portfolios of Defense and Interior, which had all along been major bones of contention among the three factions, both went to the Neutralists, but it was agreed that in the vital areas of Defense, Interior, and Foreign Affairs unanimity of the three factions would be mandatory. As the jurisdiction of these ministries could be defined as broadly as any faction wished it to be, each group thus retained in practice a veto over all important policy decisions.

24. In all, 666 Americans and 403 Filipinos were evacuated from Laos under ICC supervision.

25. The deficiencies of the ICC are analyzed and illustrated in the aforementioned study by A. L. Nutt, *Troika on Trial*. Shortcomings of the Commission's operational arrangements — the result of Communist opposition to an effective International Control Commission — included these features: (1) The Pathet Lao had accepted only three ICC checkpoints. Of these, only one was in their own zone and it was located so far West of the Vietnam-Laos border that the checking out of foreign troops could not possibly be effective, for the North Vietnamese forces were concentrated in the area between the checkpoint and the border area (particularly near the important Mu Gia Pass infiltration point). Moreover, no routes had been designated for the withdrawal of foreign forces from Laos. (2) There were no provisions for ICC supervision of points of entry into Laos or for the creation of fixed ICC teams for inspection and investigation of suspected violations. (3) In the view of the NLHS, ICC teams could only proceed to investigations at the unanimous invitation of the Lao government, which gave the NLHS an effective veto. (4) Communist opposition to any investigation of reported violations of the withdrawal agreements resulted in such lengthy delays that the Commission's activity could not possibly serve a useful purpose.

26. As quoted from Conference records by A. L. Nutt, *Troika on Trial*, p. 531.

27. According to American estimates the NVA forces involved in Laos during this period were: September 1961 — 3,200; January 1962 — 5,100; July 1962 — 9,000.

28. In a preface dated December 5, 1964, to the RLG "White Book" Prime Minister Souvanna Phouma wrote the following: "In this civil war, which has lasted for more than 20 years . . . the principal actions in these combats have been led by the North Vietnamese troops, a fact I was able to verify myself when I was at Khang Khay. The Pathet Lao, who, at the origin, disposed of only two battalions . . . could not expect to find success against the strong governmental forces of more than 20,000 men. That the Pathet Lao have not disappeared from the scene is

due to the support of its ally of the north which has supported, armed, trained, and encadred its guerrilla activities. It is not necessary to look elsewhere for reasons for this survival of a political party which gathered together at the outset only an insignificant handful of revolutionary Marxists." (*L'ingérence nord-vietnamienne au Laos* [North Vietnamese Interference in Laos], published by the Ministry of Foreign Affairs, Vientiane, December 1964, p. 3.) In this context, it is also interesting to note Souvanna Phouma's repeated assertion that he received verbal assurance from DRV Premier Pham Van Dong that Vietnamese forces would be promptly withdrawn from Laos if Souvanna would pledge not to raise this issue at the Geneva Conference. The Vietnamese Communists did not live up to their word, as only a handful of Vietnamese "civilian advisers" withdrew from Laos after the Conference.

Chapter 6

1. These commonly used terms are misleading if we attribute to them the meaning as it is understood outside the Lao context. The Neutralists were not then, nor are they today, a party, and few of them would describe themselves as occupying a middle ground, domestically, between the Rightists and the NLHS. On the other hand, most Rightists accept Souvanna's basic policy of international neutrality for Laos guaranteed by the Great Powers as the best, if not the only, hope for the survival of Laos as an independent state capable of maintaining domestic peace.

2. In the Agreements it was stipulated that each faction would continue to administer temporarily its own zone of control until such time as all military forces and all administrations were unified by mutual agreement.

3. See Robert Shaplen, "Letter from Laos," *The New Yorker*, May 4, 1968.

4. In fact, Communist propaganda increasingly stresses this theme. Typical is a Pathet Lao broadcast of October 2, 1969, which asserts that "the neutralist status of Prince Souvanna Phouma came to an end in the April 1964 coup. At present, he is only a puppet prime minister, a reactionary like other reactionary lackeys of the US imperialists in Vientiane. The Patriotic Neutralist Forces . . . have become the actual representatives of the neutralists." On reviewing the military developments in Laos during the past several years and particularly the Communist drive since 1968, one cannot escape the impression that the Communists are seeking to occupy all territory once held by the Neutralists. Success in this respect would give them a solid basis for claiming that the Patriotic Neutralists are the legitimate heirs to the Neutralist faction and thus also to their place in the government.

5. Thus, it was reported in February 1969 that the Soviet Ambassador to Laos on a visit from Vientiane to the NLHS zone (by way of Hanoi) was carrying a personal letter from Souvanna Phouma to his half-brother Souphanouvong, who replied through the same channel.

6. In March 1970, the NLHS made public a five-point peace proposal which was endorsed by Hanoi as "reasonable" and "fully consonant with the interests of peace and security in Indochina and Southeast Asia." Souvanna Phouma, however, rejected the terms offered by the Communists.

7. It had been rumored that the People's Party of Laos was officially represented at the 22nd Congress of the CPSU, in 1962. An examination of official Soviet records, however, shows no such mention (although it could well be that the party's representatives, even if not officially listed, were in attendance). The first definitely established use of the PPL label is encountered in the December 1966 issue of the Japanese Communist Party's monthly *Zen'ei* (Vanguard), which on the occasion of the JCP's 10th Convention published a letter from Laos that began, "Dear Fellow Comrades" and spoke of the NLHS and the PPL as separate entities, with the latter directing the former. It bore the notation "October 24, 1966. At Sam Neua. Kaysone Phomvihan, Secretary General, representing the Central Committee of the People's Party of Laos." The following year, on July 15, a Hanoi domestic broadcast stated that a letter of condolence had been received upon the death of Nguyen Chi Thanh. It came from the Central Committee of the PPL and again was signed "Secretary General Kaysone Phomvihan." More recently, on March 22, 1968, the East German Communist organ *Neues Deutschland,* discussing plans for the Budapest consultative meeting of Communist parties, stated that a number of "Marxist-Leninist parties born since 1960" should be invited to participate. Among those parties we find listed the People's Party of Laos (together with the People's Revolutionary Party of Cambodia). Still another reference to the PPL appeared in the summer of 1968, this time in the Polish Communist press.

8. Some reports, however, speak of larger numbers of Party members.

9. In this connection, the Vientiane newspaper *Sat Lao* on December 12, 1968, reported on the capture of a Vietnamese-language document dealing with the origins of the PPL and indicating that Souphanouvong was admitted to membership in 1961.

10. Other sources speak of only one or two Lao members of the Vietnamese Party in that early period.

11. The Lao Dong Party was actually formed in 1951, so that this informant was mistaken at least in his date.

12. For example, Arthur Dommen (in *Conflict in Laos*) and Bernard

Fall (in his essay "The Pathet Lao" in *The Communist Revolution in Asia*) have used this piece of information to construct the same thesis.

13. There is also the theory that Ho Chi Minh serves concurrently as Chairman of all three Indochinese Communist parties. In support of this contention it is pointed out that the PPL has a secretary general — Kaysone — but that there has not been any mention of a Party chairman.

14. The official RLG *White Book* of 1969 speaks of "an army more than 40,000 men strong, not counting the special armed forces (militia and others) charged with political propaganda and the supervision of villagers" (p. 24). Secretary of State William P. Rogers in a speech delivered on April 18, 1970, said: "In Laos over 65,000 regular North Vietnamese troops have invaded and now occupy large portions of Laotian territory."

15. See, for example, *Rains in the Jungle* (Neo Lao Haksat Publications, 1967), p. 43, and *Phoukout Stronghold* (Neo Lao Haksat Publications, 1967), p. 21. (No place of origin is listed on either publication, but they look similar to literature published in Hanoi.)

16. However, it appears that the Communists are rearing a new generation of leaders and cadres — men of humble origin. The sons and daughters of the more prominent families have been going for training to Moscow, Eastern Europe, and Peking, but the new cadres seem to be drawn from those who were trained in North Vietnam. Thus, one can expect to see develop in the NLHS zone a generation conflict as well as tensions caused by differences in social background and training.

17. We cannot be certain of the weight that these two representatives of the major ethnic minority groups carry in the councils of the Lao Communists, but there are indications that at least Faydang's role is that of a mere figurehead and propaganda spokesman. General Vang Pao, the Meo general who leads the fight of the Meo on the RLG side, takes a slightly different view. He too sees in Faydang a figurehead of the Lao Communists, but believes him to be essentially neutral toward them (whose interests, of course, coincide, at least for the moment, with his own). What can be said with assurance is that both Sithon and Faydang regularly figure as spokesmen of their ethnic minority groups in statements praising the NLHS.

18. The Soviet position is that the USSR is giving support to the DRV and has no control over the use that the latter makes of Soviet supplies.

19. The previously mentioned Congressional Hearings revealed much detail about the scope and nature of US air operations over Laos. According to the testimony of US Government witnesses from the State and Defense departments, the first US reconnaissance flight was flown over the southern part of Laos May 19, 1964 after consultation with Prime Minister Souvanna Phouma. The flights were extended May 21 to cover

the Plain of Jars and neighboring areas. Testimony indicated that after an unarmed US reconnaissance plane had been shot down near the Plain of Jars on June 6, 1964, armed escorts were added to the flights with the approval of the Lao Prime Minister. US bombing of Lao territory along the Ho Chi Minh Trail began in early 1965. While the number of sorties flown by US planes against Pathet Lao/NVA positions remains classified, a government spokesman before the Committee stated that such activity showed a significant increase after the bombing halt in 1968, due to the increased intensity of NVA and PL activities in northern Laos coupled with the increased availability of US aircraft. The resulting losses of US planes were given as less than 80 in northern Laos between 1964 and September 28, 1969 and as somewhat less than 300 for southern Laos, primarily along the Ho Chi Minh Trail. See Hearings before the Subcommittee on United States Security, Committee on Foreign Relations, United States Senate, Ninety-First Congress, First session, October 20, 21, 22, and 28, 1969, *passim*.

20. While this alternation of FAR and LPLA initiative has generally been characteristic of the fighting in Laos, there were of course exceptions to this rule even before 1969. Also, the Communist forces on the whole had the initiative up to mid-1964, taking in the process much of the territory previously held by the Kong Le Neutralists. Then, from mid-1964 to 1967, the FAR attempted to tie together areas difficult of access to the enemy (such as Operation Triangle in the Vang Vieng area and the Sedone Valley region). Since then, the initiative has again largely reverted to the LPLA, increasingly strengthened by a growing number of North Vietnamese forces.

21. See Ministry of Foreign Affairs of Laos, *White Book on the Violations of the 1962 Geneva Accords by the Government of North Vietnam* (Vientiane, 1969), p. 1.

Chapter 7

1. See the section "Pathet Lao Activities and North Vietnamese Support, 1954–1959," Chapter 5, above.

2. Recently, there have been indications that in southern Laos NVN advisers are also found on the district level; these are perhaps exceptional cases, although purely technical advisers occasionally also operate at the village level on a semipermanent basis.

3. In the case of Xieng Khouang Province, the administrative channel is staffed by Neutralists.

4. Other interviews showing the impact of North Vietnamese training were those with two LPLA officers (A-1 and A-17) who in 1963 received

training, along with a hundred other Lao up to the rank of captain, seven miles outside of Hanoi.

5. Interview with a former LPLA doctor (A-10), who had been chief of Attopeu Hospital.

Chapter 8

1. This refers to the North Vietnamese Lao Dong Party of which Mai Dai Hap had been a member since 1952.

2. Hap's home province, Thanh-Hoa, is in the coastal lowlands of North Vietnam. He had been serving with the 316th Brigade in the mountainous area around Dien Bien Phu, in the northwestern part of the country.

3. Vietnamese border station on the railroad from Hanoi into China located opposite the Chinese station of Ho-k'ou.

4. This was a battalion of the same brigade in which Hap had served.

5. Chinese place names will be rendered here as they appear in the Vietnamese original.

6. This is Mai Dai Hap's only reference to a briefing on the situation in Laos by a Chinese Communist cadre, although he took three journeys through China on his way to or from Laos during the years he served there as an adviser. While in Laos, Hap stated, he had no contact with Chinese Communist military or civilian personnel, nor did he observe the presence of such personnel in that country.

7. Muong Sing is a major Lao town in the Nam Tha region, only a few miles from the Chinese border. Roads and trails leading toward China, Burma, and Thailand converge at Muong Sing, making it an important transportation center for the northern part of the country.

Chapter 9

1. Until recently, the figure of 40,000 was frequently cited by both RLG and US sources. Prime Minister Souvanna Phouma, speaking to the Lao National Assembly on May 30, 1968, said that the figure included fifty-seven North Vietnamese army combat battalions. (*The Washington Post*, May 31, 1968.) Ambassador W. Averell Harriman cited these same figures at the June 5, 1968, session of official conversations between the United States and North Vietnam. (See US Department of State, *For the Press*, No. 131, June 5, 1968.) A slightly higher figure of 45,000 was being mentioned in late 1968. (See *The New York Times*, November 13, 1968.) President Nixon in his statement of March 6, 1970, spoke of 46,000 North Vietnamese troops in Laos in mid-1968, 55,000 in mid-1969, and of an all-time high of 67,000 in March 1970.

2. See Charts II, III, IV, and V.

3. The NVA units that frequently operate with LPLA forces are sometimes referred to as "mixed" NVA/LPLA units; their troop strength is estimated to be 7,000.

4. One soldier who passed through the Trail in 1965 told us that there were six defectors from his company in Laos. (AG-370, answer to question 53; one in a series of interviews with North Vietnamese prisoners and defectors conducted by a RAND team between 1964 and 1968, and now on file with The RAND Corporation.) Another North Vietnamese whom we interviewed (B-6) fled with a fellow-soldier when their infiltration group bivouacked near a supply point in the region of Attopeu Province. He had been living in northern Thailand and had been persuaded to go to North Vietnam, where he was recruited into the army. Disappointed with life in North Vietnam, and wishing to find his way back to his parents in Thailand, he took advantage of the infiltration journey to escape.

5. AG-370, answer to question 10. Similar statements can be found in AG-446, question 178: AG-202, question 57; AG-504, question 125; AG-536, question 185; and AG-447, question 72, in RAND's interview files.

6. President Nixon, in his statement of March 6, 1970, explaining US policy in Laos, indicated that the United States was supporting the independence and neutrality of Laos as set forth in the 1962 Geneva agreements and that US air power was being used to interdict the flow of North Vietnamese supplies and men into South Vietnam through the application of air power against the Ho Chi Minh Trail. He also stated that US planes were flying combat support missions for Lao forces at the request of the RLG. He further stated: "There are no American ground combat troops in Laos." (See *New York Times,* March 7, 1970.)

7. See B-8, a Vietnamese Black Tai defector, who served with an antiaircraft unit from September 1965 to December 1966.

8. First, ten men, including our informant were selected from his company of sixty-six (of whom sixty were members of the Lao Dong Party and six were members of the Labor Youth Organization) for an intelligence reconnaissance mission on which they were to scout the FAR post to be attacked. They infiltrated the FAR positions successfully, spent two days gathering details of the defenses of the FAR post, and reported back to their headquarters, where a sand table model of the FAR position was constructed. A Lao deputy commander of the LPLA battalion stationed in the area who heard the reconnaissance report and saw this sand table model expressed amazement and admiration, according to our informant, since his battalion had not gathered in four months the intelligence that the ten-man Vietnamese scout teams had collected in two days.

The Dac Cong unit attacked the FAR position several days later. According to our source, one Vietnamese soldier was assigned to take out each of the two 105-mm cannons, another to knock out the several machine guns they had spotted on their reconnaissance, and still another to blow up the barracks and some oil storage containers. They planted their explosives against their objectives and, upon signal, blew them up.

9. On a legal technicality, the Polish member refused to sign.

10. The Indian Chairman of the ICC transmitted this document to the Co-chairmen by letter as a report of the ICC investigation committee. Lacking the Polish member's endorsement, this report is not an official ICC report. Excerpts from this document can be found in *Report of an Investigation by the International Commission for Supervision and Control in Laos of an Attack on Dong Hene by North Vietnamese Troops* (no date or publisher listed). Part of the evidence of this attack at Dong Hene that was presented by the RLG to the ICC, and a segment of the ICC Report, can be found in *Livre blanc sur les violations des Accords de Genève de 1962 par le gouvernement du Nord Vietnam* [White Book on the Violations of the Geneva Accords of 1962 by the Government of North Vietnam] (Ministry of Foreign Affairs of Laos, Vientiane, August 1965), pp. 5–13, 69–100.

11. Radio Pathet Lao, on March 31, 1965, labeled the charges of North Vietnamese participation in the Dong Hene attack "groundless," calling them "merely the old puppet show which was put on several times in the past with the aim of criticizing the NLHS and the DRV." It is not clear whether the Vietnamese unit which attacked Dong Hene was diverted from its journey to South Vietnam or whether it had been sent especially from North Vietnam to launch the attack. Most of the prisoners believed that they were on their way to South Vietnam. One of them told us that his unit was only "borrowing the road" in Laos to reach South Vietnam (B-17). However, North Vietnamese troops are not always aware of the plans of their commanders.

12. See *Livre Blanc,* 1965, pp. 15–57. More recently, in 1968, the FAR succeeded in repulsing an NVA attack on Lao Ngam in southern Laos, inflicting heavy losses on the enemy. However, the Lao forces had to evacuate Lao Ngam thereafter because of the generally unfavorable military situation in the region.

13. The 1969 *White Paper* issued by the RLG states (p. 29) that the NVA then had sixty-six battalions in Laos. They were distributed among the five Lao Military Regions as follows: Region I — 8 battalions, II — 26, III — 11, IV — 21, V — 2 companies.

14. *To Move a Nation* (Garden City, N.Y.), 1967, p. 154.

15. A change of tactics in favor of greater emphasis on guerrilla activity behind the lines may be in the making, however, as indicated by a

succession of LPLA/NVA attacks against RLG airfields and the blowing up of ammunition dumps near Vientiane and in southern Laos.

Chapter 10

1. North Vietnamese broadcast of May 29, 1967.
2. Radio Pathet Lao braodcast of March 25, 1968. (Emphasis added.)
3. (1) "Memorandum" (no publisher or place listed), April 13, 1955, addressed to ICC in Laos, and consisting of a Preliminary Note, a memorandum relating to the 1954 Geneva Accords on Laos, Annexes to an RLG memo of April 12, 1954, on Communist Lao and North Vietnamese activities in Laos, letters between the ICC and Premier Katay Sasorith of Laos, and a document entitled "Position du Royaume du Laos dans les événements concernant la Péninsule Indochinoise," presented to Nehru on October 17, 1954, during his visit to Vientiane. (2) *L'ingérence nord-vietnamienne au Laos,* consisting of a Preface by Souvanna Phouma followed by a text offering proof of North Vietnamese troops in Laos (including the capture of three North Vietnamese prisoners, documents and declarations of prisoners, and letters between Souvanna Phouma and ICC). (3) *Livre blanc* of August 1965, which presents proof of Viet Minh violations in the Dong Hene attack of March 1965, the Thakhek attack of November 1965, and operations Xieng Khouang and Sam Neua in the form of interrogation reports, documents, and ICC report on Dong Hene.

Other *White Books* on the subject of North Vietnamese interference in Lao affairs were issued by the RLG in 1964, 1966 and 1968. The latest of this series, issued in 1969, covers the period from the spring of 1968 to the summer of 1969 and presents substantial evidence of North Vietnamese violations of Lao neutrality.

See also numerous official statements by Prime Minister Souvanna Phouma, such as his address to the National Assembly of Laos on May 30, 1968, and his National Army Day speech of March 23, 1970.

4. See, for example: (1) "Souvanna Says Laos Invaded by Red Troops," *Bangkok World,* April 3, 1967. (2) "Premier's Spokesman on Military Situation," Vientiane Domestic Radio Service, February 23, 1966; statement by Bouasy on location and extent of Vietnamese interference. (3) "Souvanna Phouma Speaks of Indochina Problem," Delhi Domestic Radio Service, July 27, 1965, which claims that there were then sixty North Vietnamese light battalions in Laos, each three to five hundred strong, and calls for reconvening of Geneva Conference. (4) "Foreign Ministry Protest to DRV Embassy," and "General [Sang] Interviewed on Viet Minh Prisoners," Vientiane Domestic Service, June 22, 1963, on mixed LPLA Vietnamese forces activities. (5) A series of RLG Defense

Ministry communiqués from January to June 11, 1962, Vientiane Domestic Service, on Vietnamese interference in specific areas in Laos. (6) "Sisouk Interviewed on Laos Situation," Vientiane Domestic Service, April 10, 1962, commenting on extent of Viet Minh troop involvement. (7) "Bouavan Norading: DRV Troops in Southern Laos," Singapore, Reuters, January 21, 1961. (8) "Premier Phoui Sananikone's Address to National Assembly," Vientiane Domestic Service, December 18, 1959, with comments on the DRV's inciting rebellion in Laos and protecting Lao Communists who flee to DRV.

The RLG has also frequently displayed NVA prisoners taken in Laos (see, for example, the February 14, 1970, press conference at the Ministry of Information concerning the capture of seven North Vietnamese soldiers. Hanoi in its international broadcast of February 17 promptly labeled the accusations "a calumny").

5. See, for example: (1) Charges from DRV: "Nhan Dan Refutes Souvanna Phouma Slander," Hanoi VNA, October 24, 1967. (2) "Failure of US Laos Policy Is Unavoidable," Hanoi VNA, May 17, 1967. (3) "VNA Denounces Laotian Charges of Intrusion," Hanoi VNA, December 29, 1967. (4) "DRV Envoy Denies Existence of POWs in Laos," Paris AFP, December 19, 1966. (5) "Nhan Dan Hails Victories of Lao People," Hanoi VNA, November 20, 1965, refuting "hackneyed allegations" by US and RLG of North Vietnamese in Thakhek battle. (6) "DRV Embassy Denounces US Bombing in Laos," Peking NCNA, January 25, 1965. (7) "Pathet Lao Radio Rejects Souvanna POW Claim," Hanoi VNA, October 12, 1964.

For examples of charges from the NLHS, see: (1) "Souvanna Phouma Plays Key Role as US Lackey," Radio Pathet Lao, November 4, 1967, claiming that Souvanna acted shamefully in reporting to President Johnson that North Vietnam had invaded Laos. (2) Phoumi Vongvichit speech, Radio Pathet Lao, September 9, 1966, denying the existence of supply lines between North and South Vietnam through Laos. (3) "High Command of Lao People's Liberation Army Denies 'Categorically' Presence of North Vietnamese Troops in Southern Laos," Radio Pathet Lao, February 3, 1966. (4) "Liberation Forces Deny Presence of DRV Troops," Radio Pathet Lao, December 21, 1965. (5) "Les Agents américains à Vientiane inventent la comédie sur la soi-disant capture des prisonniers nord-vietnamiens pour couvrir leurs activités au Laos," Radio Pathet Lao, April 7, 1965. (6) "Les calomnies de S. A. Souvanna sont celles que les Américains et leurs agents ont l'habitude de faire," Radio Pathet Lao, October 8, 1964, about the "so-called prisoners" presented to the ICC as being part of North Vietnamese troops in Laos.

The coordination of North Vietnamese and Pathet Lao propaganda was further advanced with the conclusion of an agreement, on January 6, 1970, between the Vietnam News Agency and Khaosan Pathet Lao (KPL) and the establishment, the following day, of a NLHS Information Office in Hanoi.

6. See J. J. Zasloff, *The Role of the Sanctuary in Insurgency: Communist China's Support to the Viet Minh, 1946–1954,* The RAND Corporation, RM–4618–PR, May 1967, pp. 36–41.

7. See US Department of State, *Aggression from the North: The Record of North Vietnam's Campaign to Conquer South Vietnam* (Washington, D.C., 1965), p. 3.

8. Tran Van Dinh, "Laos, the Fiction of Neutrality," *The New Republic,* February 24, 1968, p. 29.

9. See, for example, AG-256, a respondent who had marched with an infiltrating group through the Ho Chi Minh Trail in August 1962. See also *Aggression from the North.*

10. For example, we learned of an incident during the 1961–62 Communist offensive which shows how meager were the resources of the ICC to verify reports of North Vietnamese intervention in Laos. In 1961, the ICC headquarters had dispatched a committee of its members to investigate a complaint that North Vietnamese troops were stationed at Ban Hin Heup, between Vientiane and the Plain of Jars. Arriving at the location of the alleged North Vietnamese unit, the ICC investigating committee came upon some soldiers bathing in a stream. As the commission members drew close to them, these soldiers showed no signs of embarrassment. Since the Lao are generally more modest than this about nakedness in front of strangers, the commission deduced that they had seen North Vietnamese soldiers, but they were not empowered to make a closer investigation.

11. See Appendix D.

12. From an interview with B-22. Other relevant information came from A-3, A-17, B-4, B-11, and B-12.

13. See A-27, A-31, B-4, and B-9.

14. This was, for example, the case of Guy Hannoteaux, correspondent of the *Far Eastern Economic Review,* who was held prisoner in South Laos by the Communists. See *Far Eastern Economic Review,* November 21, 1968.

Chapter 11

1. See *Nhan Dan* of February 14, 1970.

2. Characterizing the French acquisition of Indochina, one author has written: "through their adoption of Vietnamese ambitions and tradi-

tional relationships, the French created in Southeast Asia a colonial empire that was a fulfilment of long-standing goals of Vietnamese expansionism . . . The power of France was equal to imperial dreams even greater than those of the Vietnamese." (John T. McAlister, Jr., "The Possibilities for Diplomacy in Southeast Asia," *World Politics,* vol. 19, no. 2, January 1967, p. 265.) For similar views, see John F. Cady, *Southeast Asia: Its Historical Development* (New York, 1964), p. 419, and Dennis J. Duncanson, *Government and Revolution in Vietnam* (New York, 1968), p. 5.

3. *Thirty Years of Struggle of the Party* (Hanoi, 1960), p. 27.

4. Quoted by P. J. Honey, *Communism in North Vietnam* (Cambridge, Mass., 1963), p. 170. This same document is cited by the US Department of State, *The Situation in Laos,* September 1959, pp. 2–3, and by Duncanson, *Government and Revolution in Vietnam,* p. 170.

5. Duncanson, *Government and Revolution in Vietnam,* p. 170.

Selected Bibliography
of Published Materials

A. Books, pamphlets, and documents

A travers la zone libérée Lao. Hanoi, 1968.

Budewig, Eckhard. *Wird Asien rot?* Stuttgart, 1961.

Burchett, Wilfred G. *En remontant le Mékong.* Hanoi, 1957. (Also, *Mekong Upstream: A Visit to Laos and Cambodia* [Berlin, 1959.])

────── *The Furtive War: The United States in Vietnam and Laos.* New York, 1963.

────── *Schatten über dem Dschungel.* Berlin, 1963.

Buttinger, Joseph. *Vietnam: A Dragon Embattled.* New York, 1967.

Caply, Michel. *Guérilla au Laos.* Paris, 1966.

Chae Jin Lee. *Chinese Communist Policy in Laos: 1954–1965.* Doctoral dissertation, University of Michigan, 1967.

Chaffard, Georges. *Indochine dix ans d'indépendance.* Paris, 1964.

Chalermnit Press Correspondent. *Battle of Vientiane of 1960.* Bangkok, 1961.

Concerning the Situation in Laos. Peking, 1959.

Dommen, Arthur J. *Conflict in Laos: The Politics of Neutralization.* New York, 1964.

Duncanson, Dennis J. *Government and Revolution in Vietnam.* New York, 1968.

Eden, Anthony. *Full Circle.* Cambridge, Mass., 1960.

Editions du Neo Lao Haksat. *Douze années d'intervention et d'agression des impérialistes américains.* N.p., 1966.

────── *Impérialisme américain saboteur des Accords de Genève de 1962 sur le Laos.* N.p., 1967.

Eisenhower, Dwight D. Vol. 1: *Waging Peace, 1956–61.* New York, Garden City, 1965.

Epstein, Israel, and Elsa Fairfax-Chomeley. *Laos in the Mirror of Geneva.* Peking, 1961.

Fall, Bernard B. *Anatomy of a Crisis: The Laos Crisis of 1961.* New York and Toronto, 1969.

—— *Hell in a Very Small Place.* New York, 1967.

—— *Ho Chi Minh on Revolution.* New York, 1967.

—— *Le Viet-Minh, La République Démocratique du Viet-Nam, 1945–1960.* Paris, 1960.

—— *Street without Joy: Indochina at War 1946–54.* Harrisburg, Pa., 1961.

—— "The Pathet Lao, A 'Liberation Party,'" in *The Communist Revolution in Asia,* ed. Robert Scalapino. New Jersey, 1965; rev. ed., 1969.

—— *The Two Vietnams.* New York, 1963.

Halpern, A. M., and H. B. Fredman. *Communist Strategy in Laos.* The RAND Corporation, RM-2561. Santa Monica, California, 1960.

Halpern, Joel M. *Government, Politics and Social Structure in Laos: A Study of Tradition and Innovation.* New Haven, 1964.

—— *The Lao Elite: A Study of Tradition and Innovation,* The RAND Corporation, RM-2636. Santa Monica, California, 1960.

Hammer, Ellen J. *The Struggle for Indochina, 1940–1955,* rev. Stanford, 1966.

Henle, Hans. *Chinas Schatten über Südost-Asien.* Hamburg, 1964.

Hilsman, Roger. *To Move a Nation.* New York, 1967.

Hoang Quoc. *Brief Review of the Viet-Nam Situation after 6 Years of Resistance.* N.p., 1952

Hoang Van Chi. *From Colonialism to Communism.* New York, 1964.

Honey, P. J. *Communism in North Vietnam.* Cambridge, Mass., 1963.

Human Relations Area Files. *Laos.* New Haven, 1960.

International Commission for Supervision and Control in Laos, Annual and other reports, issued by Her Majesty's Stationery Office, London.

Ivanov, N. I. *Laos boretsia* [Laos struggles]. Moscow, 1963.

Krausz, Georg. *Sous le ciel du Laos.* Hanoi, 1961.

—— *Von Indien bis Laos.* Berlin, 1960.

Katay D. Sasorith. *Le Laos, son évolution politique, sa place dans l'union française.* Paris, 1953.

—— *Souvenirs de la résistance Lao Issara.* In 16 Pamphlets. Bangkok, 1947–49.

Kozhevnikov, Vladimir A. *Sovremennyi Laos* [Contemporary Laos]. Moscow, 1966.

Kunstadter, Peter, ed. *Southeast Asian Tribes, Minorities and Nations.* Princeton, 1966.

Lacouture, Jean, and Philippe Devillers. *La fin d'une guerre.* Paris, 1960.

La documentation française. *Notes et Etudes Documentaires-Le Laos.* Paris, 1969.

Lall, Arthur. *How Communist China Negotiates.* New York, 1968.

Lancaster, Donald. *The Emancipation of French Indochina.* London, 1961.

Lartéguy, Jean. *The Bronze Drums.* New York, 1967.

LeBar, Frank M., Gerald Hickey, and John Musgrave, eds. *Ethnic Groups of Mainland Southeast Asia.* New Haven, 1964.

Le Comité Central du Neo Lao Haksat. *Les positions du Neo Lao Haksat à la Conférence Tripartite de Paris.* N.p., 1965.

Leifer, Walter. *China schaut südwärts.* Würzburg, 1961.

McLane, Charles, B. *Soviet Strategies in Southeast Asia.* Princeton, 1966.

Modelski, George. *International Conference on the Settlement of the Laotian Question, 1961–2.* Canberra, 1962.

Nuechterlein, Donald E. *Thailand and the Struggle for Southeast Asia.* Ithaca, New York, 1965.

Nutt, Anita L. *Troika on Trial—Control or Compromise?* US Department of Defense, 1967.

Pavlovskii, V. *Laos v bor'be za svobodu* [Laos in the struggle for freedom]. Moscow, 1963.

Popov, G. P. *Za nezavisimyi i neitral'nyi Laos* [For an independent and neutral Laos]. Moscow, 1961.

Randle, Robert F. *Geneva 1954—The Settlement of the Indochinese War.* Princeton, 1969.

Royal Lao Government, Ministry of Foreign Affairs. *White Book.* Vientiane, 1964–1969.

Schlesinger, Arthur M., Jr. *A Thousand Days.* New York, 1965.

Simmonds, Stuart (E.H.S.). "Independence & Political Rivalry in Laos, 1945–61," in Saul Rose, ed., *Politics in Southern Asia.* London and New York, 1963.

Sisouk Na Champassak. *Storm over Laos: A Contemporary History.* New York, 1961.

Smith, Roger M. "Laos," in George Mc T. Kahin, ed., *Governments and Politics of Southeast Asia.* 2nd ed. New York, 1964.

Sorensen, Theodore C. *Kennedy.* New York, 1965.

Takagi, Takeo. *Tōnan Ajia no yoake* [The dawn of Southeast Asia]. Tokyo, 1969.

Tanham, George, K. *Communist Revolutionary Warfare: The Vietminh in Indochina.* New York, 1961.

Third National Congress of the Vietnam Workers' Party. Hanoi, 1961.

Toye, Hugh. *Laos: Buffer State or Battleground.* London and New York, 1968.

Truong Tschinh. *Der Befreiungskampf der Völker von Vietnam, Khmer und Pathet Lao.* Berlin, 1954.

US Department of State. *The Situation in Laos.* Washington, 1959.

US Senate, Committee on Foreign Relations. *United States Security Agreements and Commitments Abroad—Kingdom of Laos,* Hearings of October 20, 21, 22 and 28, 1969. Washington, 1970.

Vietnam Central Information Service. *Cambodia and Laos Fight Hand in Hand with Viet-Nam for Freedom.* N.p., 1951.

Viet-Nam Central Information Service. *Manifesto and Platform of the Vietnam Lao Dong Party.* N.p., 1952.

Zasloff, Joseph J. *The Role of the Sanctuary in Insurgency: Communist China's Support of the Viet Minh, 1946–1954.* The RAND Corporation, RM–4618–PR. Santa Monica, California, 1967.

B. Periodical Literature

Akahata
Asahi Janaru
Asian Survey
Aussenpolitik
Bangkok Post
Bangkok World
China Quarterly
Christian Science Monitor
Current Digest of the Soviet Press
Department of State Bulletin
Far Eastern Economic Review
Far Eastern Quarterly
International Affairs (Moscow)
Jen-min Jih-pao
Journal of Southeast Asian History
Lào Presse
Le Monde
Los Angeles Times
Modern Asian Studies
Neues Deutschland
New Republic
New Times
New York Times
The New Yorker
Nhan Dan
Pacific Affairs
Peking Review
Pravda
Review of International Affairs

Revue Militaire Générale
Sekai Seiji Shiryō
(Washington) *Star*
Survey of China Mainland Press
Translations on South and East Asia (Joint Publications Research Service)
Washington Post
World Marxist Review
World Politics
The World Today
Zen'ei

Index

This index covers the body of the text and on a selective basis the appended Chronology, List of Participants in the First Resistance Congress of Laos, and Notes. Also note that proper names of Lao individuals are listed under the first name in accordance with Lao procedure.

Rightists, *see* Boun Oum; Phoumi Nosavan; Royal Lao Government

RLG, *see* Royal Lao Government

Royal Lao Armed Forces (FAR), 51, 62, 66, 67, 70, 103, 107, 138–139, 156, 157, 159, 167; battles with LPLA and NVA, 67, 103, 143, 144, 158–161, 202; morale, 160, 180

Royal Lao Government (RLG), 1, 5, 6, 9, 13, 21, 27, 55, 66, 71, 72, 80, 81, 90, 92, 143, 156, 164, 174; external support of, 11, 15, 35, 56, 66–67, 70, 71, 79, 92, 100–101, 175, 179; coalition government 1962/63, 21, 85–87, 89, 101; and Pathet Lao, 47, 56, 60, 63, 65–67, 69–70, 77, 85, 86, 90, 203; balance of power, 89–90. *See also* Geneva Conferences 1954 and 1961/62

Sam Neua, 11, 41, 53, 57, 58, 60, 63, 69, 72, 85, 90, 93, 107, 117, 120, 171, 177

Santiphab Party, 199

Saravane, 41, 91, 104

Savang (King of Laos), 16, 27, 90, 206, 212

Savannakhet, 28, 33, 34, 152, 159, 162

Schlesinger, Arthur, 78

Sedone Valley, 159

Sieu Heng, 51, 196

Sihanouk (Prince), 91, 104, 218, 222

Siho, 210, 212

Singkapo Chounramany Sikhot, 17, 99, 176, 205, 224, 236

Sino-Lao Friendship School, 102

Sisana Sisane, 93, 213, 214, 225, 235

Sisavang Vong (King of Laos), 194, 202

Sisavath, 93

Sithon Khommadam (Kommadam), 41, 46, 49, 50, 61, 99, 213, 214, 216, 217, 233, 234, 235

Son Tay, 62, 116, 118

Sot Phetrasy (Soth Pethrasi), 85, 220, 224

Souk Vongsak (Prince), 47, 50, 93, 99, 215, 217, 219, 225, 234

Souphanouvong (Prince), 21, 38, 39, 46, 47, 49, 65, 78, 85, 87, 95, 99, 176, 196, 199, 200, 201, 202, 203, 204, 205, 208, 209, 210, 211, 213, 214, 215, 216, 217, 220, 221, 222, 230, 231, 234, 235, 236, 241; as leader of the Lao independence movement, 3, 49–50, 56, 61, 63, 66, 77, 86, 93, 97, 167, 172, 193, 194, 195, 197, 206; early career, 17, 28–36, 54; and the Lao Issara, 23, 33, 38–45, 47, 194; association with Vietnam, 28, 31–36, 38, 40–45, 86, 87, 165, 172, 193, 195

Southeast Asia Treaty Organization (SEATO), 67, 70, 198, 203

Souvanna Phouma (Prince), 21, 31, 32, 35, 44, 65, 71–72, 76, 77, 78, 79, 85, 89, 100, 168, 193, 195, 198, 199, 203, 204, 207, 209, 210, 212, 216, 219, 220, 221, 239; head of coalition government, 85, 86, 88, 89–90, 196, 200, 201, 202, 205, 206, 208

Souvannarath (Prince), 29

Soviet Union, 54, 71, 72, 73, 87, 89, 97, 117, 119, 127, 160, 202, 203, 204. *See also* Pathet Lao and Soviet Union

Tai (tribes), 11, 13, 113

Tchepone, 28, 73

Thailand, 11, 15, 25, 27, 35, 39, 40, 335

Thai Nguyen Technical School, 117

Thakhek, 33, 34, 41, 160

Tham Sayasithsena, 229

Thang Binh, 112

Thao O, 193

Ton Duc Thang, 51, 196

Tran Van Dinh, 54

Udomsay, 121

United Nations, Subcommittee on Laos, 67–69, 202

United States, 48, 54, 70, 71, 73, 76, 79, 89, 91, 103, 118–119, 156, 157, 161, 162, 163, 165, 204; conflict with NVN, 1, 20, 70, 79, 156, 157, 163, 164, 179; aid to RLG VI, 15, 20, 66–67, 175; Senate, 242–243

USSR, *see* Soviet Union

Vang Pao, 104, 156, 161, 162

Vang Vieng, 72

Vientiane, 25, 27, 33, 66, 67, 85, 86, 101, 162, 175

Selected List of Rand Books

1. Gurtov, Melvin, *SOUTHEAST ASIA TOMORROW: PROBLEMS AND PROSPECTS FOR U.S. POLICY*, Johns Hopkins Press, Baltimore, Maryland, 1970.
2. Horelick, Arnold L., and Myron Rush, *STRATEGIC POWER AND SOVIET FOREIGN POLICY*. University of Chicago Press, Chicago, Illinois, 1966.
3. Hsieh, Alice Langley, *COMMUNIST CHINA'S STRATEGY IN THE NUCLEAR ERA*. Prentice-Hall, Inc., Englewood Cliffs, New Jersey. 1962.
4. Johnson, John J. (ed.) *THE ROLE OF THE MILITARY IN UNDER-DEVELOPED COUNTRIES*. Princeton University Press, Princeton, New Jersey. 1962.
5. Johnstone, William C., *BURMA'S FOREIGN POLICY: A STUDY IN NEUTRALISM*. Harvard University Press, Cambridge, Massachusetts. 1963.
6. Leites, Nathan, and C. Wolf, *REBELLION AND AUTHORITY*, Markham Publishing Company, Chicago, Illinois. 1970.
7. Leites, Nathan, *A STUDY OF BOLSHEVISM*. The Free Press, Glencoe, Illinois. 1953.
8. Leites, Nathan, *THE OPERATIONAL CODE OF THE POLITBURO*. McGraw-Hill Book Company, Inc., New York. 1951.
9. Rosen, George, *DEMOCRACY AND ECONOMIC CHANGE IN INDIA*. University of California Press, Berkeley and Los Angeles, California. 1966.
10. Scalapino, Robert A., *THE JAPANESE COMMUNIST MOVEMENT, 1920–1966*. University of California Press. Berkeley and Los Angeles, California. 1967.
11. Selznick, Philip. *THE ORGANIZATIONAL WEAPON: A STUDY OF BOLSHEVIK STRATEGY AND TACTICS*. McGraw-Hill Book Company, Inc., New York. 1952.

12. Tanham, G. K. *COMMUNIST REVOLUTIONARY WARFARE: THE VIETMINH IN INDOCHINA.* Frederick A. Praeger, Inc., New York. 1961.
13. Trager, Frank N. (ed.) *MARXISM IN SOUTHEAST ASIA: A STUDY OF FOUR COUNTRIES.* Stanford University Press, Stanford, California. 1959.
14. Wolf, Charles, Jr. *FOREIGN AID: THEORY AND PRACTICE IN SOUTHERN ASIA.* Princeton University Press, Princeton, New Jersey. 1960.